THE
AMERICAS
LOOK AT
EACH
OTHER

University of Miami
Hispanic-American Studies Series

Hispanic-American Studies Series No. 21

THE
AMERICÁS
LOOK AT
EACH
OTHER

By José Águstín Balseiro

Translated by
Muna Muñoz Lee

University of Miami Press
Coral Gables, Florida

To
Henry King Stanford
Humanist,
Educator,
Gentleman,
and
Friend

Contents

THE AMERICAS LOOK AT EACH OTHER

1 ❖ Lord Byron's South American Dream and the Greatness of Simón Bolívar

I

How did Lord Byron's character, temperament, appearance, and conduct strike his contemporaries? How did he see himself?

When we come across a certain entry in his diary,[1] dated at Ravenna, October 15, 1821, we realize the impossibility of giving full and exact answers to such intricate questions. In this passage, Lord Byron said that during the last nine years he had seen himself compared as a man and as a poet—in the English, French, Italian, German, and Portuguese languages —to Rousseau, Goethe, Young, Aretino, Shakespeare, Euripides, Harlequin, Satan . . . and the list goes on and on, so much that the poet himself found it better to recourse to a triple "etc., etc., etc."

Better than in his diaries and letters, the true Byron's personality might have possibly been revealed to us in some passages of his memoirs, *Life and Adventures,* in which he gave an account of his life up to the year 1816. These memoirs he turned over to Thomas Moore in Venice in the autumn of that same year. But, to the misfortune of history and literature, the manuscript was destroyed by the executors of Byron's will on May 17, 1824, less than a month after the death of the poet on April 19, 1824.

The authenticity of these memoirs is something that can be admitted without major objections—although Byron did warn Moore that there he had told "the truth but not the whole truth," making it clear that the memoirs were not "confessions," which to him were a very different thing. In a letter also to Moore, sent from Ravenna on July 13, 1820, Byron alluded to this document, declaring, "I only know that I wrote it with the fullest intention to be faithful and true . . ."

To such lengths did Byron go in his determination to fulfill that purpose that, despite his resentment against Annabella Milbanke—whom he married on January 2, 1815, and from whom he had been separated since she left him shortly after the birth of their daughter, Ada, on January 15 of the following year—he wrote her, also from Ravenna, on December 15, 1819, about the existence of the memoirs. It was his hope that Lady Byron would read the manuscript and mark in it any departure from the truth. He wanted his faraway wife to know everything he said about her and her family. And he committed himself to respect all her objections because, "there are two ways of interpreting facts, and both are valid no matter how different they may be."

Two years later, in a letter dated June 22 to his half sister, Augusta Leigh (who was some five years Byron's senior and whom Lady Byron accused of having been the poet's mistress) , Byron referred to his relationship with his wife as an accursed affair that was at every turn crossing the way of his fortune, his feelings, and his fame.

It was also during this period, discussing the comparison so frequently made between him and Rousseau—a comparison rejected by the English bard despite his great admiration for that citizen of Geneva—and analyzing the basic differences he found between them, that he took advantage of the occasion to hurl yet one more dart at Lady Byron in words of deep disdain: "He [Rousseau] married his housekeeper; I could not keep house with my wife."

With profound aversion, Byron would once and again identify his wife and the England that, in her isolating Puritanism, had turned against him. Adding new distinctions to his list, he contended that while Rousseau believed that the whole world was against him, his own little world thought that it was he, Byron, who conspired against his English detractors. An aversion of this type, however, often denotes emotional imbalance rather than that incurable nostalgia for things that can be neither forgotten nor unloved.

True, Byron hurled numberless invectives against England; but more than once his display of hate turned out to be nothing but mere lamentations. In a letter to his mother, for instance (from Preveza, November 12, 1809), he complained sadly that he had no one in England to whom he could send his regards and then protested haughtily that he wanted to have nothing to do with England. The key to this psychological and sentimental aspect of the expatriate Byron could be found perhaps in the following words from his letter to Count d'Orsay, written from Genoa on April 22, 1823: "For though I love my country, I do not love my countrymen—at least, not such as they now are."

Turning again to the differences he had already pointed out between him and Rousseau, Byron added yet another, this time a literary one. He observed that Rousseau wrote "with hesitation and care," while he, Byron, did so "with rapidity and rarely with pains."

This assertion, however, he contradicted at least once: in his letter to Moore of January 2, 1821, from Ravenna. He told in it that he wrote in order to clear his mind because, otherwise, he would go mad. He did it, Byron confessed, as a way of escape from inner torment, but writing never gave him pleasure. On the contrary, creative work was for him a very painful process.

II

The carefree way he spoke first suggests the impulsiveness of a Romantic. The agony he later claimed to go through when writing also affiliates him to Romanticism—which is the fruit of emotions that, on freeing themselves violently from strong repression, are transmuted into art. An art, in Byron's case, that would sometimes flow from psychological wounds and already chronic nervous illnesses, for instance:

• Childhood conflicts with his mother, who had been unkind to him as well as subject to continual paroxisms of violent rage. (The father of Catherine Gordon—that was her name—was, in turn, a suicide.)

• Recollections of his spendthrift father, who squandered the fortunes of two wives, beginning with that of Augusta Leigh's mother.

• Early memories of the unsympathetic nurse who mistreated him as an infant.

• The deformity of one or both of his feet. There are contradictory theories about this condition, some claiming a physiological origin, some a nervous one.[2] But, whatever its nature, it caused Byron to walk with a limp and exacerbated his obsessive fear of appearing ridiculous.

• The stupid treatment he underwent at the hands of an incompetent osteopath by the name of Edward John Trelawny.

• The deceitful action of Mary Ann Chatworth, who, when Byron was sixteen, fascinated him and pretended to love him, only to laugh at him and cast him aside later. This unforgettable sentimental frustration made Byron fancy himself "thrown out, alone, on a wide, wide sea."

Such were the experiences that influenced Byron's personality as he advanced from childhood to puberty, from adolescence to the first manifestations of youthhood. There lie the reasons why, as an adult, he would never be able to adjust his own inner world, remaining forever in a state of war with rankling and humiliating memories that embittered and tormented him.

When he assigned himself the mission of destroying political tyranny—whether in Italy or Greece—it was as if he would be dredging up, from the depths of his past and his solitude, the rebellious determination to overthrow every oppression that annihilates flesh and spirit, every wall that divides and isolates. The very insecurity he had experienced since so early in life strengthened his drive to escape from himself: travel and more travel, stumble from one woman's arms into another's, write, write, write . . . in short, a desperate need to reaffirm his identity in every possible way, so as to convince himself that he had a right to exist and to force the world to acknowledge that right.

Byron lived under constant tension. A note in his diary—November 17, 1813—informs us that he was tortured by seemingly endless headaches: "My head! I believe it was given me to ache with." It is very significant that, ten years later, in a letter to Augusta (August 12, 1823), he reminded his half sister that he had begun to be afflicted with frequent and severe headaches before the age of fourteen. He dwelt on the subject in that same letter, describing how his head reacted as a sort of barometer when the atmosphere became supercharged with electricity. Between those two dates, in 1819, in Bologna, the final two acts of Alfieri's tragedy, *Mirra,* sent Byron into convulsions. He told about it in a letter to John Murray, of August 12.

All these facts, and many more that could be cited, suggest that had Byron been a less virile man, had his sexual instinct been not quite so strongly developed, he might have ended a suicide, like his grandfather. For as psychiatry tells us that the idea of self-destruction is a form of revenge against the person, or the society, whom we inwardly blame for destroying our life, it also asserts that the sexual act is the most direct and intense affirmation of life.

Here we could have the explanation of the poet's libidinous excesses. While progressively embittered by the ghost of his neglected childhood, he consumed himself day after day in the flame of his indefatigable and literary production, at the same time burning out his physical capacity in the fires of impenitent lust.

When his book, *Hours of Idleness,* was published,

Brougham made him the object of a vicious attack in an article in the *Edinburgh Review* (January, 1808). This mortified and hurt Byron to such an extent that he considered committing suicide. But instead he produced a double counterattack: first, responding with a satire whose final title was to be *English Bards and Scotch Reviewers* (March, 1809); and again, three years later, with the launching of the first two cantos of *Childe Harold.*

His readers then insisted in identifying him with his hero, and London fell at his feet. Byron became the wonder of all England, whose women, in open rivalry, fought for his attentions despite his known dislike for the thin angular type. One of them was the wife of the aristocrat William Lamb (later to be Prime Minister of Queen Victoria), Lady Caroline, whom the poet fascinated and took as his mistress. She was to be only one in the series of women who, wherever Byron went, would compete for his kisses and become forever a part of his fame and his fate.[3]

III

As we study Byron's biographies and documents and read more and more of the testimony of his contemporaries, we come to extensive and cumulative evidence of his emotional instability and intense oversensitiveness.

The nature of that singular genius, subject to psychic upheavals and prey to almost perpetual anxiety, never developed the fortitude to parallel his orderly and systematic intelligence.

Benjamin Disraeli once observed, "If there was a quality that characterized Byron more than another, it was his solid common sense."

To harmonize, at least partially, that living paradox, that conjunction of extremes—the vehement and adventurous temperament as against the structured literary form of much of

Byron's work—we would have to take into account the classical basis of the culture prevailing at the University of Cam-
bridge when the poet studied there at the beginning of the last
century. For instance, Francis Hovey Stoddard, in his introduction to the 1899 edition of *Childe Harold and Other
Poems,* referred to the classical allusions, metrics, and themes
abounding in Byron's verses. Stoddard went so far as to assert
that "they form the background and suggest the scenery of the
most Romantic compositions."

Nine years after Stoddard, a scholar of a different culture
and tradition, Menéndez y Pelayo, followed a similar line of
thought in Volume VIII of his *Historia de las ideas estéticas
en España.* Said Menéndez y Pelayo:

> The last stragglers of the Romantic movement, who still
> imagine Byron as a wild-eyed, untamed, and ungrammatical
> genius who breaks the ancient molds in which classicism had
> imprisoned inspiration, would be not a little surprised to
> encounter a Byron as rigidly and austerely classical as one
> would expect of Addison or even of Dr. Johnson himself. And
> let it not be forgotten that his Byronic classicism is not
> confined to the merely theoretical, nor is simply worked out in
> a humorous aside, as those which abound in the cantos of *Don
> Juan,* nor grounded solely on Byron's aristocratic disdain
> toward most of his contemporaries.

These words, however, and others on the same subject by
the great Spanish humanist, although here and there modified,
emphasize the technical aspects of the work of Byron at the expense of his egocentric restlessness, and it was this latter aspect
that gave neither peace to his dissatisfied soul nor rest to his
body, afire with the heat of dangers, conspiracies, and intrigues.

If in the construction of his dramatic poems he carefully
followed the classical precepts, in life he preferred to trust
himself to chance and be led into the unexpected. He said as
much in a letter to his sister Augusta (Ravenna, July 26,
1819), "I detest knowing the road one is to go." Byron was a

fatalist who believed in an inexorable fate that controlled the individual.

It is imperative to cast some light also on those traits, gestures, and expressions of the poet that properly classify him with genuine stamp in the lineage of the Romantics. At the age of thirty-two, in a letter to Thomas Moore (Ravenna, August 31, 1820) he stated and defended the thesis that it is passion, not reason, that gives meaning to life. He truly believed that neither Moore nor any man of poetic temperament could escape a violent passion, and concluded, "It is the poetry of life."

In his idea that God had created him for his own misery rather than for the good of others, Byron showed the mind of a Romantic; in his proud stand upon his record of erotic conquests as upon a pedestal, he acted as a Romantic. When, at times, he would transmute his pathological melancholy into the acrimony of an exacerbated cynicism, he was like that other Romantic, Heine, who, creating in fantasy a day of perfect happiness, imagined one in which he could see five or six of his enemies hanged. In Byron the rebel we often find, together with his humanitarian impulses, or in contrast with them, the antisocial cruelty of a Romantic. His was the bitter, heartbreaking skepticism of one who early in life reached out for love and did not find in time someone who would love him truly.

Jacques Barzun, in his essay, "Byron and the Byronic History," written as introduction to *The Selected Letters of Lord Byron* (New York, 1953), observed that the poet "finds his warmth of feeling difficult to share because he thinks it unwanted or sees it undervalued."

A single one of his dramatic poems, *Manfred*, provides ample proof that Byron had from the Romantics a deep sense of suffering and a keen awareness of what sorrow can teach. Almost at the very beginning of the first act, his hero says: "But grief should be the instructor of the wise; / Sorrow is knowledge . . ."

Later (Act II, scene ii), the haughty consciousness of his towering individuality becomes apparent: his rejection of all that is mediocre and shallow. In his Romantic megalomania, Byron knew his own stature and rose alone with his emotions and his vices, with the greatness and the unwonted miseries of one who did not look upon the earth with human eyes.

Taking one of his innumerable lyric poems, "When We Two Parted," we find that it begins with a memory of silence and tears, broken hearts, pale cheeks . . . words and images bearing an unmistakably Romantic stamp. And it ends like this:

> In secret we met—
> In silence I grieve,
> That thy heart could forget,
> Thy spirit deceive.
> If I should meet thee
> After long years,
> How should I greet thee?—
> With silence and tears.

Byron's ostentatiousness and narcissism, his superstitions and nocturnal fears, his persecution complex and outbursts of rage, his personal affectations and exhibitionistic bragging, the fact that he claimed to prefer solitude to anyone's company, his periodic visits to the graveyard in Bologna in 1819, his cult of the heroic and his boastful libertinism, his knowledge that not only did he suffer self-inflicted spiritual torture but that he inflicted analogous torments on anyone who ever entered into a relationship with him, his hotly passionate love of liberty . . . and the list could be prolonged indefinitely, tell us again and again that he was a Romantic.

Notwithstanding his respect for the three unities in his dramatic poems, and despite his ardent admiration for eighteenth century poetic tendencies, as can be seen in the form of not a few of his compositions, nothing could cloud Byron's essential Romanticism or negate the irreconcilable contradictions of his nature. From a conversation with Goethe on Thursday, February 24, 1825, Johann Peter Eckermann recorded certain words of the German poet that are truly significant in regard to Byronic Romanticism. Said Goethe speaking of Byron, "Within himself he saw great darkness. He lived passionately in the present moment, giving no thought to the consequences of his actions." Goethe also expressed then his opinion that since Byron was able to produce whenever and whatever he wished, it could be said that in him "inspiration" took the place of "reflection."

In the exordium of another of his books on the poet, *Byron in Italy* (New York, 1941), Peter Quennell finds the key formula when he states that "Byron himself was a Romantic *malgré lui.*" For, as Quennell himself would explain in *Byron, a Self-portrait, Letters and Diaries, 1798 to 1824* (two volumes, New York, 1950), the more we believe we have grasped the character of Byron, the more it eludes us. So true is this that Byron himself recognized the opposites in his temperament without attempting to reconcile them.

IV

When and why did Byron first begin to feel an interest in the New World?

One of his ancestors, Commodore John Byron, came to America, took possession of the Malvina (Falkland) Islands for England in 1765, and traveled in the southern part of the western hemisphere where he founded the small colony of Port Egmont in Saunders. This act brought England and Spain to the verge of war, until Spain gave up her rights to the territory by agreement in 1771.

This great-uncle of the poet, as prone to run into storms as his immortal nephew was to be preyed upon by tempestuous passions, was nicknamed "Foul Weather Jack."

About the year 1818 wrote Byron his "Ode to Venice," in which he lamented the decadence of that Adriatic city. In this poem he also extolled the coming of freedom to America, contrasting this fact with the autocracy then prevailing in Europe. He ended his ode offering our continent: "One freeman more, America, to thee!"

By February, 1823, Byron had already completed the three cantos of "The Island." It is interesting to find in this poem a partial echo of words that he wrote in his diary, on Tuesday, January 9, 1821, while in Ravenna. In an item referring to the few things the lands discovered overseas had given the Old World, he had said, ". . . and freedom afterwards—the *latter* a fine thing, particularly as they gave it to Europe in exchange for slavery." In "The Island" (Canto II, stanza iv) he spoke of: "The Old World more degraded than the New— / Where Chimborazo, over air, earth, wave / Glares with his Titan eye, and sees no slave."

This fact becomes ever more fascinating if we compare it with a letter Simón Bolívar wrote to Bernardo Monteagudo on August 5 of that very year. In this letter Bolívar mentioned Turkey, which was then attacking the Greeks, and predicted that a war would take place between "our" Chimborazo and the Caucasus.

In Canto II, stanza xi, of "The Island," Byron returned to the paradisal vision of America's "natural man," an idea that originated with Columbus' "Letter on the Discovery" (1493) and culminated in Sir Thomas More's *Utopia* in 1516: "Of those who were more happy, if less wise, / Did more than Europe's discipline had done, / And civilized Civilization's son." For (stanza xvi), "All nature is his realm, and love his throne."

From Bologna, on August 20, 1819, Byron wrote to his friend John Hobhouse: "I have two notions: one to visit England in the spring, the other to go to South America. Europe is grown decrepit [reiteration of a feeling already expressed in his "Ode to Venice"]; besides, it is all the same thing over again; those fellows are fresh as their world, and fierce as their earthquakes."

Let us keep those words in mind. They confirm once again Byron's nomadic tastes and the psychic unrest of a man who would never feel secure anywhere. They offer added evidence of his love for the exotic, his disdain for insipid civilization, and his yearning to become one with the unknown and violent forces of nature. An earlier entry in his diary—September 22, 1816, in Switzerland—already showed the Romantic exaltation of one who found aesthetic pleasure in the rebellious might of the tempest: "Storm came on, lightning, hail; all in perfection, and beautiful."

Byron's words in his cited diary entry of August 20 are consonant with those that enliven his verses glorifying the freshness, youth, and freedom with which his imagination endowed the New World. On October 3 of that same year, 1819, he wrote again to Hobhouse, this time from Venice. Quite at the beginning of his letter, in the first paragraph, in fact, his South American dream reappeared. It was by now very specific. He had chosen a country, Venezuela (did Byron, writing from Venice, know—one wonders—that the name "Venezuela" means "little Venice"?), and mentioned Simón Bolívar by name. Byron sought to rationalize his decision by citing practical advantages to be derived from it. "My South American project," he said, "of which I believe I spoke to you (as you mention it)—was this. I perceived by the enclosed paragraphs that advantageous offers were—or are to be held out to settlers in the Venezuelan territory. . . ." He went on to explain his preference for the southern portion of the hemisphere: "The Anglo-Americans are a little too coarse for me, and their climate too cold, and I should prefer the others.[4] I could soon grapple with the Spanish language. Ellice or others would get me letters to Bolívar and his government. . . . I assure you that I am very serious in the idea, and that the notion has been about me for a long time, as you will see by the worn state of the advertisement. I should like to go there with my natural daughter, Allegra, . . . and pitch my tent for good and all."

He reiterated his intention twenty-three days later in a letter (Venice, October 26, 1819) to Douglas Kinnaird: "I want to go to South America—I have written to Hobhouse all about it."

In a diary entry for January 26, 1821, in Naples, he remembered the countries that overthrew their oppressors and praised South America in these words, "South America beats her old vultures out of their nest . . ."

V

This idea we must follow to its source if we are to find out what was stirring in Byron's subconscious mind. For, in spite of the practical cast he tried to give his arguments in favor of his overseas project, what really attracted him there was a living magnet of the purest idealism: [5] the genius of Simón Bolívar, symbol of the independence of South America. Bolívar, who, on March 26, 1812, had said, in time to prove himself against any and all adverse circumstances, "Should nature oppose us, we shall fight her and bring her to heel." Bolívar, of whom José Martí, with an eloquence in which he identified man and nature in America just as Byron had done before, was to say:

It is not possible to speak calmly of one whose life was never calm. Of Bolívar you can only speak from the summit of a mountain, or among lightning and thunder, or with a sheaf of liberated countries in your fist and tyranny lying broken at your feet. . . .

. . . his base is broad as the mountains, his roots, like theirs, mingle with those of the earth itself, and like their peaks he stands, erect and sharp, the better to penetrate the rebellious heavens. He is to be seen knocking with his golden saber on Glory's gate. . . .

. . . does he not burst the bonds of whole races of men, break the spell that held a whole continent, evoke entire peoples? Has he not ranged further, under the banner of freedom, than any conqueror under that of tyranny? Does he not, from the peak of Chimborazo, converse with Eternity, and has he not at his feet, in the Potosi, under the colors of condor-pecked Colombia, one of the most tenacious and magnificents achievements of human history? [6]

That was Martí exalting Bolívar to the heights of the Chimborazo. Byron before him, in "The Island," had already mentioned this glorious volcano. And we have noted above how the English poet said that the South American countries were "fierce as their earthquakes." It also comes to mind at this point the audacious and challenging prophecy Bolívar made when an earthquake shook the city and the people of Caracas in 1812. And we shall not forget, because coincidences are astounding, that, in his letter to Francisco de Paula Santander (Guayaquil, August 3, 1822), the Liberator compared the calm then prevailing in the south to the Chimborazo, forever ablaze underneath its icy surface.

But that is not all. Bolívar was to write his "Delirio sobre el Chimborazo" in which he told how he had wanted to climb that "watchtower of the universe." For, he said, "no human foot has left its track upon the diamond crown set by Eternity's hand upon the exalted forehead of this dominator of the Andes." The realization of his dream gave Bolívar the feeling that he had at his feet "the threshold of the abyss" and that, "in raising himself above the heads of all men," he had "surpassed them all in good fortune." And later, writing from Pativilca, on January 19, 1824, to Simón Rodríguez, fired with enthusiasm by the return of his favorite teacher, friend, and sharer of revolutionary dreams, Bolívar begged him, "Do come to the Chimborazo. Profane with daring foot this staircase of

Titans, this crown of the earth, this impregnable bastion of the universe."

These lyrical transports of Bolívar remind us of a line from *Childe Harold's Pilgrimage* (Canto IV, stanza clxxviii), "I love not man the less, but nature more . . ."

It is the same Bolívar who, nine years previously, had written from Kingston, Jamaica, to the editor of *La Gaceta Real* describing man and nature in his America: "He lives at ease in his native land, satisfying his needs and passions at a small cost; the climate does not impose the need for clothing and hardly even that of shelter." Compare this Romantic evaluation with that of the lines of "The Island" quoted before. And Bolívar had dwelt on his point further explaining that "there is no similar situation in the world; man has exhausted the whole earth; only America has barely begun to be used." Thus, the coincidence of Bolívar's vision with what Byron had expressed in his "Ode to Venice" and in his letter to Hobhouse of August 20, 1819, accentuates the well-nigh incredible parallel between the minds and characters of the Englishman and the Venezuelan.

VI

But there is more yet.

In April, 1819, Byron met an Italian countess who, having barely reached the age of twenty, had already been married for one year: Teresa (Gamba) Guiccioli. That first name happened to be also the middle name of Bolívar's wife, María Teresa Rodríguez del Toro. When she died, nine months after their wedding, and the young widower was living in Paris— where he was nicknamed "the Prince"—Bolívar took a mistress, Fanny de Villars, and chose to call her by the name of "Teresa."

Byron was in Pisa in 1822 and there ordered the construction of a schooner. To Countess Guiccioli he hinted politely that he would like to name it the "Teresa." Having dutifully made this courteous gesture, however, the *cavaliere servente* proceeded like a discreet *amico di casa* who would not compromise a lady's reputation. He decided instead to name his boat the "Bolívar," after the man who, a year earlier, had won the battle of Carabobo.

It was 1822 and three years had gone by since Byron first thought about the Liberator and mentioned Venezuela. His cult of the South American hero seemed to have increased meanwhile: the passage of time had confirmed it and made it grow. And Venezuela? Had she also become greater as a symbol of liberty, as the provider of arms and ideas for the emancipation of a whole continent?

It was from Venezuela that Francisco de Miranda had set forth upon his pilgrimage to one European country after another to promote the cause of South American independence. And, before he ever rode out into the battlefield in his own land, he had already fought against a kingdom. Under the Spanish flag, Miranda had participated in the struggle of the Thirteen Colonies against George III, fighting at the site of Pensacola, Florida. It was in Caracas, on April 19, 1810, that the cry for redemption that would definitely kindle the flame of war in the Andean region was raised.[7] From Caracas, too, started his wanderings around the world that Simón Rodríguez, the man who lighted stars of liberty in the youthful imagination of Bolívar and was, in the happy expression of Arturo Uslar Pietri, *maestro innumerable de un solo discípulo*. Venezuela was also the motherland of another of Bolívar's teachers, the humanist sage, admirer of the universal example of Humboldt, Andrés Bello, who went on a patriotic mission to London on behalf of his country and was later to be adviser to the government of Chile and first rector of the university of that hospitable republic. It was in Venezuela that the abolition of slavery was started, from partial liberation in 1821 to complete freedom in 1854. That year Byron, with favoring breezes, was sailing on the "Bolívar" over lacustrine waters. It was also the year in which the United States—two years earlier than England—recognized the republic of Colombia, a product of the Liberator's political and military as well as intellectual and creative genius.

Now we can understand fully what Andrés Eloy Blanco meant when, directing his opinion on "how America must cultivate itself" to the Venezuela that had made him suffer, he exclaimed, "Behind Bolívar, ah, what glory! After Bolívar, what anguish!"

Despite his lameness—or, who knows, perhaps to overcome this handicap by displaying his physical abilities—Byron became a persistent sportsman. He reached such high degree of proficiency that he could well take pride in his prowess in boxing, swimming, and shooting. Bolívar, sinewy and agile from childhood, was a prodigious horseman and tireless dancer. One and the other, the Englishman and the Venezuelan, seemed equally incapable of repose, of restraining the impetuous outflow of their fiery energy. Bolívar never took a rest during the times of greatest strain, not even when dictating his correspondence (more voluminous than that of Byron). Sometimes he would do it while lying on a hammock, but then could not keep from swinging vigorously in it. As it happened, it was to the rhythm of this indigenous American artifact, so dear to the Creoles, that Bolívar worked out his idea of America, the America of which he would say in Angostura (December 17, 1819), "We are neither Europeans nor Indians, but a species intermediate between the aborigines and the Spanish." For this very reason, as if looking with prophetic vision far ahead into the future, he added: "A diversity of origins requires an infinitely firm hand together with an infinitely delicate tact to manage this heterogeneous society, whose complex structure becomes dislocated, divides, and dissolves as a result of the slightest alteration."

This "diversity of origins" and this "heterogeneous society" to which the South American aristocrat confessed would not have displeased the English lord who, enamored of the exotic, traveled to Constantionople and began his *Childe Harold* in Albania. Let us remember that Byron believed a man should take to the road and travel to become conscious of his own existence. He visited Portugal and stopped in Spain, where, he learned, each peasant was proud as the noblest of dukes. Aware that Spain bordered on Europe and was within sight of Africa, being a land where many civilizations, races, and cultures left their marks in mixtures of blood and manners of life, Byron exclaimed fervently (*Childe Harold,* Canto I, stanza xxxv) : "Oh, lovely Spain! renowned romantic land!"

He then spent sometime in Byzantine and Gothic Venice and, from this amalgam of Europe and the Orient, continued to some other Italian cities. Never stopping for long anywhere, fate finally put an end to his wanderings in Greece.

The America of Bolívar was also the America of natural wonders: of great rivers, like the Amazon, the Orinoco, the Magdalena; of the Andes, overwhelming and titanic; of the Titicaca, the highest lake on earth. In his "Epistle to Augusta," overflowing as it is with almost infinite human love and tenderness, Byron nevertheless assigned a prominent place to his never-forgotten nature: "And never gaze on it with apathy." In Canto III, stanza lxxii, of *Childe Harold,* he confessed, "I live not in myself, but I become / Portion of that around me."

And, considering another line there saying that to him "High mountains are a feeling," what would his reaction have been, and in what words would have he expressed it had he come face to face with the mystery of the Andes? Indeed, a little later, stanza lxxv, the poet returned to and elaborated further on the same idea: "Are not the mountains, waves, and skies, a part / Of me and of my soul, as I of them? / Is not the love of these deep in my heart / With a pure passion? Should I not condemn / All objects, if compared with these? . . ."

Even in *Don Juan,* where satire and mockery are predominant, we once more (Canto III, stanza civ) find the Romantic vein of one who communed with nature: "My altars are the mountains and the ocean, / Earth, air, stars—all that springs from the great Whole, / Who hath produced, and will receive my soul."

VII

In Paris, at the beginning of the nineteenth century, Bolívar was no less a social "lion" than Byron was to become a few years later in London. Both these men were dandies, careful of gesture as well as of appearance, although Bolívar never carried this to such extremes as Byron. Both, in the realms of Romantic philosophy and of gallant action, shared their respective heroes: Rousseau and Bonaparte.

Upon learning that his preceptor, Simón Rodríguez, was in Vienna, Bolívar rushed there to meet him, and then they traveled together to Italy. In Milan, Bolívar witnessed the second coronation of Napoleon, who was exalting himself to the imperial throne, and thereupon lost his admiration for the French hero. In Rome, Bolívar refused to kiss the Pope's sandal, on which he saw the Cross debased. He would not temporize with opulence and showy display, nor make himself an accomplice to the degradation of a symbol that was always to be venerated.

While still in Rome, Bolívar went up to the Aventine and there swore never to rest until seeing his America free from tyranny.

Bolívar's itinerary in his many trips, although never coinciding in time, was similar to Byron's in regard to places visited: Spain, France, Austria, Italy, England, Portugal, Turkey. The two men diverged, however, in their respective attitude toward Bonaparte, whom Byron would almost constantly praise. As late as October 17, 1823, in his diary, Byron called the Corsican "Emperor of emperors." [8]

Although, on losing his devotion for Bonaparte, Bolívar became ideologically separated from Byron, he did conquer a place at the side of Byron among the Immortals.

There is an unmistakable reference to Napoleon in a letter that Simón Rodríguez wrote to Bolívar in 1827. In this very lengthy epistle, Rodríguez praised and honored Bolívar for having refused to be crowned or to allow anyone else to be crowned in South America. "It is," he said, "a greater honor to be exiled with a hero who would not be king than with a man who gave up being a hero to become a king."

Byron decided to take residence in Venice, where he remained for three years. In Venice, as in the days of the first two cantos of *Childe Harold* in London, woman after woman ran to his arms: Mariana Segati; Angelina, whose surname was the only detail Byron kept to himself in his letter of May 18, 1819, recounting this adventure; Ursula, a woman about to marry another man; Margarita Cogni (the famous "Fornarina") . . . and Teresa Guiccioli, the most impassioned of his Mediterranean lovers and the truly loyal friend among his unforgettable mistresses.

Byron's correspondence shows that he had no scruple in describing his affairs with intimate detail; an attitude incredible in a man who usually would act like a gentleman. There are instances in which his cynicism is irritating. And then we are overcome with pity on learning that he lived in fear of losing his mind.[9] Writing from Milan to Augusta Leigh, he had said, referring to women in general, "I repeat it again and again—that *woman* has destroyed me."

Byron was such an emotionally chaotic human being that it is practically impossible to tell the way he really felt about any woman in particular or women in general. He would love or hate, surrender or tyrannize, or despise in such a manner that, though he could not live without a woman or without women, he would make no secret at all of his intimacies with them. His epigrams at the expense of women might have been envied by Oscar Wilde. Notice, for instance, his comment in a letter (November 4, 1814) to Lady Melbourne, one of the few women for whom he felt any real esteem: "I like them [women] to talk, because then they think less."

Was Byron conscious of the psychological shifts and changes in his own personality?

Very interesting in this context is a certain part of a conversation he had in the spring of 1823 with Lady Marguerite Blessington, herself not so much less indiscreet than the poet. In a moment of self-analysis, Byron confessed to her that he was everything by turns and never for long, being such a strange mixture of good and evil that he was unable even to give an accurate description of himself.

And that was the Byron who a thousand times depicted the dissolute society, the licentiousness, and the libertine customs he had found in Italy, showering his English correspondents with exceedingly detailed descriptions of every adventure that would come his way.

So intensely did Byron live then that he became physically exhausted. He alternated his constant amorous affairs with the exertion of incessant writing. His years in Italy were thus fecund in literary production. Between 1817 and 1823, he finished *Manfred* and followed with seven more dramas, Canto IV of *Childe Harold,* the whole of *Don Juan,* and a number of other works besides. All this while involved also in political plots and intrigues in favor of the oppressed Italians.

As for Simón Bolívar, he, too, had time to fascinate one woman after another—including some of the most aristocratic and the most beautiful—while engaged in something else: winning victories in the battlefields of South America. In his list there were single as well as married women, the latter seeing to it that there was time and space between them and their legal husbands. Bernardina Ibáñez, Josefina Núñez, Isabel Soublette, Manuelita Madroño . . . preceded the one who came to be the Liberator's immortal passion. Bolívar, who was only forty then, seemed old. A life of constant sacrifice and heroism had left on him its inevitable marks. It took a young

woman, however, to put fiery colors in his sunset: Manuela
Sáenz, ripe with desire in the splendor of her twenty-four years.
Manuela Sáenz was a girl with some experience of her own.
Just before her wedding to an English physician by the name
of James Thorne, she had been seduced by another man, and
more than once returned, an unfaithful wife, to the arms of
that first lover. Tired of her husband, she left him in Lima
and went to Quito. Dr. Thorne had become so desperately
jealous that he even forgot that Anglo-Saxons are supposedly
exempt from a weakness currently attributed to peoples of
southern cultures.

Manuela was born in Quito an illegitimate child. Italy,
therefore, where Byron daily added to his spoils as a Don
Juan, could not call itself more tolerant. Nor was Teresa
Gamba—third consort of Count Guiccioli and of whom Byron
wrote that she cared about public opinion as little as Carolina
Lamb used to—more determined and forward than Manuela
Sáenz.

In his biography, *Manuela Sáenz, la Libertadora del Liber-
tador* (Buenos Aires, 1946), the Ecuadoran historian, Alfonso
Rumazo González, quotes from a letter of the savant Francisco
José de Caldas, written on August 12, 1802: "The atmosphere
of Quito is polluted: one breathes only sensual pleasures. The
pitfalls and stumbling blocks in the path of virtue multiply,
and one might well believe that the temple of Venus has been
transported from Cyprus to this city."

In order to separate her from her lover, the Spanish Army
officer, Fausto de Elhuyar, James Thorne took his wife to
Lima. But in that city Manuela Sáenz did not fail to notice
how Rosita Campuzano, the delicate blonde beauty of Guayaquil, made sweet the days of the Argentine general, José de
San Martín, Protector of Perú. And when, on a period of vaca-
tion, her husband took her back to her native land, where she
was celebrated as the most attractive and desirable of bru-
nettes, Manuela Sáenz happened to witness the triumphal
entry of Simón Bolívar into Quito on June 16, 1822.

As described by his contemporaries, Byron was, by English standards, a short man. General Páez made the following sketch of Bolívar:

> He is short of stature—one meter and sixty-seven centimeters —with narrow shoulders and slender limbs. A homely face, long and dark; bushy eyebrows; black eyes, romantic in meditation and sparkling in activity. His hair is also black, cropped and closely curled. . . . His lower lip is protuberant and disdainful. His long nose scarcely forms any angle with the high, narrow forehead from which it hangs. His body is small and sinewy; his voice thin but vibrant. He is always on the move: his head held high, his big ears sticking out alertly.

Rumazo González presents in his book many word-portraits of Manuela Sáenz. Here we quote the one that describes her first encounter with Bolívar:

> At the precise moment when the hero was passing by, Manuela tossed him a laurel wreath. Raising his eyes, the General met the sparkling glance of that lady of Quito and saw also her marvelous smile and her white rounded arms springing from her bare shoulders like two flames of love. Bolívar returned the smile even more obviously as he fixed his fiery eyes upon her and gave her thanks for the honor with a deep bow. . . . This encounter, which took place when Bolívar was at the height of his victorious career, could not but stimulate him into starting new and even more daring ventures. The resolute steps he took to leave his native country and set off in a long journey abroad coincided with the disturbance brought to his heart by the most beautiful woman he had ever seen.

Both Byron and Bolívar loved liberty and served its cause. And both did so with the same noble sincerity. But there was a great difference in the respective setting of their activities. While Byron moved in what could be likened to a limited stage, Bolívar acted in the midst of a whole changing world, one that rose overflowing all boundaries to put an end to one of the mightiest empires that ever existed. General Pablo Morillo, perhaps Bolívar's greatest enemy, admitted as much when he wrote to the Minister of War in Spain: "Bolívar, in a single day, does away with the achievements of five years of fighting, and in a single battle wins back territory whose conquest had cost the King's troops many battles."

VIII

Two years after his first meeting with Manuela, the Liberator won a double victory at Junín: the first, in the field of battle; the second, several months later, in the field of literature. But when, on August 6, 1824, Bolívar defeated General José Canterac in a hand-to-hand encounter and made the Spanish cavalry—in the words of their own commander—"take shamefully to flight," Byron had already been dead four months. Having died at Missolonghi on April 19, Byron never knew of that triumph, nor of the victory of Ayacucho, on December 9, nor of the fact that the South American countries did finally win their independence.

Why did the great English bard never act upon his dream of coming to the New World, of meeting Bolívar, of living in Venezuela?

Back in 1822, Byron had suffered two losses that filled his heart and his poetry with pain. Allegra, his natural daughter — with Jane Clairmont—upon whom the poet lavished all the tenderness denied him by the irreparable absence of the legitimate one, Ada, died that year. And Shelly drowned in the Bay of Spezzia; Byron was among the witnesses to the cremation of his body.

At the same time, a committee that was organized in London to aid the Greeks in the cause of their independence from the Turks appointed Byron as its delegate. And, just as he had before put his influence and generosity at the service of the Carbonari in Italy, in their struggle against Austrian oppression, he now helped the Greek revolutionaries against Turkey.

It was not Byron, therefore, who—as Alfred de Vigny used

to say about himself when his life became too complicated—
had "a game of chess with destiny." It was Byron's destiny that
involved him in a game of chess, separating him forever from
his unattainable dream.

What would Byron have thought of Bolívar and Bolívar of
Byron, and how well would those two geniuses have understood each other, had they ever met and spoken? How would
their encounter have been, having between them so many af-
finities—of temperament, of dislike for tyranny, of attraction
for women, of magnanimity to the point of charity, of selflessness in the service of noble causes, of similarity of tastes in
their cultural refinement?

Byron's worship of Alexander Pope among the English
poets is well known. He admired Pope to the extent of calling
him "the most *faultless* of Poets, and almost of men" (letter to
John Murray, Ravenna, September 4, 1820). Pope, with his
exceptional lucidity and mental energy, was perfection itself
—a condition that Byron admired all the more perhaps because he sometimes fell short of it. Also, Pope experienced deformity—as Byron did—and the pain of an invalid's life, but
he had a nervous system of exquisite sensitivity and possessed
a sense of rhythm coupled with a mastery of words that Byron
could not find equaled in his own poetry nor in that of any of
his nineteenth-century contemporaries. Pope, in short, was a
classicist par excellence who lived up to self-imposed standards
of impeccable correction.

The battle of Junín already won and the wars of independence nearing their end after the victory of Ayacucho, the Ecuadoran poet, José Joaquín Olmedo, presented to the Liberator
the definitive version of his "Canto a Bolívar." Bolívar's letter
in reply—from Cuzco, July 12, 1825—was as outstanding an
example of the classical form as of a keen knowledge of the
models of poetry, thoroughly familiar with Homer and Virgil,
Pindar and Horace, Racine and Boileau. There was even a
whole paragraph in praise of Pope, the poet who, though short
of lyric passion, almost exhausted nevertheless in the English

language all the possibilities of neoclassical satire and didactic
poetry. Then, censuring what he rightly believed to be the
greatest defect of Olmedo's poem—its forced and injudicious
reference to the Inca Emperor Huayna Capac—Bolívar observed: "The shades of many other illustrious poets could inspire you better than the Inca who, in truth, could sing nothing but *yaravis.** Pope, the poet you admire so much, can give
you a few little lessons and help you correct certain lapses
which Homer himself was not always able to avoid."

IX

The story is told that when Teresa Guiccioli was dying, in
1873, having survived Byron forty-nine years, she begged her
sister-in-law to publish all her papers. Like Manuela Sáenz,
she had once left her husband because she wanted to belong
solely and entirely to her lover. "The more Byron is known,"
she explained, "the better he will be loved." She had already
written, in French, her *Vie de Lord Byron*. Translated into
English with the title, *My Recollections of Lord Byron*, the
book had been published in London in 1869. Reacting with
impassioned loyalty against Leigh Hunt's *Lord Byron and his
Contemporaries*, Teresa valued the "treasure of kindness,
affection, and genius" left her by the poet in his love letters far
more than she feared for her reputation.

Of no less vehement nature was the devotion of Manuela
Sáenz for Simón Bolívar. He would sometimes refer to her as
"the lovely madcap," and once wrote her, "Your love rekindles
a life that was expiring." Her affection was manifested in
many ways besides the delight her company gave the hero. She
was at his side in the battlefield. She guarded his sleep, guessed
who his enemies were, kept his files. With a clairvoyant's intuition, she forestalled the treachery of his would-be assassins.

---

* *Yaraví:* a melancholic love song of the Indians and Creoles of the
mountains of Chile, Peru, and Colombia.

But, as Germán Arciniegas points out (*América Mágica II—Las mujeres y las horas,* Buenos Aires, 1961), most of the memories, which by then were Manuela's only reason for living, she "took with her to the grave, were consumed by fire, or lost with her letters." Manuela Sáenz died of diphtheria in 1859, alone and miserably poor, twenty-nine years after Bolívar had died.

The Liberator died on December 17, 1830, at the Quinta de San Pedro Alejandrino, in Santa Marta, Colombia. By then, that same America that his genius had made free had turned against him. "Opprobrium" piled upon him beyond the limit of his endurance. Always great, however, and always ready to serve even those who crucified him, Bolívar was still able to express his abnegation in his last words: "If my death puts an end to party divisions and helps consolidate the union, I shall go down to the grave in peace."

It was as if he had lived in advance the tragedy that some thirty years later was to convulse the America of Lincoln. Only Bolívar did not have the satisfaction of the Emancipator of the north, who saw his country's union consolidated and could speak to his people "With malice toward none; with charity for all"—even though in the end it cost him his life.

Byron's death did not cure either the internal dissensions among the Greeks, to whom he left his life in pledge. Just as Bolívar came to the bitter conclusion that there had been three great "nuisances" in the world—Jesus Christ, Don Quixote, and himself—so Byron confessed to Teresa Guiccioli, "I was a fool to come here," after his sense of honor and his own desire moved him to go to Greece and take up the cause of her independence.

Europe's most dazzling poet in his day and South America's most resplendent hero both came to the end of their lives believing they had labored in vain—"plowed the sea," as Bolívar said.

It has been my purpose here to bring them together—their names and their deeds, their greatness and their miseries—recalling these lines from Canto III of Byron's *Childe Harold's Pilgrimage:*

> But these are deeds which should not pass away,
> And names that must not wither . . .

[From *Expresion de Hispanoamérica*, Vol. II, San Juan, Puerto Rico: Instituto de Cultura Puertorriqueña, 1963.]

2
The
Americas Look at
Each Other

For people of the United States it is of prime importance to learn what people of the rest of the Americas think and feel when they turn their eyes to the north; and it is no less important for the peoples to the south to know about the mind and the attitude of North Americans in regard to the other inhabitants of our hemisphere.

This confrontation—impelled by sincerity and inspired by a mutual urgency to understand each other better—is a salutary and ennobling endeavor. The nearer we approach our neighbors by the disinterested paths of art, literature, scholarship, and open-hearted friendship, the sooner will we demolish the prejudices that hamper the constructive development of human nature. Men of good will intuitively know that introversion and isolation are apt to prove as barren in international as in interpersonal relationships.

Benjamin Franklin said: "God grant that not only the love of liberty but a thorough knowledge of the rights of man may pervade all the nations of the earth, so that a philosopher may set his foot anywhere on its surface, and say, 'This is my country.' " [1]

It is in this spirit that we of the Americas should regard one another. And this is the example that Andrés Bello, Juan Egaña, Domingo F. Sarmiento, Eugenio María de Hostos, Ruy Barbosa, José Martí, Eloy Alfaro, and others set for us in Hispanic America. The Christian universality of the teachings of Jesus encourages us to learn about all nations. And, among them, the ones that should most deeply engage the intellectual awareness of the New World are those of our own hemisphere. It was to the greatest glory of the University of Salamanca in the days of its splendor the fact that, transcending narrow nationalism, it did not exclusively appoint Spanish professors but opened its doors to many eminent foreigners. (Let us never forget that "university" is rooted in "universe.") Yet, when, in 1599, Spain forbade its subjects to study in institutions beyond its frontiers [2]—thus sealing off any further exchange of ideas and culture—it automatically marked itself out for decadence. We cannot draw a curtain without shutting out light and voice.

As late as the eighteenth century, that unforgettable priest, Father Benito Jerónimo Feijoo, who could so well harmonize a deep love of his country with his desire to universalize it, had to struggle against nationalistic limitations. How right is the Argentine writer, Eduardo Mallea, in saying that nothing is more terrible and tenebrous than the nationalism of men of a shortsighted mind. It is the brand of nationalism that blinds and misleads, that builds insurmountable barriers to the cooperation between men and peoples in great reciprocal need of it. When Hostos, the Puerto Rican sociologist, wished to give evidence of the intellectual progress of Chile, he told of its "affectionate adoption of foreigners dedicated to science, art, and literature." To extol Argentina in his *Canto* (1910), Rubén Darío called it "universal Argentina."

For all who long to live in freedom and at peace, America should become, as Bolívar dreamed, "the Continent of Hope." Enriched, north and south, by successive waves of diversified immigration, America was destined from the outset to develop a civilization at once eclectic and distinctively its own. What an achievement for our contemporary generations, should we be ready to obviate whatever might tend to depart from this orientation while confirming and exalting all that honors it!

As early as 1699, Cotton Mather, proposing to write an opusculum on Christianity for Spanish-speaking peoples, studied this language in North America. In the eighteenth century, the works of Benjamin Franklin were translated into Spanish and read throughout the Hispanic-American continent.[3] Alexander Garden, the South Carolina botanist, was no stranger to educated Ibero-Americans. Dr. Benjamin Smith Barton's papers on gout were translated and printed in the *Gaceta de Guatemala* in 1801 and 1802. In Colombia, Francisco Caldas, wiser and more alert than most, published scientific news from North America in his weekly, *Semanario de la Nueva Granada*.

In 1781, that Venezuelan universalist, Francisco de Miranda, fought under the Spanish flag at the site of Pensacola —then the capital of East Florida—against the English, who surrendered the garrison during the revolution of the Thirteen Colonies. Two years later, after his unjust conviction by a Spanish court in Cuba, Miranda found generous asylum in the United States. His diary (1783–1784) is rich in detailed information about the new republic.

Don Juan Egaña, born in Lima and an outstanding personality in Chile's civic life, conceived his *Plan de defensa general de toda la América* "between September 18, 1810, and November 26 of that same year," according to Raúl Silva Castro, the scholar who compiled Egaña's scattered unpublished works. In this plan, Egaña called for an America united by the commitment of every one of its constituent governments to contribute "arms, money and men in case of the slightest attack from, or sedition originating in Europe," as a remedy against disasters affecting the whole continent. Egaña thought that:

> [when] the governments of America find that a court has been set up without consulting which they cannot stir up wars against one another, they will no longer invoke their narrow

national interests but rather the interest of justice; foreigners, seeing that we are free from dissension and unable to indulge in it, will respect us . . .

Exalting specifically the republic of George Washington, Egaña wrote:

> The capital of the United States of North America, a country that was the first in our times to set the example of a people inimical to despots and by its own effort shaking off the yoke of tyranny and constituting itself into an independent nation, will be the site of the Congress of Ministers Plenipotentiary of the nations compromised in the Federation.
>
> The chief aim of this Congress will be to organize the states of the Federation within an alliance for mutual defense and for the protection of the constitutional system of each one of them, in the eventuality that any should be attacked by any power whatsoever with the intent of subduing and by force of arms compelling them to subject themselves to the government of persons other than those freely elected by them, or to be ruled by laws not in accordance with their own best interests.

As "head of the federation," Egaña singled out the United States.

On May 17, 1810, don Telesforo de Orea, a commissioner of the Caracas Governing Board, wrote to the Secretary of State in Washington, in an outburst of political enthusiasm, that "the United States had shown Venezuela the road of freedom and civic virtue," adding that the countries of South America would follow as closely as possible the Constitution of the North.

The following year (1811) saw the arrival in Washington of a commission from Bogotá, Colombia, constituted by don Pedro de la Lastra and don Nicolás Mauricio de Umaña. They brought with them a message from don José Miguel Pey, Vice-President of the Supreme Junta of Nueva Granada, to President Madison. Here is one paragraph from that document:

"We will consider ourselves fortunate if, by imitating the example of the United States, we succeed in establishing a political system based on equity, and make ourselves worthy of being an ally of that great republic."

Uruguay's José Artigas based his instructions to his country's delegates to the Constitutional Convention at Buenos Aires, April 13, 1813, on the federal system of the United States. As he himself was to explain much later, Artigas chose the northern republic as his model to insure the Provinces of Rio de la Plata an autonomous form of government.

In his Jamaica Letter, of September 6, 1815, Bolívar praised "the political talents and virtues that characterize our northern brothers." This point Bolívar stressed again at the Congress of Angostura, on February 15, 1819.

On July 19, 1817, don Manuel Hermenegildo de Aguirre (who, by the way, was Victoria Ocampo's great-grandfather) landed in Baltimore after a fifty-nine-day voyage. On behalf of General José de San Martín, Juan M. de Pueyrredón, and Bernardo O'Higgins, Aguirre asked President Monroe for United States recognition of the United Provinces of Rio de la Plata as an independent country.

In 1823, the man whom Gertrudis Gómez de Avellaneda dubbed "the wandering swan" and whom José Martí was to proclaim "the first poet of the Americas," José María Heredia, arrived in Boston. With his ode to Niagara Falls, Heredia gave a universal voice to the lyric poetry of the New World. This poem, which has been translated into every one of the modern languages, sings to an aspect of nature in the north. It is, nonetheless, deeply rooted in the poet's native Cuba, as through many allusions it evokes the Antillean landscape.

It was also in 1823 that the Venezuelan Andrés Bello pleaded, with Pan-American inspiration, for intellectual as well as politcal freedom in the New World. This seed had been already sown in North America in 1783 by Noah Webster, who had said, "America must be as independent in literature as in politics."

When the Ecuadoran, José Joaquín Olmedo, glorified Bolívar in his poem, "La victoria de Junín," he also paid high tribute to the United States, exalting especially the figure of George Washington. Witness this excerpt: "Now in fraternal friendship we are embraced / By Liberty's firstborn, that happy land / In power and glory above others blest / As on its starry flag / Virginia's star outshines the rest." [4]

Once the wars of independence had been won, however, the newborn republics of the south began a long period of difficult, painful adjustment. But in more than one of them there also arose patriots anxious to forge for their countries a solid and promising future. They were inspired by the experience of the northern republic, which had also lived through growing pains and difficult crises. One case, for instance, was that of Colonel Manuel Dorrego, who, after living in exile in the United States, returned to Buenos Aires an ardent advocate of the federal system at the Constitutional Convention of 1825.

Aside from Bolívar and San Martín, it was a Romantic poet with an acute sense of reality, the Argentinian Esteban Echeverría, one of the first to become aware of the fact that the great revolutionary ideals had not been achieved. With clear sincerity, he observed, "We are independent but not free."

In 1841, the Cuban poetess, Gertrudis Gómez de Avellaneda, wrote her sonnet to Washington, whom she ranked above Napoleon. Here are four lines of that sonnet: "By the genius of victory and strife, / Europe beheld her soil torn and made gory. / But to America's privilege and glory / The genius of good there came to life." [5]

In 1855, yet another illustrious exile, Juan Bautista Alberdi, visited the United States. His experience in ths country and his acquaintance with it were to influence deeply his ideas about public education. He said on the subject of language:

The English language, being as it is that of freedom, of industry, and of law and order, should be even more compulsory than Latin. No young man should be granted a university

degree who cannot speak and write English. This single inno-
vation would result in a basic change in the education of the
young. For, how are they to profit from the example and
civilizing action of the Anglo-Saxon race unless they have
sufficient command of its language?

And now we come upon a man who claimed to have traveled "throughout all civilized areas of the Earth." This adjec-
tive, "civilized," never absent from his pen or tongue as he
strove to "leave a lasting mark on education," reveals at once
that I refer now to Domingo Faustino Sarmiento. Also an
exile from Argentina, Sarmiento had fled to Chile, and the
government of that country was wise enough not only to welcome him, but also to commission him to go abroad and study
educational methods that might be applied in Chile upon his
return.

Sarmiento came to the United States in 1847. It was his first
visit to this country. Here the city of Boston acted as a powerful magnet on his impetuous will. He felt attracted to it for
several reasons: as the birthplace of Benjamin Franklin, whose
Autobiography, together with the Bible, Sarmiento thought
should be found in every school; as the home of Horace Mann,
his model in didactical disciplines; and, above all, as the city
that had enacted the famous compulsory education law of
1676, whereby people became equipped for their struggle for
existence.

Sarmiento was again in the United States from 1865 to 1868,
but this time not on some educational mission for Chile but as
Minister Plenipotentiary and Envoy Extraordinary of his own
country, Argentina. Dynamic as ever, he did not confine himself to his official functions in Washington. Much of his time
he spent traveling about the country, observing its laws and
institutions and mingling with its people, curious about almost everything. He promised himself that he would make the
United States better known in Argentina, while making Argentina better known wherever he went. He tried his best to
make the relations between the two countries agreeable as well

as constructive. And when, finally, he returned to his homeland in 1868, this time as president-elect, he remembered that
the nation he had had the opportunity to live in and to know
had attained true democarcy through the free exercise of
public opinion. When Sarmiento expressed this idea, he was
already familiar with the institutions of France, Spain, Italy,
Germany, Austria, and North Africa. Sarmiento was a man
who could truly say, as he did in the prologue-dedication—addressed to Horace Mann's widow—of his *Conflicto y armonía
de las razas en América,* that it was no small advantage for a
South American to have traveled to different places, as he so
often had, because that enabled him to see his own country in
a wider and better perspective. The closing paragraph of his
book was an exhortation to his fellow Hispanic Americans:
"Let us not hamper, as many in effect propose, the forward
march of the United States, but rather let us try to catch up
with it. As all seas are 'the ocean,' let the whole hemisphere become 'America.' Let us all be 'United States.' "

Besides Sarmiento, there were also in the nineteenth century other outstanding figures who favored positive inter-
American relations. Among them the Puerto Rican Eugenio
María de Hostos and the Cuban José Martí are prominent
examples.

Hostos was a man of great integrity, selfless, wise, having
faith in the future of the hemisphere. He was versed in the history of the United States and its Founding Fathers, and was familiar with the constitutional law and the social institutions
of this country. Hostos was a conscientious reader of English,
as his immortal essays on *Romeo and Juliet* and *Hamlet* make
evident. Impelled by the most exalted ideals of public service,
he traveled throughout the Americas, learned to know and
love them, and with his teachings and exemplary life awoke
everywhere a veneration for truth and justice.

As for Martí, a man of an ever alert genius, none has rivaled him in his studies, at once so broad in scope and so at-
tentive to minute detail, of the great figures of the Americas.

No matter which their country, their field of activity, or their language, Martí reached a profound understanding of each one of them. He was like a painter who not only can depict the physiognomy of his subjects in living and accurate detail, but is able as well to capture their particular states of mind and the traits that define their individualities—all against their appropriate background and in the right perspective and atmosphere.

In 1882, the Ecuadoran, Juan Montalvo, pointed out in his *Siete tratados* the similarities between Washington and Bolívar. Montalvo, who according to the Uruguayan essayist, José Enrique Rodó, "had literature for a religion," made a subtle observation about the prominent men of the United States in the eighteenth century; wrote he:

> . . . should their leader have failed, one hundred Washingtons would have risen to fill the gap, and adequately too. Washington was surrounded by men as outstanding as he, not to say even greater: Jefferson and Madison, wise and of profound thought; Franklin, genius of earth and sky, who snatched the sceptre from tyrants and lightning from heaven . . .

In Chile, two eminent Hispanic Americans later joined Egaña in his just appreciation of the United States; they were José Victorino Lastarria and Francisco Bilbao. Lastarria was a liberal, a man of reason, and a positivist. Having a conscience that rejected doctrinal conciliations, he never wrote to please anybody in particular. Political persecution forced him into exile in Peru; but when he returned to Chile, his social ideas—solvents of the indolence and ignorance of the masses —were still intact.

Lastarria's life, however, did not become fully known until years after his death in 1888. Convinced that the light of the future would shine brighter upon our hemisphere than in the Old World, he had favored immigration provided the incoming Europeans merged with the people of their adopted country—as he knew they did in the United States. So much was

Lastarria familiar with, and admired the history of George Washington's country, that he named his son after the great American patriot. Lastarria did never favor the idea of a Hispanic-American league if it was to be founded with the purpose of opposing the Anglo-Saxons. For him such a position was false, absurd, and pernicious.

The rationalist Bilbao, too, learned what it was to be attacked in his own country. But he had, in compensation, one writer, Eduardo de la Barra, who generously came out in defense of his intelligence, the purity of his motives, and his personal integrity. Very aptly, Bilbao remarked once that "freedom of thought as a natural right, as the right of rights, characterizes the origin and development of [United States] society." Comparing the revolution of the Thirteen Colonies with that of the Spanish colonies to the south, he said:

> These Puritans, or their sons, have presented to the world the most beautiful of constitutions. Thus they guide the destiny of the greatest, the richest, the wisest, and the freest of all peoples. . . . This nation has given us the concept "self-government," just as the Greek gave us "autonomy." And better still, they practice what they preach, carry out what they propose, and create the conditions necessary for the moral and material improvement of the human race.

Lastarria's objection to a league of the Hispanic nations opposing the United States shows that there existed already in South America, at least in part of the public opinion, a movement of reaction against the other America. On the other hand, the fact, truly regrettable, that the United States did not take part in the 1826 Congress of Panama, and that the delegates sent by the American government (Richard C. Anderson, who died on the way, and John Sergeant) did not join the sessions, was interpreted by some as a refusal to engage in a policy of inter-American collaboration.

There were, however, five important facts that should not be overlooked: (1) Bolívar did not include the United

States[6] among the countries originally invited (from Lima, Peru, on December 7, 1824), which were Brazil, La Plata, Chile, Colombia, Central America, and Mexico; (2) it was General Santander who suggested that Bolívar should invite the United States, and Guadalupe Hidalgo, at that time president of Mexico, insisted upon it; (3) President John Quincy Adams and his Secretary of State, Henry Clay, both favored the Panama Congress, but could not get with sufficient time the approval of both branches of the legislature to United States participation; (4) of the Latin American nations themselves, only four were present at Panama; and (5) the republics whose representatives agreed on a plan for federation failed to ratify it officially. Such a precedent explains perhaps the lack of success of yet another congress later (August 10, 1896) convoked in Mexico by another great figure of the hemisphere, the Ecuadoran Eloy Alfaro.

Like Hostos, Alfaro had traveled throughout the Americas. Argentina, Brazil, Chile, Peru, Uruguay, Venezuela, and the United States, in addition to Central America and Mexico, had been part of his crusader's itinerary. It did not take him long to grasp the nature of true Pan-Americanism, and thenceforth he gave himsef to its cause with apostolic zeal. He succeeded in reestablishing friendly relations, by peaceful means, between El Salvador, Guatemala, and Honduras; advocated Cuban independence in a memorable letter to Queen María Cristina of Spain; ignored disruptive differences in his endeavors to unite the nations of the New World on the basis of their common human elements; practiced in his own country—and eventually underwent martyrdom for it—the exalted values of personal integrity and the virtues of exemplary citizenship. The congress convoked by Alfaro had among its purposes "to discuss and decide upon propositions related to the progress and welfare of the American republics and based on justice and fraternity as well as on the political code of the Americas." Costa Rica, Ecuador, El Salvador, Guatemala, Honduras, Mexico, and Nicaragua were the only states that sent delegates to this convention—more than had participated in Panama, but a minority still. In an attempt to interpret the causes of its failure, the Spanish intellectual and statesman, don Francisco Pi y Margall, speculated that many of the governments might have taken it amiss that the initiative came from Ecuador and that the capital of Mexico should have been the one chosen as the congress' site.

The case of this last named country, by the way, takes us back to a time previous to Alfaro's project. With Federalism victorious, Mexico had a new Constitution, promulgated in October, 1824, that was inspired—except in regard to its religious provisions—by that of the United States.[7] Only four years later, however, the Mexicans were strongly censuring the United States Representative, Joel Poinsett, accusing him of undue interference in Mexico's internal affairs. And in 1828, one of the demands made by the revolutionaries was the expulsion of Poinsett. The disagreements between the two countries were barely beginning.

A few years before, a United States citizen, Moses Austin, had obtained authorization from the Mexican government to settle in Texas three hundred Anglo-American families. Under the terms of the agreement, every member of the families settling there had to be a Roman Catholic and all should become Mexican citizens. Before a decade had gone by, more than twenty thousand United States citizens were living in the north of Mexico. They had entered illegally through Texas.

In 1834, soon after becoming dictator of Mexico, General Antonio López Santa Anna had the title deeds of the Texas landowners checked in order to confiscate those which were not valid. He sent troops into Texas and imposed a tax upon all products imported there from the United States. Stephen Austin, son of Moses Austin, was then sent to Mexico as envoy to discuss the situation, but instead was summarily arrested and thrown into jail.

The problem had still another angle. As early as 1810, Miguel Hidalgo had proclaimed in Mexico the defense of the oppressed classes. It was also generally known that the southern republics, Haiti first, had advanced considerably along this road. Yet, in spite of the fact that slavery was forbidden under Mexican law, numerous settlers of United States origin engaged in the slave traffic within the Mexican territory of Texas.

In February, 1836, General Santa Anna, heading an army of three thousand, overwhelmed the garrison of fewer than two hundred men at El Alamo. Then there arose the battle cry, "Remember the Alamo!" On March 2, 1836, Texas adopted its Declaration of Independence. On April 21, the Texan Army, under the command of Sam Houston, fell by surprise upon Santa Ana's forces at San Jacinto. Four hundred Mexicans were killed, two hundred wounded, and seven hundred and thirty-one were taken prisoner. Among the latter was Santa Ana himself. Sam Houston opposed his execution and spared his life. Texas became an independent republic. Its first vice-president, Lorenzo de Zavala, was a Mexican writer and orator who had collaborated in drafting the Declaration of Independence.

It was no secret in 1845 that the United States government was planning to extend the country's southwestern boundaries. Mexico was to be forced into a war—in fact, it did start the following year. It was a war so unpopular, even in the United States, that all attempts to recruit a sufficient number of volunteers failed.

Many important voices rose expressing the national reaction. Ulysses Simpson Grant, who at the time was an army lieutenant and later became president, condemned the war as "one of the most unjust ever waged by a stronger against a weaker nation." Henry David Thoreau criticized the official policy in terms of such violent disapproval that he was arrested. Ralph Waldo Emerson, Daniel Webster, John Quincy Adams, John C. Calhoun, Henry Clay, and Robert E. Lee were among the many figures eminent in the literary, parliamentary, and military fields who spoke out against the war, voicing their disapproval of the government's attitude. When a motion was introduced in the House, on January 12, 1848, for a vote of thanks to the army and navy officers engaged in combat against Mexico, Abraham Lincoln, then a congressman from Illinois, said he had no objection to honoring the combatants, but attacked the Chief Executive, James K. Polk, saying that "the war with Mexico was unnecessarily and unconstitutionally started by the President."

Outstanding historians, Charles and Mary Beard, W. E. Woodward, and James Truslow Adams, among others, coincide in their anathema of the Mexican war. John D. Hicks, for instance, reminds us that that act of aggression against a weak neighbor was castigated as unbecoming the national honor. An exception could be, perhaps, John D. Smith, in his books, *The Annexation of Texas* and *The War with Mexico*. But even he does not show outright approval: he merely claims that the United States was not totally responsible for the conflict. William Spence Robertson summarized the situation as follows: "The United States thus gained a vast domain but aroused the apprehensions of the other countries to the south." And Texas, the territory torn away from Mexico, was not immediately welcomed into the Union despite its great extension and its splendid outlook for the future. For nine years it existed as an independent republic before being allowed to become a part of the United States.

Would it be possible to find in any other nation—whatever its history, language, or culture—another such group of representative men capable of rising above the feeling, "My country, right or wrong," men with courage enough to set truth and the sense of justice above domestic politics and nationalistic chauvinism? Would there be any other country where such opinions can be published, widely circulated, and freely quoted, and, moreover, without suppression by the government, permitted to be reproduced in textbooks and assigned as supplementary reading in elementary schools, high schools, and colleges?

Professor John A. Crow, a good friend to the peoples south of the Rio Grande, has an interesting comment on this subject. In his book, *The Epic of Latin America,* after referring to the war with Mexico as "the greatest outrage ever committed by the United States against a foreign power," he goes on to add that "Sarmiento and Mitre . . . regarded the Mexican war as a mere boundary dispute without hemispheric significance." Professor Crow also reminds us that "Alberdi, who was writing his brilliant essays from exile in Chile, did not let the Mexican war in any way affect his praise and admiration for the United States. Neither did the distinguished Chilean writers, Lastarria and Bilbao, whose panegyrics of the northern republic continued unabated."

It is also pertinent to mention that when the Mexican patriot, Benito Juárez, was imprisoned on Santa Anna's return to power in 1853, he sought and found sanctuary in the United States, in the city of New Orleans. And lastly, in strict historical honesty we must admit that there have been armed conflicts over boundary demarcations between other nations of our hemisphere, and that the contestants were by no means always equal in military strength, territorial extension, or economic resources.

Despite these realities, there have been people wanting to see in the Monroe Doctrine a political instrument advantageous only to the nation of its origin. Let just one instance suffice: the title given by the Mexican writer, Carlos Pereyra, to one of his books, *El Mito de la Doctrina Monroe.* However, there have been also some others of a different mind, like the great Colombian essayist, Baldomero Sanín Cano, who pointed out that had there not been to the north a nation powerful enough to pit itself against the old aggressive powers of Europe, the peace of our hemisphere would have been seriously endangered.

Ruy Barbosa, a wise Brazilian statesman who had a very high esteem for Anglo-Saxon culture, credited the splendid example of the United States with the fact that Brazil, at long last, freed its slaves in 1888. Speaking of the Constitution of the United States, he declared that the Brazilian one should be modeled on it, as the only other alternatives would be either the Swiss brand of democracy, unsuitable to so vast a territory, or the shifting experiments of France, incompatible with the conditions of a people naturally inclined to a confederate type of state organization.

Following Spain's final military defeat in the New World and the Far East, admirers of the might of the United States seemed to appear everywhere. In Latin America, however, a chorus of protesting voices arose, with two outstanding ones among them.

On May 20, 1898, Rubén Darío published in *El Tiempo,* of Buenos Aires, his article "El triunfo de Calibán." In it he expressed his intense love of Spain and his passionate hostility against the United States, and warned the Spanish-speaking nations to be on guard against the threat of the north.

The United States, to be sure, would commit errors in the future. But at the time he wrote this article, Darío overlooked the fact that a new nation, Cuba, had arisen as a result of the Spanish-American War. It also escaped his prevision that in due course the United States would prepare the Philippines for independence and Puerto Rico for freedom.[8]

The other dissenting voice was that of the Uruguayan, José Enrique Rodó. He also made manifest use of the Caliban image. But if its intended allusion disappeared in time from Darío's position, it did not from the sentiments of those influenced by Rodó. And it invaded many other minds when the relations between Colombia and the United States deteriorated early in our century over the Panama question. True, a new Hispanic-American republic was born—Panama itself. But the procedures utilized by Theodore Roosevelt hurt Colombia deeply.

A Peruvian, Francisco García Calderón, spoke of "the North American menace" and affirmed that there was fear of it everywhere. Another notable Peruvian, José Santos Chocano, warned in one of his poems "not to trust the blue-eyed man." Yet, Chocano would later take pride in his friendship with President Wilson, and in another poem said that "the Americas should, as they aspire to be free, imitate [the United States] first, and then try to be its peer." [9]

An Argentinian, Manuel Ugarte, called the United States the "new Rome," but added, "to hate the United States is a low sentiment that leads nowhere; to despise it, a display of rustic lack of common sense." Ugarte went on to say that "it would be madness to desire the downfall of the United States: things have come to such a point that its ruin would spell our catastrophe."

The Mexican, José Vasconcelos, declared that "it was a great misfortune not to have acted as cohesively as those of the north, that prodigious race upon which we are wont to heap insults."

Still, a number of South American countries—Haiti, the Dominican Republic, Nicaragua, Honduras, and Mexico—became involved in trouble with the United States. The fact is that, in this respect, the Wilson administration was not such as to dispel memories of President Theodore Roosevelt.

By the same token, it should be said also that the relations between not a few of the Hispanic-American countries themselves, quite independently of the United States, were not happy either. As early as November 1, 1873, in a letter published in *La Opinión*, of Talca, Chile, Eugenio María de Hostos observed: ". . . and it so happens that over questions of boundaries, that is to say, of empty space, half of Latin America neglects the present, which should be filled with work, and forgets about the future, which should be of union for work, to engage instead in an arms race and in going to war and fighting one another in fratricidal conflict." [10]

In 1922, during the administration of Warren G. Harding, Colombia and the United States officially put an end to their dispute, with the latter paying the former a compensation of $25,000,000.

President Hoover recalled the Marines from Port-au-Prince and Managua. His successor, Franklin D. Roosevelt, inaugurated the Good Neighbor Policy.

Then, the American states, meeting first in Chapultepec and later, with the other nations of the world, in San Francisco, made memorable progress in the field of common interests and responsibilities. The Rio de Janeiro Treaty, signed in 1947, strengthened at the time the Monroe Doctrine, asserting that an attack against any one of the American republics would be considered an attack upon all.[11] In 1952, Puerto Rico became a Commonwealth with the approval of the majority of its voters and the ratification of both branches of Congress, at the time controlled by the Republican Party, and of President Truman, of the Democratic Party.

One of President Eisenhower's earliest decisions was to appoint his brother Milton, then President of Pennsylvania State University, to lead a group that would officially visit ten of the southern republics—a twenty thousand-mile trip—to study the problems affecting the entire American hemisphere. Shortly thereafter, the Chief Executive of the United States and President Ruiz Cortines of Mexico met at a point on the frontier. The occasion was the inauguration of a hydroelectric project serving both their countries.

Not only did Dr. Milton Eisenhower, by then president of Johns Hopkins University, make a second study and investigation trip to Latin America, but the United States president himself visited Mexico again for a meeting with President López Mateos in Acapulco, 1959. One of the results of their exchange of views was the purpose of fomenting other mutually beneficial enterprises.

A resolution approved in Caracas, on March, 1954, could serve as a guidepost for a hemispheric policy. Thanks to the prompt and efficacious mediation of the Organization of American States in January, 1955, when it was admitted that Costa Rica had been attacked by aircraft with bases in a foreign country, "war in Central America," as the then Secretary General of the O.A.S., the Chilean Carlos Dávila, declared, "was prevented."

During February and March, 1955, Vice-President Richard Nixon made a goodwill tour through the Caribbean region. The friendly welcome Nixon was then granted fooled those who look upon the countries to the south without sufficient knowledge of their problems and thus fail to recognize the symptoms of their ills. These people were unable to foresee the show of frustration, irresponsibility, and protest—opportunistically and viciously exploited by the Communists—that greeted Nixon three years later with a dramatic showdown in Peru and Venezuela.

This unfortunate situation, carried as it was to unforgivable extremes, created great concern among honest and conscientious government leaders. They wondered about how a climate that would permit the peoples of the hemisphere to understand and help one another on a basis of sound solidarity could be propitiated.

We know that seventy-five percent of Hispanic Americans who studied outside their countries between 1928 and 1953 attended schools in the United States. And let us remember, too, what a considerable number of works in the fields of history, geography, archeology, psychology, economics, architecture, painting, and Spanish-American literature, outstanding by their splendid quality as well as by their noble motivation, have had their source in colleges, universities, or foundations of the United States.

The failures of the past should be used only to prevent their recurrence in the future, not to keep alive debilitating and destructive resentments. Especially at a time of world crisis, when the Antichrist goes around rampant, bent on giving unto Caesar even that which, being the soul's heritage, belongs to God. Ironically, this power is incapable of providing in return, even when imposing its rule upon a people so industrious as the Germans (as evidenced by the eastern zone of that country), neither bread for the body nor freedom for the life and the activity of the spirit.

Projects like those of sanitation and public health successfully completed in Panama through the cooperation of Americans of diverse nationalities; services like those rendered to more than one republic by initiative of the Rockefeller Foundation; experiences such as that of the Organization of American States, diligently acting as an instrument for the prevention of international conflict—all witness to what an extent the human condition can be bettered when we fully realize that what benefits one benefits all.[12]

Inspired by such realities, each setting aside prejudices that do so much harm, regarding the other fairly and drawing support from mutual esteem and respect, thus complementing one another, we will be able to diminish material poverty, relax the psychological tensions that beset the entire world, and help to keep alive for mankind the Christian essence of our civilization.

[From *Expresión de Hispanoamérica*, Vol. I, San Juan, Puerto Rico, Instituto de Cultura Puertorriqueña, 1960.]

3*
Rubén Darío and the United States: (A) Ariels and Calibans

In 1907, in the poem, "La canción de los pinos," from his book, *El canto errante,* Rubén Darío published the briefest of his manifestoes: "Romantics we are—who who is is not a Romantic?" [1]

Then and there did he confirm himself as a lover of dreams who had his sources in the remote past and advanced toward the future.

Darío was forty then.

In 1889 he composed his sonnet to Walt Whitman, which saw light the following year in the second edition of his book, *Azul,* published in Guatemala. The very first line of this sonnet, "In his iron land . . ." already gives us a hint of Darío's preconceptions about the United States.

Four years later, in 1893, Darío stopped over in New York for the first time. He was only twenty-six. His Romanticism had not yet been filtered through the many-layered culture that he was to accumulate gradually with the fine intuition of a self-taught genius. Life had not yet matured his spirit to that point he reached later when, with a broader mind, he recognized that the verbal cliché is harmful because it encloses the mental cliché—which perpetuate a rigid immobility. [2]

The metal with which Darío's imagination had armored the country of Whitman now met his eye in the architecture of

Manhattan, which was to him not only "the iron island" but also "the gory, the cyclopean, the monstrous capital of the bank note." [3]

From former fancies and actual observation, Darío went on to reflections of a different kind. It was no longer a question of a superficial sketch: almost at once he began to work on a new outline: "One gets the impression that from the ground of Manhattan a colossal Uncle Sam will suddenly arise calling the nations to an unprecedented auction, and that the auctioneer's mallet falls upon cupolas and roofs with a deafening metallic thunder." [4]

To Darío, New York was a monster. Looking at Broadway, he fell prey to a nightmarish anxiety. In the murky palette with which he depicted Manhattan shines only one exceptional hue of clear approbation: in that very place he had seen "extremely beautiful women."

Darío's scope extended itself later beyond the limits of Manhattan. His canvas became wider. It was not long before he used an epithet that has been often quoted and much discussed in Hispanic-American letters ever since. "Caliban reigns in the island of Manhattan, in San Francisco, in Boston, in Washington, in the whole country," said Darío. His generalization has been applied to the entire panorama of the United States.

Without himself realizing it then, this reference to Caliban provided a clue that would recur significantly in the future. With this clue, and with another one that Darío released on May 20, 1898, he not only anticipated a symbol later used by José Enrique Rodó but also the genesis of the negative aspect of the latter's book, *Ariel,* regarding the first of the American republics. For Darío continued in this vein: "He [Caliban] has succeeded in establishing the empire of matter, from its mysterious state with Edison to the apotheosis of the hog in that overwhelming city, Chicago. Here Caliban soaks up whiskey as he soaked up wine in Shakespeare's play. He grows and expands. No longer the slave of any Prospero, no more tortured by any airy spirit, he fattens and multiplies: his name is Legion." [5]

Two of the epithets used by Darío, "cyclopean" and "Caliban," had already been hurled at the United States by other writers. He himself tells about it in his book, *Los raros* (1896) : " 'Those cyclops . . .' says Groussac; 'those ferocious Calibans,' writes Peladan."

This example shows how Darío was influenced by the Francophile viewpoint of Paul Groussac, who was born in Toulouse and went to Argentina at eighteen, and by the pugnacious and eccentric Joseph Peladan, writer of fiction and founder of the Rosicrucian Order. It also tells us that when Rodó, as we shall see, took the same line, his was already a fourthhand version.

Born in Uruguay on July 17, 1872, Rodó was five years younger than the Nicaraguan Rubén Darío. His book, *Ariel,* published in 1900, is that of a young man, well-read for his twenty-eight years, but still falling short of the intellectual maturity his theme required. The author takes here a bold stance, but continually brings in other people's opinions to prop up his own arguments.

I have already mentioned that clue Darío gave us on May 20, 1898. Spain having been defeated by the United States, Darío published his article, "El triunfo de Calibán" (Caliban's Victory) , in *El Tiempo,* Buenos Aires.

Epithets, hostile and impassioned, crowd in it one upon another. The men of the United States are "buffaloes with silver teeth," "haters of Latin blood," "barbarians." "Red faced, heavy, and gross, they walk down the streets of their cities pushing and rubbing against one another like animals in their hunt for the dollar. . . . They eat and eat, calculate, drink whiskey, and make millions." [6] Not even the women, whom he had spared in 1893, escape Darío's lash in 1898: "Among them [the Americans] even gaiety is hard, and the female, while very beautiful, is made of elastic rubber." [7] [The Americans] are "stupendous gorillas . . . all the winds of the centuries will be insufficient to polish their enormous Beast." [8] Darío winds up with an emphatic conclusion: "No, I cannot side with them; I cannot be for the triumph of Caliban." [9]

At the very beginning of *Ariel,* in the third paragraph of the book, Rodó explained that his spirit of the air represented "the predominance of reason and sentiment over low, irrational impulses," [10] for it corrected in the superior man, "with life's persevering chisel, the vestiges of Caliban, symbol of sensuality and baseness." [11]

It is very interesting to note that, while Darío gave credit for his symbols to Groussac and Peladan, Rodó did not relate his with Darío's, which preceded them—not even when referring specifically to Poe, who happened to be the first in Darío's book, *Los raros,* and in whose praise Darío had first alluded to Caliban:

> By God's will, there occasionally springs from among these powerful monsters a being superior by nature who takes wings and flies toward the eternal Miranda of the ideal. When that happens, Caliban mobilizes Sycorax against him, and he is exiled or killed. This the world witnessed in the case of Edgar Allan Poe, that unhappiest of swans who has best known of dreams and death.[12]

Compare the following passage from Rodó's *Ariel:*

> And this supreme energy with which the genius of North America—daring hypnotist—seems to lull the Fates to sleep and bring them under its sway, is to be found even in the particular instances that seem to us exceptional and divergent in that civilization. Nobody will deny that Edgar Poe is an anomalous and rebellious individual among those people. His select spirit is like one unassimilable particle in the national soul: no wonder it went about among the others with a sense of infinite loneliness.[13]

When he wrote *Ariel,* Rodó had already read *Los raros.* He had also corresponded with Darío. And it was in that very year, 1896, when he wrote the critical essay on Darío's *Prosas*

profanas that would serve as preface to the 1899 edition of
that book. Moreover, in a letter written on January 16, 1899,
Rodó lamented that when Darío stopped over in Montevideo
—where the ship "Vittoria" touched port—it had not been
possible for him "to clasp that friendly hand." [14] In this same
letter Rodó expressed the opinion that the best of *Azul* is in its
prose, while the chief merit of *Prosas profanas* lies rather in its
poetry.

He might well, when he, too, commented on Poe's case,
have mentioned Darío's essay. But, ever more of a Francophile
than Darío then was, he did not make reference to what he
had read in *Los raros*. Instead, he went to Baudelaire, who
had "profoundly" pointed out, as a fundamental trait in Poe's
heroes, their "superhuman courage and the indomitable
strength of their will." [15]

In his article, "El triunfo de Calibán," Darío raised his banner of protest against Yankee power. He commented then:
"There have been in Peru manifestations of approval for the
triumph of the United States; and Brazil, sad to say, has made
more than manifest its interest in playing games of give-and-
take with Uncle Sam." [16]

Had Rodó read this article and had he its words in mind
when he wrote the following in *Ariel?*: "That powerful federation [the United States] is achieving a sort of moral conquest
over us. A feeling of admiration for its greatness and power is
rapidly infusing the spirit of our leaders and, perhaps even
more, that of our masses—impressionable and easily fascinated
by victory as they are." [17]

Also in his "Triunfo de Calibán," Darío once again turned
to Poe while dwelling on his charges against the United States:
". . . their Poe, their great Poe, poor swan drunk on pain and
alcohol, was a martyr to his dream in a country where he will
never be understood." [18]

And Rodó in *Ariel*, still not mentioning Darío: "True art
has managed to exist in such an environment only as a form of

individual rebellion. Emerson and Poe are there like members of a species ejected from its true medium by a geological cataclysm." [19]

Let us keep in mind that *Ariel* was published in 1900. This happens to be the year in which Darío and Rodó were to find themselves in fundamental disagreement. Said Rodó in this book:

> When Tocqueville wrote his masterpiece, however, there still glowed in Boston, that Puritan citadel and city of learned traditions, a glorious constellation that shines in the intellectual history of this century with the magnitude of universality. And, what heirs have Channing, Emerson, and Poe left? Mesocratic leveling, hastening its devastating action, tends to dilute to the vanishing point what little character was left to that precarious intelligentsia.[20]

But by that time Darío had lived longer and seen more.

Earlier, looking out upon Manhattan, not having yet seen the capital of France, he had ventured this comparison: "One seems to hear the voice of New York, the echo of a vast soliloquy of figures. How different the voice of Paris must be as one gets near—pleasing like a song of love, poetry, and youth!" [21]

At last in Paris, Darío looked forward to the realization of one of his "great desires": that of talking with Verlaine.[22] Here is how he described the encounter:

> Certain evening, at the Café D'Harcourt, we came upon the Faun himself; he was surrounded by equivocal acolytes. He had the same distorted appearance with which Carriere simulates his looks in his marvelous portrait. Obviously, he had drunk his fill. Now and then he would answer a question put to him by his companions, intermittently banging his fist on the marble tabletop. We approached with [Alejandro] Sawa, who introduced me as "a [Spanish] American poet, an admirer, etc." I murmured something in bad French with all the devotion I could muster, ending my little speech with the word "glory." That did it. Who knows what might have happened that afternoon to the unfortunate genius: the fact is

that, turning to me and without stopping his table-banging, he
said in a low, guttural voice: *La gloire . . . la gloire . . . M*
—— *M*—— *encore!* . . . I thought it prudent at this point to
leave and wait for a more propitious occasion. It never came.
Several times I saw him again, but always pretty much in the
same condition. It was truly sad, painful, grotesque, and tragic.
Poor *Pauvre Lelian! Priez pour le pauvre Gaspard!* . . .[23]

How could Darío, after having lived in 1893 this unforget-
tably pathetic experience, commit again, in 1898, in "El
triunfo de Calibán," the error of blaming the whole of
United States society for Edgar Allan Poe's personal tragedy?
But then came the year 1900 and, while Rodó reiterated the
ideas he had expressed in *Ariel* about "the precarious intelli-
gentsia" of the United States, Darío, back in Paris, where he
had seen the sad sight of "Pauvre Lelian," visited the World's
Fair. He went to the United States exhibit. He wanted especially to see wherein lay "the superiority of the Anglo-
Saxons," [24] as he confessed in his article of August 27 entitled
with those words. And, what did he see there? How did it
affect his thinking? Let him tell us: "This adolescent and colossal people has once again shown its plethoric vitality. As farm-
ers, the North Americans have fairly won many prizes; as
mechanics and industrialists, they rank with the first; as culti-
vators of the human body's grace and beauty, their athletes,
disc-throwers, and high-jumpers deserve to have their glories
sung by a present-day Pindar; . . ."
The material, the mechanical, the physical—was that all?
No; next came the complete reversal that brought him in ideologic conflict with Rodó, who, remember, had already published his study on Darío's *Prosas profanas*. Darío had a good
deal more to say about the people of the United States. He
went on:

. . . as artists, they have shown us Latins, who are wont to
deny them ability and taste for the arts, such painters as
Sargent and Whistler, as well as several sculptors with daring

thumbs and valiant chisels. At the Fine Arts Palace here, new names have been revealed, such as those of Platt, Winslow Homer, and John Lafargue. The latter's canvases on Samoan themes make him the R. L. Stevenson of painting. No; those strong men from the north do not lack the artistic gift. They, too, can think and dream.[25] We Latin Americans cannot as yet display to the world constellations in our intellectual firmament with stars as bright as Poe, Whitman, Emerson. Over there, if the majority are consecrated to the cult of the dollar, it also flourishes, within the plutocratic empire, an intellectual minority of undeniable excellence. So vast is that ocean, that there are upon its bosom isles that bear the rarest blooms of the most exquisite spiritual flora. (Where in Europe can one find a publication superior to the *Chap Book?*) Whistler has influenced one of the currents of contemporary French art now in vogue. Two of the most outstanding names in modern French poetry are those of two North Americans, Villié-Griffin and Stuart Merril. The Yankees have a school of their own in Paris as well as in Athens. Amongst these millions of Calibans, the most marvelous Ariels are born. Their language has evolved rapidly and vigorously; the Yankee writers resemble the English less than do the Latin Americans those of Spain.[26]

Darío knew then, and said it, that it is not easy to love the Anglo-Saxons; but he also knew, and confessed, that it is impossible not to admire them.[27]

Rodó's question—"What heirs have Channing, Emerson, and Poe left?"—already answered by Darío, would be answered also again and again by the Nobel Prize Committee on Literature, which, up to the year 1962, had chosen six United States writers: Sinclair Lewis, Eugene O'Neill, Pearl Buck, Ernest Hemingway, William Faulkner, and John Steinbeck. Moreover, the people of the United States themselves had something important to add to the matter when they made Robert Frost's last book, *In the Clearing*, a best seller while the poet was still alive.

Appropriating Lincoln's words, "With malice toward none, with charity to all," one could yet point out that poets of the stature of José María Heredia, José Asunción Silva, Porfirio

Barba Jacob, Delmira Agustini, Alfonsina Storni, César Vallejo, and Leopoldo Lugones, to name just a few, were never
any luckier than Poe in their own countries.

As for Europe, were we to take a census of artists of genius
who were misunderstood, abused, and driven to desperation,
of poets unfortunate, reviled, persecuted, and condemned, the
list would not be a short one. It was in France, that very
France from whose literature Rodó constantly sought nourishment and with which his *Ariel* is saturated, where Villon
would cry, *"Je ris en pleurs."* And this bitter, tearing voice has
not, after five centuries, been stilled, nor will it ever be wherever the Greco-Roman cultural heritage still lives. Let the
guillotined head of the classicist André Chénier bear witness
to this. Gerard de Nerval, too—a scholar of languages dead
and alive, Oriental and European, writer of comedies and
dream-enchanted poet—when he hanged himself in a Paris
street. Let Alfred de Musset, poisoned by lovelessness and ab-
sinthe, tell us. Take the evidence of that deliberate and scru-
pulous stylist, possessed of so acute an esthetic sensibility,
Flaubert, when he was haled before a court to defend himself
and his book, *Madame Bovary,* against charges of pornogra-
phy and offenses against religion. At this trial, the author was
exonerated but his book was severely censured in the judges'
sentence. Let Baudelaire bear witness: he, too, was tried on the
publication of his *Fleurs du Mal,* and in his case the prosecu-
tor, Ernest Pinard, was successful. The book was withdrawn
from circulation, and a majority of its readers were attracted
to it only because of the morbid themes publicized by scandal
during the *cause célèbre.* But that was not all: even after many
years had elapsed, the poet was deprived by his relatives of the
right to administer his own property. Is it any wonder that
Baudelaire, lost between the images of the Madonna and
Satan, beaten down by official France and crushed by his own
family should have become a drunkard and an opium addict?
Let alcoholic, miserably poor, imprisoned Paul Verlaine bear
witness too. See him looking for shelter in paupers' hospitals,

which with melancholic irony he would call his winter
palaces. . . .

I have mentioned Lincoln once already. It is especially significant now, in this context, to recall that his prose was of
such high literary value, so imbued with profound religious
feeling and noble spiritual vigor, that Walt Whitman regarded it as a new dawn of poetic revelation. The deep affection felt by the author of *Leaves of Grass* for Lincoln and his
grief when Lincoln died find tender manifestation repeatedly
in "When Lilacs Last in the Dooryard Bloom'd":

> O how shall I warble myself for the dead one
>   there I loved?
> And how shall I deck my song for the large sweet
>   soul that has gone?
> And what shall my perfume be for the grave of
>   him I love?
>
> . . . .
>
> I'll perfume the grave of him I love.
>
> . . . .
>
> To adorn the burial-house of him I love? [28]

Was it because the martyred president was his countryman
that Whitman invoked and mourned Lincoln that way?

In January, 1898, José Martí confessed in a letter to his
friend, Angel Peláez, that he had wept and trembled on learning of the death of two men personally unknown to him: one
of them was Lincoln.[29]

Why bring up Lincoln when speaking of Poe? Because both
were born in the same year, 1809, and because Lincoln, being
the son of poor country folks and self-educated, was twice exalted by his and Poe's fellow citizens and contemporaries to
the presidency of the United States.

On November 20, 1903, Rubén Darío wrote to Juan Ramón
Jiménez from Paris—the Paris where he lived and suffered,

whose voice he no longer found pleasing as a song of love, poetry, and youth. This time he said he was disgusted with men of letters and with all the rubbish of the so-called literary life.[30] In that same year, 1903, his book, *La caravana pasa,* was written. In its first chapter Darío said: "Poetry is at a low level now in France. Although they have made a divinity of Hugo, books of verse do not sell in the bookstores. Even the new poets cannot break the ice. This cannot be a symptom of progress; in England and in the United States there is no family who does not keep the works of their favorite poet in their living room bookcase." [31]

Years later, in *El canto errante* and in the "Epístola" (addressed from the island of Majorca to the wife of the Argentinian poet Leopoldo Lugones), Darío told how unhappy he felt in Paris:

> So I returned to Paris, that fearsome enemy,
> Neurotic city, center of madness where I'm free
> To play out at will my role of *sauvage*
> In this focus of every *surmenage.*
> Shut up in my cell at the Rue Marivaux,
> Trusting only myself, my ego guarding from every foe.
> And if, señora, I could protect it there,
> Were it not for my being what Parisians call a *pear!*
> I creep into my corner, but intrigue finds me out,
> Petty miseries, friends' betrayals put me to the rout,
> As does ingratitude. My accursed sentimental view
> Of the world constricts my heart anew,
> And so every rascal can exploit me as he would.[32]

It seems strange, therefore, that in a reference to the Cuban-French poet, Augusto de Armas, Darío, who called his verse "a flower of France," [33] should overlook the fact that de Armas had suffered extreme poverty and misery while living in that same Paris.

Again, writing about "Paris and foreign writers," in *Letras* (1911), Darío would insist on the subject in a manner that we might call definitive: "I was more passionate and wrote more "Parisian" things before coming to Paris than during the time I lived in Paris. I could never help but feeling like a stranger among those people. And, whatever became of those old-time cute stories?" [34]

Just as Musset, who lamented that he had arrived too late in too old a world—*Je suis venu trop tard dans un monde trop vieux* [35]—Darío lamented and protested that he loathed the life and the time into which he had been born.[36]

It was this same Romantic mood that prevented him in his youth, evoking Poe in Manhattan, and again being somewhat older and mourning over *fin de siècle* Spain, from asking himself: Where have there not been, where will not there always be both Ariels and Calibans? For later on, when the hour of reasonableness came to him, Darío was willing to make amends, as in that occasion in August 27, 1900, in which he recognized that in the United States "amongst those millions of Calibans the most marvelous Ariels are born."

[From *Seis estudios sobre Rubén Darío*, Madrid: Biblioteca Románica Hispánica, Editorial Gredos, 1967.]

4✤
Rubén Darío and the United States: (B) "Let not hate shoot its bolt"

The amends made by Rubén Darío in "Los anglosajones" were not to be definitive. His appreciation and judgments of the United States were still to fluctuate, to undergo many ups and downs.

Before writing that article, his rejection of the republic of the north seemed often the manifestation of "Latin" solidarity; some other times, of esthetic sensibility. Then, in 1904, his poem "A Roosevelt" showed definite political reaction. Darío did not think himself to be a poet for the masses, but he was well aware that he would have sooner or later to go to them. He offered this explanation: "If there is politics in these songs, it is because politics is universal. And if you should find here verses addressed to a certain President, it is because they express a continent-wide clamor. Tomorrow we may well be Yankees; in fact, we probably shall be." [1]

To Darío then, Theodore Roosevelt was the embodiment of the United States, and as such "the future invader": "Of confiding America whose blood is partly indigenous / Which still prays to Jesus and speaks the Spanish tongue." [2]

The poem "A Roosevelt" dates from 1904; the preface to *Cantos de vida y esperanza* from 1905. In this book he included the poem, "Los cisnes," which may have been written the same year as his ode to Roosevelt. From "Los cisnes" are

the following lines: "Shall we be given over to those fierce barbarians? / Shall we, so many millions, speak the English
tongue?" [3]

Had Darío's doubts set in a definite mold by that time?
Hardly: "Los cisnes" was preceded in the same book by "Salutación del optimista." He said in this poem: "Abominate the
lips that predict endless misfortune, / Abominate the eyes that
read only zodiacs of grief, / Abominate the hands that stone
magnificent ruins, / Or grasp the arsonist's torch or the dagger
suicidal." [4]

Still in another poem from *Cantos de vida y esperanza*,
"¡Carne, celeste carne de mujer!" in which he exalted the "ce-
lestial" flesh of woman, even such a universal subject came out
tinged with politics: "Useless is the cry of the cowardly legion
/ Of self-interest; useless Yankee / Progress if it disdains
you." [5]

It is very interesting to compare Darío's position in regard
to Spanish America in his ode to Roosevelt with that he had
manifested on the same subject in 1892. In the 1904 poem he
came out as a defender, exalting and glorifying his continent:

> But this, our America, which had her own poets
> From the old times of Netzahualcoyotl,
> Which still bears the imprint of the foot of great Bacchus,
> Which learned the Panic alphabet in centuries gone;
> Which consulted the stars and knew the lost Atlantis
> Whose name comes from Plato resounding to us,
> Which from its remote moments of life
> Lives on light and on fire, on fragrance and love;
> The America of the great Moctezuma, of the Incas,
> The fragrant America Columbus praised so much,
> America the Catholic, America the Spanish,
> The America where said the noble Cuauhtémoc:
> "Bed of roses mine is not"; . . . [6]

Yet, in his 1892 poem, "A Colón," he had denounced, re-
buked, and cried out his inconformity with what he saw, four

centuries after the Discovery, in the peoples of Hispanic America, his own America. Here is part of that poem:

> A spirit of disaster pervades your land:
> Where once the tribe, united, brandished their maces,
> Now flames between brothers perpetual war,
> And carnage among men belonging to the same races.
> The idol of flesh, enthroned, replaces
> The idol of stone of yesteryear,
> And day by day the white dawn gazes
> On fratricidal fields of blood and ashes.
> Disdaining kings, we made our laws
> To cannon clamor and clarion cries,
> And now, in our black kings' sinister favor
> The Cains with the Judases fraternize.
>
> . . . .
>
> Perfidious ambitions no barriers own,
> Our dreamed-of liberty in fragments lies:
> Thus would our caciques never have done
> Who sought their arrows from the mountainsides!
>
> . . . .
>
> Would to God the waters' once intact glaze
> Had never mirrored those fateful sails;
> Nor the stars ever looked in amaze
> Down on the shoreward course of the caravels!
>
> . . . .
>
> The Cross you brought us is on the wane,
> And after many a rabble-born revolution
> The writing rabble has smeared its stain
> On the tongue of Cervantes and Calderón.
>
> . . . .
>
> War, horror, incessant fever most grievously
> Fate upon our path has set:
> Columbus, poor Admiral of the Ocean Sea,
> Pray God have mercy on your New World yet.[7]

If we notice that "A Colón" was never included in a book until its publication in *El canto errante* in 1907—three years after "A Roosevelt" and two after "Los cisnes" and the preface to *Cantos de vida y esperanza*—the full significance of the contrast becomes more apparent. In other words, Darío did not mean his address to the Admiral of the Ocean Sea to be merely timely or applicable only to one specific set of circumstances, that of 1892. Might it not be correct, then, to interpret it as an intended confirmation of what he had already said in the final decade of the nineteenth century?

The "Dilucidaciones," or elucidations, published at the beginning of *El canto errante,* are extremely valuable evidence of the ambivalent attraction that the figure of Theodore Roosevelt exercised upon Rubén Darío. In 1904, he had seen Roosevelt as only "a hunter—primitive and modern, simple and complex." Yet, in the first two paragraphs of "Dilucidaciones" we can read the following:

> The highest praise recently accorded to Poetry and the poets has been expressed in the "Anglo-Saxon" tongue and comes from a man who cannot be suspected of unusual indulgence toward the nine Muses. A Yankee: Theodore Roosevelt. This President of a republic judges the harmonious lyre-bearers more favorably than did the philosopher Plato. Not only does he crown them with roses, but he asserts that they are useful to the state and demands for them public esteem and national recognition. All of which goes to show that this fearsome hunter is a sensible man.[8]

Such words were written by the Rubén Darío who in that same article considered himself a "citizen of the [Spanish] language" and one of "those who fight for our ideals on behalf of the amplitude of culture and freedom." [9]

Also in *El canto errante* Darío included his "Salutación al Águila," a salute to the symbolic bird of the United States. Addressing himself to the American eagle, he said in verse:

> Welcome, magical Eagle, of strong and
> wide-sweeping wings,
> To cover the South with your great
> continental shade;
> To bring in your claws, with red
> brilliance ringed,
> A palm leaf of Glory, as green as
> measureless hope,
> And in your beak the olive branch of a
> vast and fecund peace.[10]

In other words, Rubén Darío's image of the United States at that time—when the Rio de Janeiro Conference was held—was not merely that of a big power with which it would be wise to live at "a vast and fecund peace"; he also cast it in the role of a senior brother who can show his younger ones the ways of "constancy, vigor, and character."

Could it be simply a coincidence that in his "Salutación al Águila" Darío should have honored the United States with a poem similar, as regards technique, to the "Salutación al optimista," with which he had earlier honored Spain? Both poems are written in hexameters and, moreover, as the titles indicate, both are "salutes."

Those who despised or disliked the United States reacted by condemning Darío's welcome to "the eagle" and apostrophizing the author of the poem. Rufino Blanco-Fombona, for instance, is said to have called it a "divine and infamous" poem. On the other hand, one seldom hears quoted that part of the article on the Argentinian Manuel Ugarte in which Darío himself called his ode to Roosevelt "a blast, albeit a rather inoffensive one." [11] Again, in his splendent "Epístola" to Mrs. Leopoldo Lugones, which dealt with his life in Majorca and with events in the recent past, Darío declared, speaking of the Rio de Janeiro Conference and of his second "Salutación," that "I panamericanized / With a vague fear and very little faith / On the land of diamonds and tropical bliss." [12]

Then came the year 1912. In a new book, *Todo al vuelo,* Darío published a series of articles, one of which dealt with Theodore Roosevelt's visit to Paris. There he called the former president "a marvelous example of free, untamed humanity," adding in another paragraph that that "superman" had, for the time being, superseded D'Annunzio and Rostand.[13]

Having thus spoken about such *pas ordinaire* personage— the expression is Darío's—he went on to present Paris, but not necessarily as the capital of enchantment:

> And with this Paris is overjoyed. Paris doesn't know much about the United States but it does know the American dollar and has heard about the forty-story buildings; it has become acquainted with Buffalo Bill and Bostock, and on one memorable occasion it heard Sousa's band play marches and dance tunes at the Place de l'Opera itself. Paris is well aware that the United States has millions to spend and that every year arrive in this Capital of Pleasure a number of tourists who leave behind a goodly portion of those millions. And all these things Paris considers excellent.[14]

To Darío, Roosevelt was no longer, at that particular place and moment, the "primitive hunter" of 1904. No longer was the former American president "one part Washington to four Nimrod." This last name he would apply to Roosevelt again, but in a very different mood: "The jovial Nimrod has had a good press," he said.[15] Then he proceeded in a tone that actually neutralized the protest once voiced in *Cantos de vida y esperanza:*

> He is praised and acclaimed. His phrase about the "big stick" is remembered but by a few, and then only to explain that, as happens with many phrases, the public has changed its meaning, taking one thing for another. Here is the explanation given: that with so much talk about the "big stick," many people have become convinced, and not insignificant people, to be sure, that the slightest lapse would bring down upon other nations a drubbing from Cousin Jonathan. But nothing could be farther from the truth. The words that have caused

such a flurry, especially, and with good reason, among the
Spanish-speaking nations, are these: "There is a homely adage
that runs, 'Speak softly and carry a big stick; you will go far.' "
If the American nation cares to speak in a conciliatory tone
and at the same time decides to build and keep at a pitch of
the highest training a thoroughly efficient navy, the Monroe
Doctrine will go far. What Roosevelt did was simply to para-
phrase in his own fashion an old Roman saying: *Suaviter in
modo, fortiter in re.*[16]

But Darío went on, still heaping praise upon Roosevelt:

He is a force of Nature. And then, people here, some people at
least, were familiar with John Morley's statement: "In the
United States I saw two prodigious natural forces: Niagara
Falls and President Roosevelt, and I cannot decide which of
the two is the more powerful."

This last passage Darío topped off with a bit of light witti-
cism: "And, as you know, John Morley is not a native from
Andalusia." [17]

In his poem, "La gran metrópolis," 1914, Darío told his
readers about his "meditations at dawn." The great metropolis
was New York, a big city that he summarized as "pain, pain,
pain." But as he went deeper into his subject, contrasting what
was sordid and painful with the glamour of pleasure and with
the munificence of the Maecenas, and even while declaring
that there "crowded living had killed all love and feeling," he
did make, as we shall see, capital amends.

In his poem, "A Roosevelt," shaken by the fear that that
"proud and strong exemplar" of the northern nation could be
a living symbol of "the future invader," Darío ended up with
the warning that he might have everything, but "lacked one
thing: God!"

In his interpretation of New York ten years later, Uncle
Sam would be portrayed as one not exactly bent on conquest.
Darío did realize that God was present within the people of
the United States, moved as they were to charity, and loving
healthy joy as they did:

Tall is he and fierce of eye,
On his waiscoat Stars and Stripes
As on his tailcoat and his hat;
For conquest he does not care
But the world is well aware
He's alert, ready to dare
In repose as in bivouac.

In this place all love and feeling
Have been killed by crowded living
But in all there is a God;
And I've seen great tenderness
Reaching out to boys and girls
From the sledded and befurred
Old Santa Claus.

For the Yankee loves his golf
And his horses and his dogs
And his yacht and his football;
But much more loves he joy
With strength and harmony:
A happy, laughing boy
And a girl bright as the sun.[18]

Darío's last important poem was also conceived and written
in New York. Grieving for the destruction of Europe, he
thought of Petrarch's poem to war-torn Italy, *Io vo gridando
pace, pace, pace,* and with these words began his own unforgettable plea, "Pax." The Old World he saw sunken in blood and
broken down with grief, and his poet's cry went out to "the
countries of the dawn"—the peoples of America. He recognized no geographical barriers between them, no separation by
sentiment or duty. It was like a transcendent testament with
which he was resurrecting the idea of union among all the
peoples of the New World; an idea that, as seen in Chapter II,
the Peru-born Chilean, Juan Egaña, had proposed in 1810 in
his *Plan para la defensa general de toda la América.* No word

of negation rose this time to the lips of Hispanic America's greatest poet: Darío's voice now was wholly affirmative:

> O, peoples of ours! O, peoples of ours! Unite
> In hope, and in work, and in peace.
> Seek not out darkness, pursue not chaos
> And do not drench with blood our fertile earth.
> Enough that of old our forefathers fought
> For Country and Liberty, that a glorious clarion calls
> Through all time, under the heavens' vault,
> Washington and Bolívar, Hidalgo and San Martín.
> See the bitter example of Europe undone:
> Her graveyard trenches, her blood-soaked soil
> Where Pity and Sorrow together weep.
> No; let not Hate shoot its bolt—
> Bring to the altar of peace honey and roses.
> Peace to the immense America. Peace in the name of God.
> And as we have the focus of a new culture here,
> Let its principles flow to the South from the North,
> Bringing to life the union that to new triumph leads:
> The Star Spangled Banner with the white and the blue.[19]

No longer was he "panamericanizing with little faith." Darío was never again to write on this subject: he died in 1916. The words of this poem stand as the last will and testament of a man who, struggling through doubt and inner conflict, reached finally his ultimate vision of hemispheric peace and harmony.

There are those who will ask themselves if Darío did **not** write "Pax" under the fleeting influence of emotions, anguished by the bloody war in Europe and his own loneliness in New York. For it is true that he was then living one of his bitterest moments. Yes, we might well question what impulses really led the poet to write in this instance, were it not for the fact that at an earlier time and in different circumstances he had, imbued with the same love of peace, written a similar call to inter-American fraternity. It was in 1909 when Darío composed his *Canto a la Argentina,* written to celebrate that republic's centennial, which occurred the following year. In this poem, six years before "Pax," he wrote:

> Blood soaked the soil of the North
> As it soaked the meridional soil.
> The centuries in such wise
> Ordained that for what is to come,
> To make, if not Paradise,
> At least the happy worker's home,
> With a fullness of citizens' rights,
> An inner link should unite
> And an outer force make one
> The Anglo-Saxon race
> And the Latin American.[20]

These verses are evidence of how, in the poet's mind, the idea of a union of the whole western hemisphere grew and became stronger. They prove that his 1915 poem is indeed his testament, definitive and mature, and with a continental scope: a living legacy from Rubén Darío to the civic conscience of the Americas.

No; let not hate shoot its bolt.

[From: *Seis estudios sobre Rubén Darío,* Madrid: Biblioteca Románica Hispánica, Editorial Gredos, S. A., 1967.]

5 ❋ Some Political Trends in the Literature of Hispanic America

There are millions of human beings, from the Rio Grande to Patagonia, whose language is Spanish and who have a literature of their own. Many of their writers incline to their art just for art's sake; but there are also many poets, essayists, and novelists in Spanish America whose work shows the marks of evident political intention.

In Central and South America, examples of freedom-loving, orderly societies can be seen abiding side by side with nations afflicted with dictatorships or presenting a picture of anarchy. There, many aspirants to public office have forwarded their ambitions by setting off revolutionary explosions, and in most of those countries the coup d'etat has often been used as a shortcut to the highest executive post.

A number of scholars have tried to analyze this state of affairs from an exclusively politic-economic angle. This approach will never be sufficient. Speaking in general, the Spanish heritage, with its egolatry and nomadism, has been a most determining factor in the making of the character and personality of those peoples to the south.

The Spanish conquistadores arrived in the New World subject to no moderating influence, with neither family nor religious ministers to hold them in check. They did not bring their wives with them, and, in his first voyage, Columbus did not include a priest among his crew. Restless, goaded by his own audacious spirit, arriving at exuberant lands whose women were to him exotic and enigmatic, the Spanish adventurer must have felt that he had come upon a whole continent created especially to please his senses with its natural splendor: lands that were his to take as chance offered.

The "Mayflower" Pilgrims, in contrast, set out with their wives and children, determined to secure for themselves the right to practice their religious creed according to the dictates of their Puritan outlook. The whole atmosphere savored of respectable domesticity, and it was from such elements that the Pilgrims evolved and lived out their epic, in extremes of violence and piety, superhuman endeavor and selfless charity.

Against this picture of austere discipline and Bible-cult in the north, the south presented the unpredictable: the Spanish passion for extemporaneous political domination by individuals and for planting the Cross in every corner of the earth.

The exuberant and vital Spaniards were further inflamed by the victories of Ferdinand and Isabella under the banner of Castile. In comparison, the New England colonists seem just a drab group of men and women with a rigid conscience strictly oriented toward their religious aims, the bearers of the civil rights tradition of the Magna Charta. The Spanish, after centuries of fighting the Moor and mingling with them in the same environment—centuries of struggle, coexistence, fraternization, and intermarriage—were free from racial prejudice and arrived in the New World ready to mix their blood with that of the aborigines.[1] The English settlers originated in an island whose sons carry their insularity with them wherever they go. Unlike them, the Spanish set sail from one of the lands most often invaded by foreign races and cultures—Jews, Arabs, and Gypsies among others. So opposite are the two backgrounds that, once we analyze their differences, it is easy to understand why the Spanish did not hesitate to interbreed with the Indians, while the English, as a rule, remained endogamous within their restricted family circles. Bound as they were by these family ties, the settlers of the north explored rel-

atively small areas. The Spanish, fired and spurred on by their
freedom of action as individuals and, in some cases, by the eu-
phoria of extreme youth,[2] scattered over the continental lands,
moved by individual prowess rather than by collective organization. We can and do speak of "the Puritans" in the plural,
but we cannot think of Cortés, Pizarro, Balboa, De Soto, or
Ponce de León except singly, as individuals. And just consider
the vast territories they conquered: from Mexico and California to Panama; from Florida to the Mississippi; from Chile to
Venezuela and the Greater Antilles.

The Puritans did not have to worry about pleasing the
Stuarts, whose world they had firmly and deliberately left behind. The Spaniard, on the other hand, had to ingratiate himself with his sovereigns, whose authority over him persisted
and upon whose favor he depended. Because of this ineluc table necessity, the Spaniard generally tried to impress upon his
rulers the momentousness of every one of his enterprises. This
is probably the reason for one of the most obvious traits of the
earliest Spanish letters and chronicles from the New World:
their exaggeration. The Discoverer himself set the example.
Writing in 1493 to his friends at the Spanish Court after having taken possession of several Caribbean islands, Columbus
extolled his discoveries with hyperbolic wordiness: those were
the richest, most fertile of lands; their landscape was incompa-
rably beautiful; their climate, the mildest; their inhabitants,
the most hospitable, as well as the readiest to embrace Christianity and the most eager to submit to their Sacred Majesties,
the Catholic King and Queen of Spain. This habit of hyper-
bole proved contagious and developed into a tradition of
fraudulent claims.

The Puritans gloried in their self-sufficiency. Men and
women were proud of being able to satisfy their needs with the
work of their own hands. Anxious not merely to earn but also
to deserve their daily bread, they lived lives of exemplary aus-
terity. The Spaniard, on the other hand, would rather starve
than plant and harvest his own food. When forts had to be

built, he sturdily bent his back to the task. But this was part of his duty as a soldier no less than a need of his instinct for self-preservation. Feeling himself to be an aristocrat, he looked down on menial tasks as debasing and injuring to his personal dignity.[3]

Yet, contrary to what one would expect from the approach of each to manual labor, it was Spain, not England, which left in her colonies works of architecture that are the wonder and admiration of all foreigners who see them, albeit not always appreciated as they deserve in their own countries. Attempting to estimate the cost of all of Spain's important architectural works in this hemisphere—not counting fortresses and fortifications—one comes more and more to doubt that her treasury could have been finally enriched by the vast enterprise of the colonization.

Quite often the Spaniard would try to deceive his own countrymen—from the King on down—both in the metropolis and in the new possessions. Many times, too, in his greed for power and command, he would become insubordinate. Yet, not as many heads fell under the executioner's axe by royal order in the Spanish colonies as did in Henry VIII's and Elizabeth I's England, where more than one subject found death the penalty for personal integrity, no less than for failing in his ambition.

A typical example of the rivalries and conspiracies of sixteenth century Hispanic America can be found in one of the viceroyships. Francisco Pizarro, conqueror of Peru, murdered his comrade, Diego de Almagro. Almagro's son thereupon killed Pizarro, only to be in turn decapitated by Vaca de Castro, who was then imprisoned by the viceroy, Núñez de Vela. Gonzalo Pizarro then killed the viceroy. At this point, Valdivia, disregarding his great debt to the Pizarro family, came from Chile to put an end to the power of his former friends.

Of course, this group of scoundrels, rebels, and troublemakers was not representative of Spain as a whole. To offset such an impression of cruelty and duplicity one needs only point to many noble and generous deeds. But that kind of situation shows, first, that the seeds of sedition and violence were sown early and grew fast in Spanish America; [4] and, second, that men who so ruthlessly exterminated one another could hardly be expected—despite the missionaries' selfless intervention— to treat the Indians fairly.

In most of that vast territory, and very especially in Mexico and Peru, the apologists of the Indian and those of the Hispanic tradition sharply disagree. The former assert that the Indians had built a great civilization that was brutally destroyed by the invaders. The latter uphold the theory that, in her New World, Spain created a better and more important empire in lands that had previously reached no significant degree of spiritual development and did not constitute a language community. They point out that some of these peoples were bloodthirsty and superstitious practitioners of witchcraft and sorcery, which in some cases, as witness the astronomy and artistic skill of the Mexicans and the agriculture and architecture of the Incas, startingly contrasted with their knowledge.

There is a heated conflict between the partisans of these two extreme viewpoints. Yet, looking at the picture in its historical perspective, we find that conflict and rivalry are by no means a new development here. It existed among the Indians; was not Huáscar the victim of his own brother, Atahualpa? And, among the colonists, was there not conflict between cruel exploiters of the natives and the apostolic missionaries who braved the powerful in order to love, protect, and instruct the aborigines? The Uruguayan, Zorrilla de San Martín, painted a simplified representation of this situation in his narrative poem, *Tabaré*. In this work, the Spanish commander, don Gonzalo de Orgaz, represents the conquistador who looks upon the Indians as contemptible enemies. His power is defied by Father Esteban, who risks his life in defense of the oppressed, exemplifying the insight and mercifulness of his ministry as it was understood and practiced by countless priests and friars during the Conquest.

It is true that the Spanish demolished beautiful temples and great fortifications; that, worse still, they destroyed established and prosperous kingdoms like that of the Incas. But it is no less true that even the Incas lacked an alphabet and the wheel, and that the succession to their throne, based as it was on brother-sister marriages, seemed a monstrous perversion in European eyes. We might add that, at this time, Spain, having just saved all Europe from the infidels, was approaching the peak of her splendor. The first grammar of a Romance language the world had ever known, Antonio de Nebrija's, had already been produced; a whole new continent had been discovered under Spanish auspices; *La Celestina,* one of the great masterpieces of literature, was soon to appear; and Spain's literary golden age was about to bloom. In this hemisphere, Spain built thousands of costly and beautiful churches, universities, in Mexico and Peru, equal to her own, and public buildings unmatched in number and grandeur by any other empire in history.

The conciliatory and analytical stance assumed by Justo Pastor Benítez in his work, *Formación social del pueblo paraguayo,* is worthy of note as, expounding upon the diverse linguistic and racial elements in his country, he contrasts the original Guaraní groups with the Inca state:

> Those who would stress the importance of our Guaraní heritage try to show Paraguayan culture as simply an indigenous development with European technology superimposed, when in fact we have here a process of transculturation, assimilation, and creation, to which the autochthonous tribes contribute their diverse elements as do the Spanish, who attained primacy because of their culture, their arms, and their introduction of tools, plants, and animals, which together changed the cultural landscape, bringing a new style of life into being. The Indian becomes incorporated into the bloodstream and history of his conquerors. Had the primacy in fact been his, we would now have an autochthonous culture, marginal to Western civilization, albeit with a thin European veneer. Or we would have become one big settlement, like in the Far East. If, on the

other hand, the Indian element had been eliminated, we would now have a republic with no Indian admixture, like the United States and Canada. The Guaraní was not exterminated; he was incorporated. This process is not merely one of hybridization; it is transculturation, the assimilitation to superior forms. . . . The Guaraní lacked the conditions required to become a nation. First of all, they lacked established rights over a well-defined territory. They occupied areas of uncertain extent, were continually at war with other tribes, and their rudimentary institutions did not have the conditions necessary for state formation. To illustrate the idea, we could just say that they never attained the Incaic degree of organization. In a comparison of the two aboriginal cultures, we could add that the Incas had a state, while the Guaranís lived in groups similar to the *ayllus*, the basic unit of Inca organization.

A statesman of the political stature of Hernán Cortés, who was capable of conceiving Mexico as one among many kingdoms under the dominion of one imperial crown, was not a common thing, even among the conquistadores. It is also amazing to discover that, in addition to the Law of Burgos (1512) and the new legislation of the Indies (1542), by 1593 Philip II of Spain had decreed a forty-seven-hour work week for the New World's laborers. Understandably, these principles and laws were often flouted and disobeyed: great distances and the lack of rapid means of transportation were not the best allies to the cause of justice. Ots Capdequí, himself Spanish, points out that there was a true divorce of law and action. But, in what other colonial empire of that time can we find even one law showing such responsible conscience and alert sensibility? When Columbus engaged in the slave trade, Queen Isabella reacted indignantly in defense of the Indians, and asked, "In what way have I empowered the Admiral to give my vassals to anybody?"

Spanish Americans who side with the Indians as victims of Spanish avarice are aggressive in their attacks. We find this attitude in José Carlos Mariátegui, author of *Siete ensayos de interpretación de la realidad Peruana;* we find it again in Luis

Valcárcel, who wrote *Tempestad en los Andes.*[5] In Mexico there is possibly no written work so radical, sarcastic, and biased as Diego Rivera's murals. These three men just mentioned—Mariátegui, Valcárcel, and Rivera—are evidence that the Indian problem in Hispanic America is not one to be relegated to history, but one that presently demands serious political and social thought. This becomes the more obvious when we recall that Mariátegui and Rivera are among the foremost exponents of Marxism in their respective countries.

The consequences of such a situation are as evident as they are dangerous. Communist propaganda is directed to the South American Indians in understandable and seductive tones: they are wheedled into believing in a return to a golden age similar to the Inca empire. The Indian is promised that the land—the land torn from his ancestors, the land he deeply and passionately loves—will be redistributed; that the capitalist system, which has exploited him, will be destroyed; and that he will be redeemed by getting his share of the total economic production.

Do not forget that over sixty percent of Peru's population is Indian, and that this means that at least five million human beings are being urged to get ready for the reconquest of their land. Valcárcel expresses this hope in his *Ruta cultural del Perú.* If to the five millions in Peru we add the teeming aboriginal masses of Ecuador, Bolivia, Guatemala, Venezuela, Colombia, and other countries to the south, we can begin to see the full scope of the revolutionary message.

At the opposite extreme, the selfish indifference of ultraconservatives and the harshness of foreign capitalists established in some of these southern countries invite and exacerbate rebellion.[6]

Equally dangerous are the double-dealing demagogues who, posing as liberal defenders of the Indian, are, in fact, as bad as the heartless traffickers who exploited him, wearing away his miserable life in their plantations and industries. All these exploiters were later joined by politicians of the same stamp who used the Indian to keep themselves in power. They granted the Indian rights for which they had not even begun to prepare him; they took advantage of the ignorance of the indigenous masses and unscrupulously fomented social hatreds. In one South American country, not Peru, I saw ragged, starved-looking men with an expression of unfathomable loss in their eyes, armed by the government with rifles to defend the "rights" it had granted them. Meanwhile, in this same country's so-called "autonomous" universities, the Marxists, alert and militant as always, participate in academic elections in which they manage to fill all posts—from that of rector on down—with their followers. Instead of education, conscientious leadership, and a policy for their progress as a social class, all that the Indians actually get is a demagogic farce. As for the universities, Marxism predominates in them and is reflected in the ideology of their directors as well as in the philosophy of their publications.

As a rule, the Indian has been ignored when not trampled upon and degraded. Public education policies, except in Mexico, have hardly been concerned with him. In Brazil, an attempt has been made toward a rapprochement with the Indian tribes, thanks initially to the advice of a statesman, José Bonifacio de Andrada e Silva, and later to the magnanimous intervention of Colonel Cándido Mariana da Silva Rondón as president of the National Council for the Protection of the Indians.

Many Hispanic-American countries lack a middle class to serve as a backbone of the national economy, as is the exemplary case of Uruguay.

All these various elements of discord and dissolution stimulate radical discontent and deep-rooted individual and social frustrations. In consequence, these countries lay themselves open to communism, which often thrives on the extreme nationalistic zeal present in a number of them.[7] Instead of the wise utilization of raw materials and natural resources by exploring virgin lands that might legitimately be distributed to those in need, many already productive lands have been taken away from their owners. In countless cases, there is no attempt to search honestly for available social remedies and no thought except for making a political impression and calculating its effect upon the unwary masses.

The abuses against the Indians, often analyzed and commented on in essays and studies, are also dramatically reflected in the Spanish-American novel. Granted that certain novelists have been more interested in making propaganda than in depicting reality, yet the thesis can be illustrated with works of fiction such as *Raza de bronce* by the Bolivian Alcides Arguedas; *El mundo es ancho y ajeno* by the Peruvian Ciro Alegría; *El Indio* by the Mexican Gregorio López y Fuentes; *Huasipungo* by the Ecuadorian Jorge Icaza; and *Caos* by the Guatemalan Flavio Herrera, to mention only a few.

Opening at random the first of the above mentioned novels, we come upon the following passage:

> In this way had don Manuel Pantoja established the valuable property that was now being exploited by his son, who squeezed the ever discontented tenant farmers to satiate the lust for gain he had inherited with his blood. Isaac Pantoja was a miser, and, like his father, he treated the Indians brutally. For him, Indians lacked the most rudimentary feelings, and were distinguishable from animals only by their ability to express their needs in words. He neither saw nor wished to see any difference between using beasts of burden and commanding the services of men.

And quoting from the last book of that list:

> They come and go. They stir about; move as in a shadow play. They are born, love, suffer, and die at our side. They are among us but we are unaware of them. A wall separates them from us. And yet, they are the sap and soul of this land—our land, their land. They trudge up and down these montains; they were who cleared these jungles; they are who work these fields. They built these roads with their toil, with their blood, in silence. We do not wish to know these things. We look, yet

refuse to see. We will not acknowledge that we are molded from the same ancestral clay and that our umbilical cord was cut from the same primordial ancestry as theirs. Saint Francis will come back to earth one day and teach the "whites" his lesson of love. Indian, close to us, yet remote. Brother and victim. Stone of flesh. Scrap of glory. Indian: unrecorded, tortured, betrayed, exploited as a "national industry" by the cacique, the *encomendero,* the peddler, the doctor, the lawyer, the artist, the writer, the tourist, and the politician. Indian: butt of mockery, derision, vituperation, and abomination. . . . Protoplasm of the Americas, festering wound in the continental conscience.

About the Indians of his country, José de la Riva Agüero wrote: "Reserved and tradition-loving, this race, above all others, has the gift of tears and practices the cult of memories." This melancholic trait, however, is not exclusive to the Indians of Peru. Although there are inevitable exceptions, that is the general cast of temperament of the New World's aborigines. To some extent, it might be the result of the existence of slavery—even before the Conquest—in some of the Indian peoples. The Aztecs, for example, made their *tlamenes,* or proletarians, work as beasts of burden. There were tribes that fattened up and ate their captive enemies; and others where honored guests, like Cortés in Coyoacán, were supplied with women slaves for their pleasure. Still others, as in Tenochtitlán, used to honor or appease their gods by countless human sacrifices. But, did the Indians' lot improve after the wars of independence with the birth of the new republics? Let a Colombian essayist, Germán Arciniegas, give us the answer to this question:

Today, four centuries later, in those regions where the Indians have survived, they still cultivate the land with pre-Columbian implements. The same hut houses them; the same earthen floor is still their bed. Their feet are yet unshod. The native dress, in hot climates, is still what Adam wore, just as in the highlands it is the same cotton cloak that the Chibchas taught their children to weave when Columbus was not even a premonition in his parents' mind. The same dwelling, the same bed. The same fare: the same bread to eat, the same *chicha* to drink. The same old techniques.

The great social importance of the literary movement that concerned itself with the Indian question was further accentuated by the Mexican Revolution of 1910. The unfinished altruistic endeavors of the sixteenth century missionaries and the Jesuits' projects in Brazil and Paraguay were then just a memory of the remote past. The participation of José Santos Chocano added significance to the movement. He outlined his position in 1913 in three lyrical poems: "¡Quién sabe!," "Así será," and "Ahí, no más," all under the title of "Tres notas del alma indígena." The incitement to rebellion was evident in the first poem of the group:

> Indian, toiling with fatigue
> Upon another's land so long,
> Do you know it should be yours,
> Earned with your sweat and with your blood?
> Have you forgotten brazen greed
> Tore it from you in ages gone?
> Don't you know you rightly own it?
> "Who knows, *señor!*" [8]

In Spanish America, large segments of the population are keenly sensitive to the spell of the lyre, to any message expressed in poetry. Poets, therefore, are held in high esteem. If we bear this in mind while noticing that some of the best poets of our time—César Vallejo, in Perú; Pablo Neruda and Pablo de Rokha, in Chile; Nicolás Guillén, in Cuba—promote vital social ideas of the extreme Left, we will realize that this is not a symptom to be glossed over.

Vallejo, according to Luis Monguió, is "the pioneer in the expression of solidarity with the sorrows of all men." This solidarity, in the opinion of the author of *La poesía postmodernista peruana,* is wholly emotional: it arises from sorrow, turns to rebellion, and finds expression by attacking "the causes of that common sorrow." Persecuted by the law and jailed for one hundred and thirty days in the city of Trujillo, Vallejo, once released, left Peru for good. Exiling himself to France, he visited Russia in 1928 and 1929. During the Spanish civil war he sided with the "Loyalists" or Republicans. He died in Paris in 1938. His last book of poems, *España, aparta de mí este cáliz,* was published posthumously two years later. In "Los nueve monstruos," from *Poemas humanos,* published by his widow in Paris in 1939, there is this warning: "Misery grows, oh men, my brothers, / Faster than a machine, than ten machines, and still grows," / [9] and perhaps a threat: "Ah, unhappily, humane men, / There is, my brothers, a great deal to be done." [10]

Jorge Carrera Andrade, from Ecuador, not primarily a proletarian poet, at times writes verses vibrant with protest. Furthermore, as John Peale Bishop reminds us, "He himself dates his true beginning as a poet from his 'Song to Russia' and the 'Lament on the Death of Lenin.' " In one of his poems, "Indiada," from *Boletines de mar y tierra* (1930) , we find these two highly significant lines: "The Indian mass carries the morning / On the protest of their spades." [11]

Besides its social elements, these lines also express the *indigenismo* * present in Carrera Andrade's poetry—despite his cosmopolitan travels through Russia, Germany, France, Spain, Japan, China, and the United States.

Pablo Neruda (the pen name of Neftalí Ricardo Reyes) praises the Spanish Loyalists with exalted and commanding words in his "Oda solar al Ejército del Pueblo," from his book, *España en el corazón* (1937) :

> Onward, bells of the people,
> Onward, apple-orchard regions,
> Onward, banners of grain,

* *Indigenismo:* literary and political movement, widespread in Spanish America, idealizing and attempting to revive certain traits of the indigenous cultures of the Americas.

Onward, capital letters of the fire,
For in the midst of battle, on the sea-wave,
    in the plain,
In the mountains, in the twilight, heavy with
    acrid smells,
You bring a birth of permanence, a thread
Of difficult toughness.
Meanwhile,
Root and wreath arise from the silence
Awaiting mineral victory:
Each tool, each reddened wheel,
Each saw-handle and plowshare,
Every extraction from the soil, every thrill
    of the blood
Longs to follow in your footsteps, People's Army:
Your organized light searches out the poor
Forgotten men, your clear-cut star
Sinks its hoarse rays into death
And establishes the new eyes of hope.[12]

Yesterday's poet of passion, who infused a new vitality into the romantic poetry of his language, turned into just a propaganda instrument of the Marxist creed and Soviet Russia. He has been showered, from Moscow and its satellites behind the Iron Curtain, with invitations and honors. So great and exceptional poet is Neruda that, at times, not even the fact that he is writing propaganda can mute his lyricism; but, in serving the Soviet Union, he refuses to encompass the whole truth of the contemporary world. The crimes against Hungary have never been condemned in Neruda's verse. Yet, the United States he does anathematize, as for example, in this poem on the subject of Chilean copper, from *Odas seculares:*

Chile,
Mastered crude matter,
Tore loose from stone
The quiescent mineral

> Which was then taken for a ride
> To Chicago
> Where copper
> Is forged into chains
> And ghastly
> Crime machines;
> After my country labored
> To bring it forth
> And brought it forth in glorious
> Virgin birth,
> They have made it death's adjutant,
> Hardened it, labeled it
> Murderer.[13]

But Neruda has no poems for the slave laborers of Siberia: they are only the slaves of Moscow. He has nothing to say either about peoples in Europe and Asia subjugated by violence: not as long as the crime is perpetrated by the Communists. Yet, he was quick to cry out about the "North American invaders" of Arbenz's Guatemala.[14]

Another poet who flies the red flag of socialism and anti-Yankeeism is the Cuban, Nicolás Guillén. Also indulged and flattered by the Marxists, he often travels in Europe and the Americas, where he is feasted and where some of his works are translated by totalitarian Leftists and haters of the United States. Take, for instance, this "Diana" (Reveille) from his book, *Sóngoro cosongo y otros poemas:*

> The bugle call of reveille
> With red pins pricks sleeping eyes,
> Bidding the soldiers to rise
> The bugle call of reveille.
>
> Its sound lifts the barracks high,
> It hefts the barracks entire.
> The soldiers stumble out, tired.
> Its sound lifts the barracks high.

Ah, bugle, but you shall sound,
At the dawning of some day,
A rousing, rebellious lay.
Ah, bugle, but you shall sound.

You shall call, "My friend! My friend!"
Thrilling by the hard, rough cot
Where the beggar's left to rot.
You shall call, "My friend! My friend!"

You shall roar with new-freed throat
By the silken bedside too:
"Get up! Get out! You're through!"
You shall roar with new-freed throat.

Bugle of fire at reveille,
Fierce, untrammeled and strong,
Rouse blind and poor with your song,
The bugle call of reveille.[15]

And these rather vulgar lines from "Cantaliso en un bar":

Every one of these red-faced Yankees
Is a boiled shrimp's son,
And they were borne by a bottle,
Borne by a bottle of rum.[16]

Or these from "Maracas":

Two by two
The *maracas* advance to greet the Yankee,
Saying:
"And how are you, *señor?*"
When a ship heaves into sight,
The *maracas* are waiting at the port,
Their gestures lively, their eyes greedy
          and bright,
To catch their prey leaving the tourist boat.

Maraca, you turncoat!
Güiros that on the tourist dollar gloat!
But there is a *maraca* of another sort,
With a certain decorum almost anti-imperialistic,
And that is the *maraca* that's artistic
And has no business ever at the port.[17]

By now, Juan Marinello's enthusiasm for Neruda, Guillén, and Mariátegui should be easy to understand. Marinello, whose literary career began in 1927 with the publication of a book of poems, *Liberación,* was president of the Communist Party in Cuba. In his book, *Literatura hispanoamericana* (1937), he heaps unconditional praise on Mariátegui:

. . . leader in his day, he proclaimed a *world* as yet unborn. He affirmed when all others doubted. . . . To José Carlos Mariátegui, Marxism was the absolute. This is the reason why his work—every single line of it—is a call to battle, and every battle in his books is fought for the establishment of socialism in Latin America. . . . Now mixed-blooded America must again be freed from strangers' talons without, this time, forgetting to grant the Indian and the Negro—losers in all American wars—full stature as men. . . . In a Peruvian setting, Mariátegui gives us the dimensions of the tragedy we are living through. . . . Cheap land and cheap exploitation of men who, in cultivating the land, give it its value. An uninterrupted feudal tradition. The unscrupulous steward who insures the absent master's comfortable enjoyment of his income far away from his feudal holdings. Perú, Cuba: Indian America. . . . He knew that the southern part of the continent was living an economic moment that other countries had left behind, but that there, from that mess of slaveries, was slowly emerging the impulse to overleap the moment of triumph now enjoyed by the North. He pointed out that each blow dealt by capitalistic imperialism to Spanish America weakened the aggressor's arm. He was convinced that the breakdown of the great northern machine would coincide with the awakening of Indian America. He had evidence that, while the blond bourgeoisie accelerated the decline of an economic stage that has already received its death blow, the anxieties that on the morrow shall bring to both North and South the reign of definitive justice rub elbows by their sickbed.[18]

About Nicolás Guillén and his *Cantos para soldados y sones para turistas* (1937) , Marinello wrote:

> There is in these verses a daring deed and a unique achievement. It is no exaggeration to say that they display a new and most unusual mode of revolutionary poetry. . . . He has not been able—and it is a great event—to introduce his white culture within the ways of a vagabond, aseptic, sybilline art. The voice of the jungle within him has radically prevented it. . . . There is in the poet who wrote *West Indies* a miraculous capacity to pour his natural force into molds of the best traditional quality. A perfect marriage between primitive inspiration and the cultured expression of ancient wisdom is the clue to the value of these poems. . . . At the edge of the most abysmal depths of the Afro-Antillean soul, political enlightenment comes to Guillén: if the Negro is to live free of oppression, it is necessary to create a society where human relationships are such as to make oppression impossible.

How true, if only Marinello would also speak out in defense of the white men suffering oppression in Russia and her satellites, and in red China!

It goes without saying that Guillén hates the "Yankee" as much as he claims to hate soldiers and imperialism. But he never cares to mention the fact that the Soviet Army, with its one hundred and seventy-five divisions in 1939, has subjugated small civilized nations like Finland and oppressed later on every people it has dragged behind the Iron Curtain.

Another poet, Carlos Díaz Loyola, better known by his pen name, Pablo de Rokha, in his "Elegía de todos los tiempos" pairs Lenin and Jesus, in that sequence, calling the Communist master and the great Master of Christianity "the great banners of all times." In another poem, "Los días y las noches subterráneas," from *Morfología del espanto* (1942) , de Rokha wrote: "And as you understand why the Bolshevik hero is / Essential to enter, in flesh and blood, into / History, understanding it." [19]

Like Neruda, this other Pablo is Chilean, too. Born in Licantén in 1894, he is ten years older than the author of *Las furias y las penas.*

In more than one of the Hispanic-American republics we find the audacious usurper, the politican spurred on by his ambition for personal power, the so-called "strong man." In some cases, the dictator finds his support among the ultra-conservatives (who in the long run fail to conserve even their own position) ; in others, having demagogically taken advantage of a situation of anarchy, the "strong man" keeps an ace up his sleeve: the support, if not the absolute command, of the army. The former kind of dictator is afraid of sane, honest liberalism —and so is the latter. This is not as paradoxical as it may sound. A vigorous liberal movement would make the dictator's pretense of being a "benefactor," his contrived prestige as an indispensable figure or a messianic redeemer, his very existence, superfluous. Commenting on the subject, the Argentinian, Carlos Octavio Bunge, wrote in his *Nuestra América* (1903) : "In a cacique's career there is always an initial stage in which he deceives the mob with imaginary or superficial virtues. . . . Once he has consolidated his power, he usually divests himself of these appearances as one who frees himself from clumsy garments that hamper his movements."

A story told about one of these despots would apply equally to many others. On his deathbed, this man asked for a priest to hear his confession. The priest advised His Excellency to forgive his enemies, that he, too, might be worthy of forgiveness. "But Father," cried the dictator, "that is impossible for me to do!" "Why not, my son?" asked the confessor. "Because," the sick man answered, "I already had every last one of them shot."

There are dictators who do not think the firing squad to be the only deterrent for their opponents and resort to techniques of mental and physical torture as well as to more or less disguised concentration camps. Some, once they have seized the most prosperous businesses and the best industries, are crafty enough—as well as eager to satisfy their personal vanity

—to turn their capital city into a showcase. The visiting foreigner, who sees this display but is unaware of what goes on inside the national tragedy, is impressed by it as a real manifestation of progress and order. Other dictators, however, despise their own people too much to take even the trouble of improving the physical aspect of their metropolis, and concentrate only in extending the amount of their holdings. They enrich themselves, their relatives, and their friends at the expense of the people they remorselessly fleece while pretending to serve. The list of dictators answering one or another of these description could be prolonged ad nauseam.

In his enlightening essay, *Nuestra América,* Martí asked: "Where has a man a better right to feel proud of his fatherland than in our suffering American republics, raised, amid the voiceless Indian masses and to the clash of the battle between book and censor, on the bloodstained arms of a hundred apostles? . . . Never, from such discordant elements, have nations so advanced and unified been created in so short period of history."

The *montoneras* * of the Argentine plains, for instance, were blind instruments of anarchy and of hostility against the metropolitan city; but this barbarism did not prevent Buenos Aires from growing, as Sarmiento predicted as early as 1845, into one of the three largest cities of the Western Hemisphere, all in roughly one century. On the negative side, however, this same Argentina lived through four revolutions in less than a quarter of a century: in 1920, in 1942, and twice, in June and September, during the year 1955—these last two against the Perón dictatorship. It can be said that while the pampas still echo to the hoofbeats of the gauchos' mustangs, Buenos Aires can make us fancy that it is Second Empire Paris reborn.

In Brazil the exuberant natural coloring of South America reaches its climax in an orgy of vividness and subtlety, but the daring works of engineers modify the landscape here and there

* *Montoneras:* bands of armed horsemen that harassed the government troops.

with building projects in which concrete structures markedly predominate. The dazzling wonders of Rio de Janeiro contrast with the bold impetus of São Paulo, which in turn is rivaled by the dynamism of present-day Caracas. At the same time, how different psychologically are the Brazilians from the Venezuelans!

The republic of Colombia, which is as large as California and Texas together, has a population of twelve million, of which two and a half million are white, and two thirds of its territory is covered by jungles that are all but impenetrable to civilized man.

In Bolivia, whose average altitude is fourteen thousand feet above sea level, we find only eight human beings per square mile, eighty percent of them Indians.

Thousands upon thousands of Indians throughout the Spanish-American countries do not speak Spanish, and a large percentage of them do not speak any mutually intelligible language. And the personalities and temperaments of men in the different zones are as varied as the climate and the geography.

If Lima, for example, is like some meridional Spanish city, the gigantic peaks of Peru, with their hidden ruins and the mysteries of Lake Titicaca, take us back to the remotest past and the most fascinating aspects of the entire South American continent.

Each frontier is seen as a challenge, and many have been turned into actual battlegrounds by the exacerbated nationalisms of the countries they divide.

The Hispanic tradition of these republics speak of Catholicism but, despite the baptism of many million Indians, there is among them widespread indifference to and abandonment of Christian dogma. In his book, *El perfil americano,* the Honduran, Arturo Mejía Nieto, laments that, in Hispanic America as a whole, "there is lack of a religion that would teach us moral principles."

A nation of such high human quality as Chile must live with the agonizing fact that only one-fourth of its soil is arable. And it struggles in noble anguish on a narrow strip of land squeezed between the Andes and the sea.

War after war has bled Paraguay, a country so gentle in its hospitality and so fierce in battle, so generously endowed with land and so reluctant to make it come alive by the development of industries.

In another country, Honduras, innumerable acts of violence have been perpetrated since the time of the Spanish conquistadores. One of her sons and best authorized spokesmen, the late Rafael Heliodoro Valle, made this moving synthesis: "The history of Honduras could be written on a teardrop. Land of pines in perpetual springtime and of craggy mountains, through which endless rivers of blood have run in a long night of hate and pain."

There we have some of the "discordant elements" that Martí spoke about, from which these nations, so admirable in so many ways, have been forged.

To the enduring honor of Hispanic America, and as an accent to its dramatic and well-nigh unbelievable contrasts, if at one end of the scale we find the greedy *caudillo* subjecting everything to his tyrannical will, at the other end we find the writer who opposes and denounces him with integrity and incorruptible courage, fearless of financial ruin, persecution, physical torture, or death. Some of the finest pages of Spanish-American literature have been penned in political exile. Witness the writings of the men proscribed from Argentina during the rule of Juan Manuel Rosas: Echeverría, Alberdi, Sarmiento, and others. Of such quality, too, are the works of Juan Montalvo, who could not live in his own country, Ecuador, during the periods of García Moreno and Veintimilla. Also the books of Rufino Blanco-Fombona, who, undefeated, attempted to overcome the dictator of Venezuela, Juan Vicente Gómez, with words as hard and searing as red-hot iron.

Revolutions have borne important literary and artistic fruits. Especially rich is the yield of the Mexican Revolution. We have, for instance, the novel *Los de abajo*, by Mariano

Azuela, a physician who fought under Pancho Villa, and *El Aguila y la Serpiente,* a fictionalized chronicle of the Mexican Revolution, by Martín Luis Guzmán. Equally expressive of that movement are the striking paintings of José Clemente Orozco and Diego Rivera, as well as the anonymous songs composed by the soldiers in the midst of the struggle.

It is interesting to recall that Francisco Madero was living as an exile in Texas when he organized the revolution against Porfirio Díaz. And it was also in Texas that *Los de abajo* was first published—in installments (October–December, 1915) — in the newspaper, *El Paso del Norte.* This realistic novel is rich, like *El Aguila y la Serpiente,* in vigorous sketches and psychological insights. Part of the action of this latter book takes place—again in Texas—in the city of San Antonio and among the family circle of José Vasconcelos. There, the author of *La raza cósmica* and future minister of public education was heartened by his conviction that the triumph of the revolution was assured, for in Pancho Villa it had found a man—¡*Ahora sí ganamos! ¡Ya tenemos hombre!*

Such an ideological union of civilization and barbarism could not last. Near the end of *El Aguila y la Serpiente,* we hear Pancho Villa assert that Vasconcelos was nothing but a traitorous intellectual.

In his book, *Este pueblo de América,* the Colombian, Germán Arciniegas, put the question very aptly: "Looking realistically at the panorama of nineteenth century America, it cannot be said that there is democracy. But, should this be taken to mean that America is not for democracy?"

Although in the years that have already elapsed of the twentieth century democracy has not seemed to develop in the desirable measure, Arciniegas' question is still valid. It is a serious and important question: one that every conscientious inhabitant of the western hemisphere would do well to keep alive. And, better still, try to find an answer to it.

[From *Expresión de Hispanoamérica,* Vol. I, San Juan, Puerto Rico: Instituto de Cultura Puertorriqueña, 1960.]

6✤
Eugenio
María de Hostos,
A Public Servant
of the Americas

Here we are facing an essentially vigorous personality, a fighting thinker whose ideas never had a price tag. Unmoved by personal ambition, he gave himself, day by day, to the cause of the Americas. To be of service was for him the dutiful mission of the human being. He advocated, against all historical tradition, that we of the Western Hemisphere should prize the useful man above the hero.

It is this quality that has made Hostos a vital part of the Hispanic-American conscience. To teach Hispanic Americans to think was his goal; his watchword was "civilization or death." However, his view of the future of the New World was not limited by a nationalistic kind of ethics: the whole vast expanse of the continent was not broad enough to contain his thought. Chapter XXI of his *Moral social*, which deals with the duties of men to mankind, begins:

Social morality would be not only incomplete but confiningly narrow in its scope and petty in its aims if it merely related men to their own national society. It has a broader scope and a higher purpose: to study and define the relation between each man and every one of the groups that immediately contain him. For a group constitutes a part of mankind and, therefore, when a man does his duty to one particular society, he has

done his duty to mankind. It is thus clear that, far from
excluding the individual's relation to humanity, social morality is bound to include it. So much so that the first truth to be
learned from it and applied throughout is that individuals are
a part of humanity and that the natural source and sustenance
of each man is society as a whole.

For Hostos, the history of civilization, in its moral implications, was nothing but palpable proof of the unconscious
brotherhood of human beings. His tenets, disregarding individual phenomena, honored universal ideas of good. On April
27, 1870, he wrote in a letter: "Should the day ever come when
I lower myself to deal in personalities and do myself the injustice of backing personal interests, my patriotism shall have
sunk to the personal level. And the average stature of five feet
is too low for my ideas."

He was always eager to serve those in need of education or
victims of some injustice, whatever their national origin or
race. In another letter, dated January 16, 1868, he said that
whoever suffers in the cause of truth and justice is his friend.

There are few men whose lives show words and deeds in
such harmonious balance or so congruently paralleling each
other. He expressed this in 1888 when some of his students
urged him to go ahead and published his *Moral social*. He refused to let himself be hurried, explaining that one's own life
is his best example, and that he who thinks or speaks wrongly
lives a wrong kind of life. He concluded that what is important is to lead an ethical life, as the merit of a good deed resides in the act itself, not in its being understood, approved, or
rewarded with gratitude.

According to Hostos, there had been in Hispanic America
every kind of revolution but one: a revolution in education.
He admitted that the "Latin imagination" allowed itself to be
seduced by "blind force." As a man who, where the cause of
freedom was concerned, neither retreated before his enemies
nor made allowances for friendship, he proclaimed and defended these values wherever he went—for to him there was

no greater cowardice than to be silent when one should speak out.

He demanded that the world should be built on truth. Without truth the world can be destroyed, but with truth, he felt, it could be rebuilt after every destruction. In his world of truth, he would have men taught to serve not only the concrete reality of their nations but that abstract fatherland that includes the whole of the human race. He believed that all men on earth should communicate in thought as well as share in labor: ". . . because the future is the sum of the ideas, feelings, and deeds of mankind and is therefore best served by the most humane people: those who most freely and generously work at the universal task, supporting it with their ideas, their affections, and their actions, all made further known through their efforts."

From this thesis he went on to the following, which should always be kept in mind by the men of the New World: "America is situated where it is and appeared in history at the propitious moment in which it did appear because it is called to be the universal intermediary of human progress: the moral and intellectual modifier of civilization."

Eugenio María de Hostos, son of Eugenio María de Hostos y Rodríguez and María Hilaria de Bonilla y Cintrón, was born on January 11, 1839, in Río Cañas, a suburb of the city of Mayagüez on the west coast of Puerto Rico. He attended elementary school in San Juan, the capital of the island. In 1851, he traveled to Spain and there enrolled at the Instituto de Bilbao. At the age of eighteen he was studying law at the Universidad Central in Madrid. Later on, he was to meet some of Spain's representative men of that period: Nicolás Salmerón, Francisco Giner de los Ríos, Nicolás Azcárate, and Francisco Pi y Margall.

Toward the end of 1863, despite the fact that works of fiction aroused in him "a pitying sadness," he published a novel, *La peregrinación de Bayoán,* in which he attacked the Spanish government's abuses both on the mainland and in its Antillean colonies. Years later, looking back upon that period of his life, Hostos said that he was then twice a child: once, by reason of his youth, and, again, because of his exclusive preoccupation with ideals. To write fiction, he felt, was to cut himself off from what the world needs most, logical men. Although his novel was one with a thesis—its hero judged and condemned colonial government—and in spite of the fact that the well known Spanish novelist, Pedro Antonio de Alarcón, wrote him a letter praising it, Hostos still believed that "literature is the craft of the idle." Thus, rejecting his literary vocation and conscious that he had a great deal of work to do, he turned aside from the purely creative genre.

On the evening of Saint Daniel's Day, April 10, 1865, University of Madrid students demonstrated against the government's suppression of academic freedom. There were several armed clashes between the students and the police. In the Ateneo, where the most prominent intellectuals and liberals met, Hostos protested with vigorous and incisive eloquence against the official action. The future great novelist, Benito Pérez Galdós, who was in the audience, told later about this occasion in his historical novel *Prim,* where he recalled Hostos as a young man of "very radical ideas, talented, and vital." Hostos himself, in a letter to Práxedes Mateo Sagasta (Barcelona, March 18, 1868), alluded to the episode: "Do you remember our campaign of '65? I was, thanks to God and to my own indignation, the first to protest against the infamous Saint Daniel's Day killings. To protest was dangerous, and I signed my name to that protest, defying danger."

Three years later Queen Isabel II was dethroned, and Hostos, who had worked for the republican cause, was offered a post in the newly created government. But Hostos was not interested. Such an offer did not measure up to the promise made to him, which he had cherished with such anxious expectations. For he was not seeking—then or ever—his own personal advancement. He had been promised that, should the Republican cause be victorious, Cuba and Puerto Rico would be granted autonomy. And he demanded of General Serrano, President of the Provisional Government, that the promise be fulfilled. Emilio Castelar, who had pledged his word, failed to keep it, taking refuge in a rhetorical evasion: "I am a Spaniard first and a Republican second."

Thus betrayed and while still on Spanish soil, Hostos defied the Spanish government by publicly denouncing the deceit practiced upon him and the cruel flouting of the colonies' hopes. He further predicted that Cuba and Puerto Rico would be forced to cut their ties with the metropolis. Hostos was no longer merely a youth with noble ideals—he proudly displayed what, as he himself would say years later, few men ever develop: strength of character.

He left Spain because, as he said, "Where there is no room for my country, there is no room for me," and went to New York where he joined the Cuban Revolutionary Committee. There he also published the newspaper La Revolución.

By August, 1870, Hostos was convinced that the men among whom he found himself did not understand him and that he could no longer collaborate with them in their separatist movement as he would have liked to. He was overcome by the feeling that his sacrifices had been in vain and that he was like a wanderer who clamors in desert after desert. He decided that it was pointless to keep on struggling when he could see no object worthy of struggling for. It was at this juncture that he resolved to carry his message of independence for Cuba and Puerto Rico throughout South America.

It is amazing that, with just such a brief stay in the United States, Hostos should have become so imbued with the spirit of the American people. His writings are filled with glowing praise for the republic that was to apply the soundest doctrines of freedom. He wrote then: "For the first time in history, full freedom resulted from complete independence. For the first time, great men were eclipsed by the greatness of a people, outstanding individuals by an extraordinary community."

He believed that no society in the world was ever as free, as powerful, and as strong as that of the United States. This nation he considered "the most complete of all existing social organisms."

Hostos was, therefore, the first great man of the Antilles who, being acquainted with the institutions of the United States—after having known those of Europe—visited the countries of the south well equipped with universal ideas to serve the Hispanic-American mind.

He went to Cartagena de Indias, Colombia, and there founded the Society for Antillean Immigration. From Cartagena he went to Callao, via Panama, and from there to Lima, Peru.

Like Sarmiento before and Martí after him, Hostos was able to earn his living as a journalist anywhere he went. In Lima, together with Federico Torrico, he founded *La Patria*. Hostos made this newspaper a vehicle of his liberal ideas, his rationalist creed, and his civilizing endeavors.

During Hostos' stay in Lima, three notable events took place. All three brought out his moral acuteness, his philanthropic nature, and his manly integrity. The Chinese mine laborers in Peru were shamefully exploited; from a civic, social, and moral point of view, they were slaves. Hostos advocated the complete cessation of the infamous trade that "hypocritically disguises itself as 'Asian immigration.' " His always lively interest in schools led him to found a society to promote elementary and secondary education. It was no secret that Hostos never had enough money to cover the minimum necessities of living. But this situation never prevented him from being more concerned with the needs of others than with his own. While he was writing articles that commanded for him the greatest respect and made him increasingly influential in Lima, his wallet nevertheless became thinner and thinner. He was a poor man at the time the Peruvian government was considering the public works project for the Oroya railroad. A man who hoped to be awarded the contract offered Hostos

$200,000 "for the Cuban cause," if only Hostos would write "one single article" favoring this man's claims. The idea was to influence government officials. Disregarding the thinly disguised bribe, Hostos carefully studied all the bids and, seeing that the conditions proposed by his would-be "benefactor" were the most onerous of all, conscientiously opposed him. Once again Hostos proved that he was guided by duty, not by personal interest. Man of uprightness that he was, he never trafficked with his ideas nor with the legitimate interests of others—both were sacred to him.

In 1872, the wanderings of this pilgrim of duty, justice, and freedom had taken him to Valparaíso, Chile, where he was employed by a newspaper. But, as with Rubén Darío in days to come, Valparaíso was only a way station en route to Santiago. This hospitable capital city, in 1829, had welcomed the Venézuelan Andrés Bello, who founded and became first rector of its university. Later, Chile warmly and generously received Domingo Faustino Sarmiento, who, in turn, could claim the honor of having organized there, in 1842, the first teachers' college in South America. Chile, which so magnanimously welcomed educators, writers, and civic leaders, became the congenial refuge of yet one more foreigner. Here Hostos found so propitious an intellectual climate that in the course of a single year, 1872–1873, he wrote some of his best works on a wide variety of subjects: a biography and critique of the Cuban poet Gabriel de la Concepción Valdés ("Plácido"), Biografía crítica de "Plácido"; a plea on the scientific education for women, La educación científica de la mujer; a memoir on the 1872 Fair, Memoria de la Exposición de 1872; and his masterly essay on Hamlet.

Hostos' look at the past of his own country, Puerto Rico, did not in any way limit the scope of his vision. The clear and penetrating insight of Chile revealed in his Memoria won for this work the first prize in a contest to which many other entries were also submitted. And, as he went from the subject of his little island to that of a country of continent-wide prestige, he also turned to the question of the education of women, arguing that they should be admitted to universities and allowed to work for degrees in law and medicine. Then, having pioneered in the field of pedagogy, he moved on to the dark and complex world of the Prince of Denmark, plumbing its depths and bringing it into focus for us with a winged pen and a mind surcharged with wisdom.

Hostos' works and life are living proof that the more deep-rooted our patriotism, the more pressing becomes our intellectual obligation to explore the multifaceted realities of other nations and cultures, so that we may understand men better and be able to find the soundest solutions to the problems of mankind.

In September, 1873, Hostos stopped over for a day in Montevideo and then proceeded to Buenos Aires. The people of this city received him well, but he was nevertheless attacked in the editorial page of *El Correo Español*. Hostos replied cuttingly, in turn making accusations. Only the intervention of Cuban friends prevented a duel between him and the editor.

A man dedicated to the service of the Americas, Hostos was, once again, to prove his usefulness to the republics of the south. In letters written from Buenos Aires and published in *La Opinión*, of Talca, he attempted to establish closer relations between Argentina and Chile. In order to accomplish this, he explained, it was necessary to make the two countries known to each other in every one of their characteristics. He knew that the peoples of our hemisphere need one another, that they "mutually complement one another." Joining the empirical to the theoretical, he proposed the construction of a trans-Andean railroad that would unite the two republics. The project was carried out, and in his honor the locomotive of the first train to cross the mountain range was named the "Eugenio María de Hostos."

When Hostos later returned to New York, he was quite familiar with the landscape, the society, and the individual and collective idiosyncrasy of several South American countries. In

1874, in collaboration with the Cuban critic Enrique Piñeyro, he was publishing *La América Ilustrada*. But the distance and physical separation from Chile by no means cooled Hostos' affection for that land. From the north he began sending ideas and suggestions for the International Fair of 1875.

Then the Cubans in New York organized a revolutionary expedition under the command of General Aguilera, and Hostos promptly enlisted. On April 29, 1875, the rebels sailed off in the "Charles Miller," but the ship was in such poor condition that the invasion project ended in failure.

However, the prospect of new adventures was for Hostos like a constant magnetic pull. He then decided to go to the Dominican Republic. There he began to write articles for *Las Dos Antillas,* a newspaper founded by the Cuban Enrique Coronado. But before long the government suspended its publication, whereupon Hostos started a new one, *Las Tres Antillas.* This title was meant to express one of Hostos' most fervent political ideals. For he was convinced that Cuba, Santo Domingo, and Puerto Rico—the three Antilles—must survive or perish together.

How could it be that this thinker, usually guided unerringly by his knowledge of the history of the Americas and his logical rigor, should in this instance have strayed from his rationalistic course? This seems the more strange and contradictory when we read what Hostos himself had written long before, in an article published in 1847:

In spite of Bolívar's influence; in spite of the fact that almost every one of the Founding Fathers of Latin America and almost every one of the military leaders of her wars of independence, no less than the liberated peoples, favored a union; in spite of the experimental union of Venezuela, New Granada, and Ecuador into a political unit named Colombia; in spite of the unification of the five Central American republics; in spite of the ephemeral Peru-Bolivian Federation; in spite of the federal form of government adopted by the Provinces of Río de la Plata and by the sections of the Mexican state; the principle of unity in diversity, which all circumstances seemed to favor in that vast continental mass that our race occupies, did not prevail. The Colombian Union was broken; the Central American Union was dissolved; the Peru-Bolivian Union failed; the Panama Congress' unifying effort was unsuccessful. And only with superhuman trial and after serving a gory apprenticeship on the character and objectives of a federation, was the federal form of government finally established in Venezuela, in the United States of Colombia, in the United States of Mexico, and in the Argentinian Provinces.

Like its predecessor, *Las Tres Antillas* was soon suspended by executive order, and Hostos returned in 1876 to New York.

The indefatigable knight of noble pursuits headed next for Venezuela. Little did Hostos guess that during his twenty-month stay in that country he would, somewhat belatedly, come to know the joy and the enchantment of love. In Caracas lived the most charming fifteen-year old girl that he had ever seen: Belinda, the daughter of an exiled Cuban physician, don Filipo Carlos de Ayala.

It came to pass that Belinda fell in love with the Puerto Rican apostle of freedom. He, in turn, was fascinated by her silvery voice, which echoed in his ear as it went deep into his heart. So unconditionally did he surrender that, in his *Páginas íntimas,* he wrote, rather inaccurately, that this had been his only love, adding that everything about it was to him transcendental. Hostos must have forgotten the July 14, 1870, entry in his diary where he tells of his love for a young Colombian lady named Cara. And what about Nolina, the Peruvian, and the Chilean Carmen Lastarria? But be it as it may, there is no doubt that this time Hostos was deeply and definitively involved. It is refreshing to notice that he was able to relax, however briefly, his severe discipline of austere thought and persevering and almost exclusive dedication to "duty," meaning Puerto Rico and Cuba. Under the overwhelming sway of his feelings, he would even play lightly upon a few chords, in a manner reminiscent of a scherzo in Beethoven. Writing to the girl he loved on April 4, 1877, Hostos said: "How well my Belinda thinks, and how badly she punctuates! As if wanting to imitate with her blessed scrawls the locomotive-like speed of our affections, she uses neither periods nor commas; she makes no pause and allows no rest, so that one must follow her like the poor wagons dragged by the strength of steam, panting for breath."

Belinda's parents forbade Hostos to court their daughter, fearing to have her share the hazardous nomadic existence of that wise and virtuous but impoverished knight-errant. True, Hostos had been hired by the Colegio de la Paz, where he not only taught but was also assistant to the director. But the Ayalas, who knew about his quixotic nature, learned that he had resigned the post. And, why had he made this decision? One of the instructors, a Cuban immigrant, had been dismissed. He was a man of not much worth, but his dismissal had been arbitrary. And Hostos, who by that time was also fully aware of the discrepancy between his educational ideas and methods and those of the head of the school, resigned as a matter of principle. But Belinda's parents felt, besides, that Hostos' commitment to the Cuban revolution loomed over and eclipsed all his other duties. Hostos answered that Belinda was not only willing to allow him to honor his ideals but encouraged him to pursue them. She was made, Hostos told them, "of that marble from which perfect statues may be chiseled." But the Ayalas were adamant—they even thought of shutting Belinda up in a convent in Curaçao.

Meanwhile, Hostos had been writing articles for *El Demócrata* and *La Opinión Nacional*. Then, on June 7, 1877, he learned that he had been appointed headmaster of a school in the city of Asunción. This brought a critical situation for him. He feared that should he leave Caracas alone then, he would remain alone forever. (His self-imposed sentimental renunciation in the past—Cara, Nolina, Carmen—prove this point conclusively.) So, on July 9, 1877, Belinda de Ayala y Quintana, in defiance of her elders, was married to Eugenio María de Hostos by the Archbishop of Caracas. Their witnesses were two Puerto Rican friends, Bonifacio Tió and his wife, the poetess Lola Rodríguez de Tió. Hostos was thirty-eight years old then. He had, however, this comment on the occasion, "Joy was a new state of mind for me."

On August 5, Belinda, who had fallen ill, returned from Asunción to Caracas. She rejoined Hostos the following year at Puerto Cabello, where he was teaching at the Instituto Comercial. In May, 1878, Belinda went to stay with her husband's family at Mayagüez, Puerto Rico.

In June, while in Saint Thomas, Hostos heard that the Spanish and the Cubans had signed the Pact of Zanjón. He was shocked and frustrated. For him it meant that the revolution had been crushed, and that he, the rebel, must cut short his dramatic struggle.

Saddened and cast down, Hostos yearned now for his family. He found himself living in absolute moral solitude and became hypersensitive, inclined to mistrust everyone.

Belinda would write to him from Puerto Rico. The thought of her was his one constant companion. He also had memories of his mother—who had died in the very year of Belinda's birth. On May 10, 1878, he wrote in his diary that, in his desperation, he had often thought—and that day more than ever —of returning to Puerto Rico. His feverish thoughts were a seedbed of anguish and uncertainty. He had also considered going to Curaçao, and another possibility was Santo Domingo, where he had friends and might perhaps be given the opportunity of reorganizing public education. But it was the hope of rejoining Belinda that gave him fresh energies.

In June, 1878, he went from Puerto Cabello to La Guaira, in Venezuela, and from there sailed off to his birthplace in Puerto Rico, Mayagüez. His wife was there, as well as his father and his sister, Rosita. But his father sent word to him that if he should come ashore the Spanish authorities would arrest him. So, he stayed aboard until the "Lotharingia" left for San Juan, without having seen any member of his family. The sight of his land seemed to him far lovelier than he had ever remembered it, so much so that he could find no words to describe it. Yet, beautiful as it was, and many as the years were that had passed since he had last seen his country, he now had to leave without even setting foot there on the beach. Sadly, he asked himself, "Who, in so short a life, has consumed such monstrous amount of pain as I?"

In Saint Thomas, Hostos met the Cuban general, Vicente García, one of the men who had acquiesced to the peace of Zanjón. García's explanations left Hostos full of bitterness and confusion.

Irritable and dejected, he now regretted not having gone ashore in Puerto Rico. The thought of continued separation from Belinda was unbearable, and, defying danger, he decided to go to Mayagüez if only for a short visit. In 1879, he went to Santo Domingo.

In his history of Dominican literature, *Panorama histórico de la literatura dominicana,* Max Henríquez Ureña devoted the whole of Chapter XVII to the activities of Hostos and to his influence as an educator from the year 1880, when he founded the teacher's college in Santo Domingo, until 1888, when he accepted the Chilean government's invitation to return to Chile and reform public education in that country. Henríquez Ureña referred to Hostos' experience in Santo Domingo with words like these: "Having lovingly observed and studied the conditions of the Dominican people, he encouraged them to persevere along the path of civilization and pointed out errors and deficiencies that could and should be corrected. . . ."

Four years after the teacher's college had been functioning, Hostos, as part of the first graduation exercises held there, delivered a speech that was to become famous, one that the Mexican philosopher, Antonio Caso, considered the masterpiece of independent moral thought in Spanish America. But the political atmosphere of Santo Domingo became so intolerable under the oppressive dictatorship of Ulises Heureaux that

Hostos decided to take advantage of the Chilean invitation and leave the country.

In Chile the cause of public education made great strides under the influence of his pedagogical ideas. At the end of ten years, however, a situation developed that made Hostos feel unhappy once again. There was much talk of war between Chile and Argentina. In a letter to his sister Rosita (April 4, 1898) referring to his firstborn, Eugenio Carlos, Hostos left a telling example of his Pan-American sentiments: ". . . I would not leave him here alone; nor could I approve that he, as an officer in the Chilean Army, should fight against his brothers of another republic. I have, therefore, made him abandon his military career."

These feelings, here expressed in private, he also discussed openly in public. His frankness wounded those in Chile who could view the question only from a nationalistic angle. But such was not Hostos' position. Years before he had told a man who had enviously criticized Chile, "You see this through Argentinian eyes, while I look upon it as an American—a citizen of the continent as a whole."

He became desperately homesick, but his nostalgia was not for Puerto Rico alone. Sometime before, on August 20, 1895, he had confided to his Dominican friend, Gregorio Luperón, that enforced absence from "his" Antilles made him so anxious and restless that, were it not for his family, he would have gone there "to be near the center of the events."

Several months had passed since the Cuban patriot, José Martí, had died in Dos Ríos, Cuba. But Hostos, who had never paused in his struggle for the independence of this country, was never able to visit it. Three years later, on March 19, 1898, he said that he was afraid there was not one single place left where an Antillean of integrity could hope to find peaceful hospitality.

It happened then that Belinda's mother fell seriously ill in Caracas, and Hostos thought it was time to leave Chile. Behind remained friends he would never forget: José Victorino Lastarria, Benjamín Vicuña Mackenna, Pedro León Gallo, and others. One of them, Guillermo Matta, even proposed to Hostos, by way of compromise and hoping that the Puerto Rican would return, that he should just take a leave of absence. Hostos arrived in Venezuela in June, 1898, and on July 6, he informed one of the Dominican patriots, Federico Henríquez y Carvajal, that he had resolved to proceed to New York at the request of a group of Cubans and Puerto Ricans. Two days later, from Curaçao, aboard the "Abydos," he wrote his wife a letter that showed him no less a wise man than a humble laborer—always on the move in search of ways to earn his bread:

> Since, in addition to the political purpose of this trip, I also have, as you know, an urgent domestic one, I shall, from the very day of my arrival in New York, try to find a job that will allow me, should my mission fail, to return to you with some kind of occupation, such as that of translating science textbooks, out of which I was able to make a living back in 1875 and 1876 in Puerto Plata (Dominican Republic), earning approximately a hundred dollars with my translations.

In a letter to his son, Eugenio Carlos, from New York, July 19, 1898, Hostos showed that he had already some significant impressions to discuss. Santiago, Cuba, had been occupied by the United States Army. Hostos commented in giving this news, "And Puerto Rico will soon, perhaps, provide a safer asylum than could be found anywhere else." He added that both the people and the government of the United States had such self-mastery that they harbored no hate for Spain nor any desire for revenge, and that they already felt—and rightly so —fully satisfied. He said further, "I want you and your little brothers and sisters to come up here, so that your minds and characters may be formed in this noble social environment."

On July 27, 1898, Hostos was in Washington. In a letter written on this date, he indicated that he would have gone to his country to advise the Puerto Ricans to receive the Americans as liberators, and the latter to recognize the independence of Puerto Rico.

The men with whom Hostos talked in the nation's capital —among them the Cuban patriot Enrique José Varona—were convinced that the United States would end up by annexing Puerto Rico. Spain, having lost the war, was doing all she could to keep from losing Puerto Rico too. But, as President McKinley had twice informed Spain through the French Ambassador, this gentleman being a spokesman for the Madrid government, the annexation of Puerto Rico was a *sine qua non* for the signing of a peace treaty.

Hostos faced now what was, perhaps, the most critical problem of his life. For thirty years he had been a firm supporter of, first, autonomy and, later, independence for his country. During this time he also repeatedly expressed his admiration for the form of government of the United States and for its people. Hating colonialism as he did, and believing in human rights as they are defined in the American Declaration of Independence, he was shocked and indignant at seeing Puerto Rico under military rule. However, dejected as he was by this turn of events, he asserted that he would not let himself be overcome by discouragement.

The visit to Washington left him "practically cleaned out." If he could only find a job, he wrote to his wife, "you and the children could come and live with me here." He felt certain by now that "even if no shot is fired, the United States will take possession of poor Puerto Rico."

Two days later, in a letter to his son, Eugenio Carlos, on July 29, 1898, Hostos declared: "I have been most deeply hurt by the North Americans' determination to take hold of Puerto Rico—which is now confirmed by the preliminary peace talks; but the truth is that Puerto Rico will gain a great deal, and that very soon."

The impact of the events shook Hostos, he said, out of his melancholy. He wanted to go to Puerto Rico. He had a double

objective in mind: to help his country to become a small republic under United States protection—thus bringing to an
end the undefined situation of the island—and to establish a
great educational system. He believed that among the historical obligations of his generation of Puerto Ricans was that of
"learning from the example of the American people, that we
may cease to be representatives of the past and become men of
our own time as well as a society of the future."

Expounding on the first of his aims, Hostos said his idea
was to accept United States protection for a number of years
and, at the end of that period, establish the republic of Puerto
Rico (letter of August 4, 1898). From another letter—to his
daughter Luisa Amelia, written on August 22, 1898—we learn
that he was in a mood of "near hopelessness" in regard to the
attainment of "the free Puerto Rico I have labored for." It is
not surprising, therefore, that, in his letter of September 10,
addressed to all Puerto Ricans, Hostos is found proposing an
alternate solution:

> The means granted us by the letter of the law to pass from
> military to civilian rule, to request from the Congress of the
> United States the recognition of our capacity to be a state of
> the Union, or to enable us to gloriously serve the future of
> America without the need for servile submission to the conse-
> quences of a war that we did not initiate and which was not
> fought against us, are indeed powerful means. Just as in the
> very warp of the federation the right of everyone to act for his
> own good and of all to act for the common good are powerful
> strands.

On September 27, 1898, Hostos rejoined his family in
Ponce, Puerto Rico. He was hopeful that his compatriots
would help him "to prove the possibility of creating a great
strength" in spite of the weakness left in the body and soul of
their society. He was ready to work wholeheartedly and with
patriotic devotion for the present and the future of his island.
However, enchanted as he was by the beauty of the Puerto

Rican landscape, his impressions "of the country and its men were not very agreeable."

In the southern town of Juana Díaz, where Hostos made his residence, he was appointed, together with Drs. Julio Henna and Manuel Zeno Gandía, member of a commission to represent Puerto Rico in Washington. He felt that "to organize our country is basically the same thing as to have fought for its independence" (December 12, 1898). On January 17, 1899, the commission arrived in the federal capital, carrying with them carefully phrased petitions to President McKinley. Of the three, Hostos was the one who had worked the hardest, but Henna was the spokesman for the group. Having conscientiously studied the English language and with a clear understanding of it, Hostos lamented nevertheless that he was not able to speak it fluently, concluding that it was foolish not to try to acquire its command.

The commission's first proposal to the president was that, after twenty-five years of contact with United States government institutions, Puerto Rico should be allowed to hold a referendum to determine its own political future. McKinley, Hostos said, though willing to consider every suggestion offered, "made plain the [United States] government's intention to keep Puerto Rico as already an integral part of the union." The other two commission members, Henna and Zeno Gandía, were jubilant; Hostos, on the contrary, said, "Frankly, we have gained nothing from this interview."

On his return to Puerto Rico, Hostos gave all his time to the activities of the Liga de Patriotas (Patriots' League). He explained to the Puerto Ricans the political and constitutional structure of the United States. He once again acted as the great teacher that he was.

Two new political parties were organized: the Federal and the Republican, and both included in their platforms the aspiration that Puerto Rico should be one day a state of the union. This was one of the alternatives proposed by Hostos in his above mentioned letter of September 10, 1898. Yet, neither of the two parties made any overture to him. One of them held its convention at the Municipal Theatre in San Juan, and Hostos attended as a private citizen. A moment came in which he rose and asked to be allowed to speak, eager to express his opinion. But, under the ruling on a technicality—he was not actually a delegate—he was denied the opportunity.

Hostos was later to refer to this incident as "that uneasy hour when I lost my country." In a letter written on February 22, 1899, he complained bitterly that Puerto Rico was in such a condition that he found his duty as a patriot incompatible with his duty as head of a family.

Meanwhile, in the Dominican Republic, the bloodthirsty Heureaux, better known as "Lilís," was killed by Ramón Cáceres, who thereupon was made Vice President. The new government, headed by Horacio Vázquez, invited Hostos to return. He accepted the invitation and left Puerto Rico, this time forever.

In a letter dated January 15, 1900, Hostos hopefully wrote: "Judging by the continual expressions of happiness that my coming here has called forth, my prospects are of useful work for this country. If this should really come to be so, I shall be happy for the rest of my life, which, to be satisfactory to me, must be filled with activity fruitful for others."

He worked tirelessly for three years. His goal was the preparation of civic leaders inspired by the noblest ideals of democracy. But one morning, on March 23, 1903, he learned that a new revolutionary uprising had broken out and that among its instigators were some of his students. On April 20, he wrote that the years since his arrival—"in an evil hour"—in the Dominican Republic had been lost. He reflected sadly on "how the edifice I strove to build can be destroyed when it is based upon men like these," and concluded that "it is absolutely useless to attempt to do any good in a country dominated by evil." He himself felt "surrounded by animosity."

President Vázquez had had to leave and take asylum in Puerto Rico. Hostos then declared that Woss y Gil was one of the few Dominicans capable of exercising executive power; he had spent many years in the United States and had learned there the workings of government. Hostos wished to resign his post and leave Santo Domingo. Woss y Gil begged him to stay. But Hostos insisted that there was no longer a place for him there: he had done all he could to impart education and felt that he had failed. It was no secret to him that many powerful men in the Dominican Republic disliked him. His salary had been cut again and again. On May 5, 1903, he made the following entry in his diary: "Even through hunger have they assailed me! My friend Horacio's Minister of the Treasury docked my salary by thirty-something percent; now the Minister of the Treasury of my friend Woss y Gil has cut another thirty percent of what was left."

At a critical point in the revolution, Hostos was compelled to accept the hospitality offered him by the Commander of the "Atlanta," a United States Navy cruiser. Commented Hostos, "The 'Atlanta' saved us from anxiety, dereliction, or even death." His melancholy seemed to have no end: "How sad, how painful it is," he said, "to have sacrificed so much life, so much spirit, so much thought for so little!"

Spiritually as well as physically, Hostos, now sixty-four, was a very sick man. Overcome by hopelessness, like the Liberator Simón Bolívar when he uttered his heartbreaking, "I plowed the sea," Hostos declared that he was "convinced of the uselessness of every altruistic effort in these countries."

The last entry in his diary, August 6, 1903, shows that he was obsessed by the idea of the futility of life. Five days later, the great crusader for the cause of the Americas, the champion of the persecuted and the oppressed, was at rest for the first time.

His remains repose in the Dominican Republic, under his own statue.

In San Juan, I promoted the idea of raising a monument to Hostos. Happily, the idea was carried out under the direction of an eminent compatriot, don Emilio del Toro, at that time

Chief Justice of the Supreme Court of Puerto Rico. The statue was made by the Spanish sculptor, Victorio Macho, and unveiled at the campus of the University of Puerto Rico on August 14, 1926.

In 1939, on the occasion of Hostos' centennial, his complete works were published by the people of Puerto Rico. Busts of this great man are to be found in many places of the New World, from New York to Chile. Many articles, essays, and books dealing with his personality and achievements have been published in Europe as well as in America.

Did not Balzac say that glory is the sun of the dead?

[From *Expresión de Hispanoamérica*, Vol. I, San Juan, Puerto Rico: Instituto de Cultura Puertorriqueña, 1960.]

7 *
The
Sense
of Justice in
José Martí

A preacher of justice and love wherever he went, surpassed by none in equanimity: such was José Martí.

A man whose passionate and merciful spirit, unmindful of frontiers, embraced all of humanity, his life teaches us many lessons of civic morality and sets for us an example of unwavering Christian virtue.

Martí's justice was not the one doled out by the magistrate, an uninvolved observer secure in his official post, who probably has never suffered in his flesh the hardships of poverty nor in his spirit the thrusts of relentless anguish. His was the august justice of a man who, heroically stifling his feelings, bore the abuse of enemies as well as the disloyalty of many of his own associates who unfairly and unreasonably insulted and harassed him.

Driven out of his Cuba, and from other and equally beloved American countries as well, Martí, unlike Pushkin, never took refuge in sarcasm while malnourishing his spirit on the bitter bread of exile. Although he lived in continual exodus as if torn in two, the objectivity of his judgment was never impaired. Asserting that the intellect is only half the man, and not the best half at that, he did not judge merely with his brain and never forgot that, in being fair to others, a man does justice to himself.

Martí sensed the beauty of serenity, but could never remain serene when wrong was done. To do so, he felt, would be to become an accomplice of wrongdoing. As he once said of Byron, wherever he saw an injustice, he lashed out against it.

Martí preserved his sense of justice even in situations that confused many other men among those who fought for freedom in the Americas. The fine precision of his judgment and his daring grasp of opportunity disturbed many lesser individuals. He affirmed that justice admits no delay and that he who detains its fulfillment turns it against himself.

The concept of justice in Martí, as he saw it then, was obviously not political: it came from deep inside his own conscience and existed on a higher religious level—just as is the case with all those who love, who defend, and who lay down foundations.

Compare Martí's attitude with, for instance, José Joaquín Olmedo's complete rejection of Spain: "What do we owe her —lights, customs, religion, our laws?" Even while he was fighting tyrants, Martí did not allow his hatred of tyranny to blind his eyes to the existence of a Spain worthy of being loved. "If I hated anyone," he once wrote, "I should hate myself for it." He was a man privileged to write from the depths of sorrow rather than in the heat of anger.

Surpassing those who would divide, Martí was a defender of outraged virtue and unprotected reason. In his search for truth he came very close to the eternal light. The greatness of his spirit and his logical intelligence led him unerringly to the just solution, enabling him to extract from human confusion the serene, clear, enduring truth.

Olmedo, like Bolívar, was hampered by negative passions arising from transitory situations. Martí freed himself forever from this limitation through a love of humanity that made him a brother to all men. No wonder he believed that man, who carries within himself the seeds of permanence, should cultivate that which is permanent.

He was still a young boy when he first rebelled against the

political evils that beset Cuba. Soon he suffered what he termed "the most devastating of griefs," that of being imprisoned and mistreated by men enraged with hate. Exiled to Spain, he tried to shake up the conscience of the Spanish government officials by telling them the stark truth, thus making it impossible for them to plead ignorance. He, then, challenged them to sanction, if they dared, "the most iniquitous violation of morality and the most thorough disregard for every feeling of justice."

But, even while condemning all that was evil and retrograde in Spain, he knew there was another Spain that he loved and respected: the Spain of selfless missionaries, liberal minds, and immortal books; the Spain that won his heart with the courage, hospitality, and loving kindness he found during his stay in the city of Zaragoza. Knowing that fools would not understand without an explanation that in honoring Spain he honored himself, he wrote:

> **For Aragon in Spain**
> I have set a place apart,
> For Aragon, in my heart,
> Free, brave, loyal, without stain.[1]

In the closing lines of this poem, he expressed his love for "this blossoming land where the short-lived flower of my own life bloomed."

Jailed, physically mistreated, exiled by the Spanish government in Cuba, Martí rose above bodily and spiritual torment when he wrote, "Spain can be loved, and even those of us who still feel the sting of the lash upon our backs love her well."

Here the integrity of José Martí is on a level with that of Andrés Bello, who asserted that the South American wars of independence were the fruit of the elements of Spanish culture in those countries. To Bello, this was proof that Spain was not as evil as she was reputed to be: she could produce the men who fought for freedom in the New World. Remember

that Miranda, that tireless forerunner of the revolution, and
San Martín, one of its best soldiers and perhaps the man of
greatest integrity among its leaders, both received their early
training in the Spanish army, in which they were officers. And
let us not forget that a Spanish priest, José Matías Delgado,
was prominent in Guatemala's fight for independence.

In words that are fully applicable to himself, Martí described Walt Whitman as a man who loved the humble, the
fallen, the hurt, and even the wicked. Anxious himself to cast
his lot with the poor and the oppressed, Martí wanted to free
the Indian from "stagnation" and to make a place in society
for the "self-sufficient Negro."

For him there is only one inferior race: the "race" of those
guided primarily by self-interest. As one who felt the misfortune of others and believed in the spiritual unity of mankind,
Martí affirmed that a man acquires no special rights by the ac-
cident of having been born into a particular race, for "when
you say he is a man, you have said that he is the inheritor of
every right."

For Martí, everything that discriminates, separates, or con-
fines men is a sin against humanity.

Sparked by that selflessness which, as he himself once said,
is the unfailing mark of greatness, Martí (who was himself
white, the son of Spanish parents) gave renewed hopes to the
masses, forgotten and helpless in the cruel indifference of the
white man.

His magnanimous nature shows clearly through in the anecdote in Rubén Darío's autobiography regarding his only meeting with Martí:

> We had walked only a few steps when we heard someone
> calling, "Don José, don José!" It was a Negro workingman
> who, approaching him, said humbly and affectionately, "Here's
> a little gift for you," and handed him a silver pencil case. "You
> see," Martí commented, "the affection these poor Negro to-
> bacco workers have for me. They know how I work and suffer
> for the freedom of our poor country."

No wonder Darío praises Martí so highly in *Los raros:*

> This great, kind-hearted man lived in communion with God;
> this man who abhorred pain and evil, this amiable, dove-
> hearted lion who had the power to smash, crush, wound, bite,
> and tear, was always silk and honey even to his enemies. And
> he rose to this communion with God by climbing up to Him
> by the firmest and surest of all ladders: the ladder of pain.

Martí achieved a profound knowledge of every nation he
studied. One of the amazing facts of his brief and hazardous
existence, subject, among other things, to the chances and in-
conveniences of incessant traveling, is how he was able to preserve his serenity and write with such objectivity and precision
about all the peoples he alluded to.

Even as founder of a new nation Martí remained un-
touched by sterile nationalism. This attitude of his transpires,
for instance, in the admiring way in which he quoted the Venezuelan writer, Cecilio Acosta, on the latter's saying that the
light that benefits a nation most is not the spotlight but that
which shines all around. He also approved of Acosta's assertion that "to cut oneself off from the new wave because of race
prejudice, pride of tradition, or habits of caste is a crime
against society."

Martí believed that to know the literature of different nations is the best way to free oneself from bondage to any single
literary tradition. His intuitive insight and cultivated judgment make us wonder when and how did he find the time to
accumulate so much knowledge; and, furthermore, how did he
manage not merely to arrange it into conscientious collections
of data but to organize it into a brilliant and unmistakably
personal synthesis. Innumerable are the instances that can be
cited of his searching intelligence, his many-faceted interest in
aesthetics, his universal vision as a statesman, his solid and fac-
tual program as an indoctrinator, and his transcendental,
guiding voice!

How was Martí able to produce such vast amounts of work of such high quality in spite of his never having found peace, companionship, or understanding in his home life? On what inner security did he base his moral strength? How could it be that his work was never slipshod; that he never went astray, wasted his talents, or showed any symptoms of frustration?

The spiritual joy he derived from the constant exercise of love saved him. When he said that fame can never satisfy a man completely without a woman's loving smile, he was complaining of his sad and lonely life; but he was also expressing his belief that there are women who can give a man's soul wings to rise up to the luminous skies of happiness.

Martí's inexhaustible capacity to love was both his burden and his reward. To him, a woman without tenderness was a vessel brimful of poison. He felt that where Nature writes "greatness" she really means "tenderness." A man who can understand this becomes, according to Martí, one of those compound and comprehensive beings who are the living consciences of humanity.

The diversity and quality of his interests made Martí a superior man: the universality of his culture kept his mind alert and his heart compassionate. From this happy combination his noble sense of justice was born and nourished. Many European and American countries—their representative men, their political institutions, their social problems, and their science, literature, and art—come alive for us through Martí's warmth and versatility. He unveiled the particular psychology of each as if reading from a book written in letters of fire, and analyzed their collective characteristics with the same subtlety that he grasped their distinctively individual traits.

Here is, for example, how he interpreted the English character as shown by England's attitude in regard to Oscar Wilde: "[England] prefers pleasing wit to consuming genius. Too bright a light distresses her: she prefers a warm, subdued glow. She likes elegant poets who make her smile, not poetic geniuses who force her to think and make her suffer. She always opposes the solid shield of her traditions to any man whose vigorous voice disturbs the placid sleep of her spirit."

And here is what Martí wrote when Darwin died: "The expression of his eyes was benevolent, as of one living in creative contact with nature, and his hand soft and loving, as if made to care for birds and plants."

As early as 1880, Martí predicted that unless the Russian Crown revolutionized the monarchy, a revolution would overthrow the crown. Of Dostoevski he said that the Russian novelist wrote with "a steel-tipped pen" and "had the look of an eagle and the heart of a dove." Speaking of Corot, forerunner of the French impressionists, Martí observed that he "expressed in painting, with all the vibrations and mysteries of the lyre, the hidden voices that fill the air." In an evocation of Goya, he saw the genial Spanish painter go down, wrapped in a dark cloak, into the very entrails of the human being and with their colors depict his return trip. He called the Colombian poet, Diego Fallon, his "modest teacher of languages." And Martí, a Hispano-Antillean, reached new heights of universality when he said: "There is nothing like knowing other languages to help us speak our own well: the contrasts we find make us love our own all the better, and the knowledge we acquire enables us to borrow from other tongues what ours lacks and to cure any defects it may have from which others are already cured."

Here we have the ferment, which Martí perhaps borrowed from Walt Whitman, of the attitude of the Spanish-American *modernista* movement in regard to the language of poetry.

Such examples, although only a few, of his objective appreciation of the styles and sensibilities of diverse nations make us think that Martí was unconsciously describing himself when he called another poet "a man of all times and all nations—an intrinsic man whose breast encompassed the universe."

Martí wrote copiously about the United States, where he lived for fourteen years. His *Escenas norteamericanas* run to fourteen volumes, and his *Norteamericanos* to three. Seventeen volumes on North Americans and North American scenes, and yet they represent only a part of his activity during those years. For, while writing those essays, he was also engaged in a variety of other occupations as well as beset by numberless worries and concerns. Our admiration grows when we consider, aside from the dizzying number and diversity of his themes, the amount of learning he brought to his task, the authoritative way in which he discussed his subjects, and the masterly individuality of his style.

In a synthesis about the Founding Fathers and their role in the birth of the American nation, Martí expressed the following: "Washington pacified, Madison prepared, Hamilton administered, Franklin advised, and Jefferson urged." Just a few words, and yet they fully describe the psychogenesis of a country. As for the man who saved the Union and kept the nation strong and indivisible, Martí felt that "every one of his acts assured him a place in what is best of every heart." "Who," he added, "could fail to be overcome by Abraham Lincoln's saintly greatness?" The United States itself Martí called "freedom's best home." Tributes like these appear quite often in his writings.

But when it came to questions strictly within the bounds of inter-American politics—especially when he was shaken by the thought that his native Cuba might fall before the onslaught of the United States—he was, momentarily, no longer the universal man nor the citizen of the world. At such times, he found it easier to remember the United States' imperialistic blunders than to recall that it was "the best home of freedom." Then he abandoned the vantage point from which he so often looked out with clear and prophetic vision to give way to his patriotic concern. "Once the United States is in Cuba," he once wrote, "who can drive it out?" He did not foresee that the United States would one day become the most powerful ally of Cuba in her fight for independence.

Martí feared that, once having gained a foothold in the Antilles, the United States would proceed with greater force against the other countries of the hemisphere. "I have lived inside the monster and I know its vitals," he said.

Nationalistically minded North Americans take offense at these words, just as the enemies of the United States take malicious pleasure in quoting them. Both forget the painful occasion in which they were uttered: it was Martí's angry reaction because the United States had confiscated three ships loaded with arms for the Cuban revolution. He was also suffering at that time, as Jorge Mañach reminds us, from a recurrence of an old ailment: "an inguinal infarct that got sore with long walks and prevented him from moving or taking up arms." He was, above all, overwhelmed by feelings of anxiety that, as Félix Lizaso has pointed out, became habitual with him during the last years of his restless life.[2]

In all justice to a just man, we should bear in mind all these circumstances. We should remember, too, that Martí once said that no man would ever dare look in the United States for a place to sow the seeds of tyranny. Martí did occasionally criticize the United States, and in so doing he did commit some errors of judgment, but he also voiced many justified protests against expansionist policies that the best minds in this country were among the first to recognize and condemn. In short, his negative reactions to the United States— some justified and some not—were far outnumbered by his many expressions of sincere, enduring respect and admiration for the land of Emerson, Lincoln, Whitman, and Longfellow.

Hardly a praiseworthy event took place in what he called *nuestra América* that went unnoticed by Martí. On the occasion of the anniversary (September 30) of Guatemala's declaration of independence from Spain, for instance, Martí recalled how it was achieved "without spilling a single drop of blood." And commenting on the triumphal entry of the liberal revolutionists (June 30) in Guatemala City, he said that they did so only after having first decreed, from the battlefield, the free exercise of all human rights, which had until then been restricted.

With all the warmth of his magnanimous heart, Martí brooded protectingly over his sometimes misunderstood America, lovingly and zealously defending it. Never from so much conflict and misfortune, he said, had more generous and more precious peoples been born. With fervor almost religious he recalled words of the Argentinian Rivadavia saying that those countries would be saved. Martí was proud of them, and lived to honor and serve them. He felt, in consequence, that he had a right to admonish those peoples, and he said that their arms would be those of reason, which overcome all others. This almost maternal feeling added accents of sincerity to his words. "Where could a man have a better right to be proud of his motherland," he asked, "than in our suffering American republics?"

And, what kind of government should these countries have? ". . . it should be born of the people; its spirit should be the spirit of the people; its form congruent with the constitution of the country as a whole. Government is simply the equilibrium of a country's natural elements."

Martí's most significant words on the subject of justice and hemispheric solidarity are, perhaps, those he dedicated to José María Heredia in an article written in 1888 and then in a speech delivered in November, 1889.

Why so? For one thing, Martí spent more years of his life in the adversity of exile than he did in his own country. After his disappointment with the government of Spain's First Republic, he never made overtures for a possible reconciliation with the Spanish rulers. He was convinced that the surest way to victory is patience and that the ability to wait is a sign of strength. He took good care to live in such a way as to deserve the esteem of his fellowmen. And, although fate had it that he should set out on the seas of life with black sails on his ship, white was the color that he chose to symbolize his arduous existence:

A fair white rose I do tend
In January as in July

> For the man who loyally
> Gives me his hand as a friend.
>
> And for that cruelest of foes
> Who would see my heart all torn,
> I grow not bramble nor thorn:
> I grow but the fair white rose.[3]

Heredia, also a lover of liberty, became involved in the political conspiracy known as "Los Rayos y Soles de Bolívar" and had to leave Cuba in 1823 in order to avoid imprisonment. He went to New York, but there he found the life of an exile intolerable. In one of his letters he told of how deeply depressed he felt. The thought that the best he could hope for was to live in New York for the rest of his days, he said, made him long for death.

Year after year Heredia maintained his integrity. Then came the year 1836 when the Spanish government granted amnesty to many who had opposed it—but not to Heredia. Heredia made friendly overtures to Spain, but to no avail. It was then that he wrote his famous letter of retraction—the letter so many have since refused to forgive him—addressed to don Miguel Tacón, the Spanish *Capitán General* of Cuba.

When at long last Heredia could return to his homeland, on November 4, 1836, his former friends repudiated him. One of them called him "a fallen angel." Heredia left Cuba again, became a Mexican citizen, and spent the rest of his life in Mexico.

The grief of Martí for his country made him take, as he once said, his first steps toward Heaven. In one of his letters he protested: "But don't you know that there is in me no particle of egotism or vanity, no thought for nor cultivation of my own ego; that death is my pillow and Cuba my only dream; and that I keep and use myself only to smooth over difficulties for my country and to serve it?"

These words show us how deeply Cuba's bitter plight had entered into his soul and how it tortured him. Any threat to

Cuba made Martí tremble; nothing brought him happiness unless it brought honor to Cuba. Long before a Spanish bullet killed him, he had already received his death wound from vicious slander and malicious misrepresentation.

How did Martí—who fell only to rise again, at once, into immortality—regard Heredia, who had fallen before only to take refuge in the forgetfulness of solitude?

Heredia's adoption of Mexican citizenship did not disturb Martí, who deeply loved the land of Benito Juárez. His comment on this question was that Heredia "had felt drawn to Mexico, the land of hearts of gold and welcoming arms, where they are not afraid to offer shelter to a stranger." For Martí, Mexico was a land where all noble sentiments take root, a part of the Americas of which he was a son and to which he felt he totally belonged. So profound were his feelings in this respect that Cuba and *nuestra América* became as one in his hopes and affections. Such open-mindedness of continent-wide solidarity permitted him to rise above geographical boundaries and nationalistic pettiness. This trait had already been evident in him when he said of General San Martín that his greatest glory was that "he never looked upon the nations of the Americas as separate entities, but rather, with a flaming passion, he saw the whole continent as one single American nation."

Who, among Martí's compatriots, would have had a better right to condemn Heredia, had Heredia really deserved the scorn of posterity? Yet, Martí was the one who with the greatest kindness and tolerance forgave him. And, how did Martí do it? By trying to find excuses for Heredia's weaknesses? No: he simply dwelt on Heredia's virtues and strengths.

Here, as in everything else, Martí lived up to his own moral maxim that "compassion is the mark of select souls"—one more aspect of his personality, which Alfonso Hernández Catá cited in his book, *Mitología de Martí,* with these apt words: "[Martí] was one of those echoes of Divinity who from time to time appear upon this earth, nobody knows whether before or after their time." It was precisely because he, too, felt keenly that to live away from his native land was a kind of death that Martí was so generously fair to Heredia. With his "Ode to Niagara," Heredia earned for Cuba all the praise universally heaped upon his immortal poem. And Martí, like a dutiful son admitting his debt to his father, declared that it may have been Heredia who awoke in his soul, as in that of all Cubans, "an inextinguishable passion for liberty."

This particular aspect of José Martí's sense of justice, which has been barely touched upon—as many other aspects to be found in his work—is almost inexhaustible. No matter how deeply we might delve into this mine, even working all together to extract its treasures, we could not grasp them all at one time. What Martí once said of someone else he might justly have said of himself: that "he was one of those who have gathered unto themselves a great sum of universal life and know everything, for they themselves are a compendium of the universe in which they live."

The work of Martí is a work of genius. It is one whose message grows significant with time and projects itself into the future, quenching with its refreshing juice the thirst of justice of each new generation. For, as Paul de Saint-Victor said of Marcus Aurelius, this man "had a mind of bronze, but was all human flesh in love and tenderness."

[From *Expresión de Hispanoamérica*, Vol. I, San Juan, Puerto Rico: Instituto de Cultura Puertorriqueña, 1960.]

8
The Immortal Message of Andrés Bello

In Chapter VII of his *Letras y hombres de Venezuela*, Arturo Uslar Pietri wrote about the poet Juan Antonio Pérez Bonalde: "Born in Caracas in 1846, he had hardly reached the age of adolescence when the upheaval of the Federal War sent him with his family into exile. His father decided to establish himself in Puerto Rico, one of the traditional refuges of exiled Venezuelans."

The family of this masterly translator of Poe and Heine were neither the first nor the last of their countrymen to find sanctuary in Puerto Rico. As early as 1821, prominent members of the Venezuelan upper classes, fearing the new regime established after the wars of independence, left their country to make their home in Puerto Rico.

One of those refugees was the girl who later became the mother of the Puerto Rican poet, José Gualberto Padilla, better known by his pen name, "El Caribe."

Puerto Rico, being neither indifferent nor inclined to violence, was a kind of little Switzerland in America where the exiles found an atmosphere conducive to the healing of political wounds and the easing of material problems. The hospitable and cordial Puerto Ricans provided for the Venezuelans a peaceful environment and offered them the opportunity to earn a living. In return, many of the Venezuelans accepted their welcome with friendly gratitude while serving their adopted country well and honorably.

It is therefore not strange that, among the many unforgettable messages left us by the great men of the Americas, I, as a Puerto Rican, should choose as a theme the enduring aspects of the poetic genius of that Venezuelan humanist, Andrés Bello, especially since he voiced ideas so congruent with my people's idiosyncrasy and traditions.

Spanish America has its immortal triumvirate in the field of arms: Bolívar, San Martín, and Sucre. Bolívar gave wings to his ideas with the ardor typical of his extraordinary and passionate temperament. Endowed with prophetic vision, he accurately foretold, as early as 1815, many of the situations that would arise and events that would later take place in the Spanish-speaking nations of the Americas.

A man possessed of such insight into as yet remote situations cannot always put his mind to the task of winning the support of those who demand immediate results. More than once Bolívar had no other alternative but going into exile—a decision that, although it often seems voluntary, almost never is.

Bolívar's passion was not a thoughtful but a dynamic one. It was beauty and danger joined together like in a spark: it would sometimes burn with a bright light, sometimes with an all-consuming flame.

Everything Bolívar did, he did impulsively. Evidence of this can be seen, for instance, in his farewell letter to Fanny de Villars, written while he was still in Europe. His lack of planning and method is notorious also in his political actions, as when, years later, he went to London as his country's representative and startled the Foreign Minister by not defending the cause of the king of Spain, Ferdinand VII, as expected, but instead demanding support for the independence movement in his native Venezuela.

If Venezuela wore like a crown the splendor of the living flame of revolution, she did not lack the light of wisdom and mature thought. While Bolívar's cry for freedom unleashed the oppressed hearts of the Creoles, Andrés Bello's serene and clear voice reminded them that peace should be a goal and an ideal to be served in an orderly and constructive way.

Thus Venezuela, as the homeland of Bolívar and Andrés Bello, gave the Americas two stars of the first magnitude, yet remarkably contrasting.

That the two men were essentially different becomes obvious when we recall that the wise and scholarly Bello was not Bolívar's favorite teacher. The young genius preferred instead Simón Rodríguez, whose romanticism enlivened the fire of his spirit and instilled a noble unrest into his youthful impulses. It was Rodríguez who opened up vast panoramas for his pupil and inspired him with his wanderlust, with the desire, as he said, not to be rooted like a tree, but to be in perpetual motion like the water and the wind.

This love for being constantly on the move, this search for one's true self in foreign lands, was by no means unique in the splendid Venezuela of that time. It was Venezuela that produced the first universal personality of Hispanic America. It is, therefore, no wonder that Francisco de Miranda—after a cosmopolitan life in Spain, France, England, Prussia, Austria, Italy, Russia, Turkey, Greece, the United States, Cuba, Jamaica, and other countries—should have become the forerunner of the independence of the southern republics. Every climate was propitious to his adventurous spirit and inquiring mind: they all served to confirm him in his passionate love of liberty.

The great men of that period of South American history were not provincial souls: not one of them was restricted by chauvinistic ideas. Heroes of a whole continent, frontiers to them were only stepping-stones to broader fields of thought and action in the service of freedom for the New World. Their vision was not narrowed by the blinders of nationalism. They dreamed of wide horizons, and believed in making their continent great in unity, not weakened by sterile divisions. They dreamed and fought, created and served, not for this or that section of their America, but for the whole of it, which they saw as a vital unit.

San Martín, returning to Argentina after having completed his military training in Spain and fighting as an officer of high rank and distinction in the Spanish army, did not lay down his sword once he won the independence of his country: he fought in Chile and offered his protection to Peru.

Bolívar's oath at the Aventine, like a lightning bolt, showed in one fiery instant the whole future of the Americas. It was not in his own Venezuela but in a foreign land that the Liberator made his definitive commitment to freedom.

Andrés Bello's eighteen years in England were years of learning, teaching, and meditation—and classical in tone. Bello was only two years older than Bolívar, but, in a way, he felt himself to be living in the past, while Bolívar dreamed of a future yet in gestation in his universe of passion and violence, of prophecy and creativity.

The work of the Liberator spread from the north to the south of his continent. Five republics sprang from it: Venezuela, Colombia, Ecuador, Peru, and Bolivia. He lived for them, and for them he died. For them he enjoyed the taste of glory and suffered the pain of sacrifice. And, toward the end, he said bitterly, "I have plowed the sea."

Once again we find Puerto Rico and Venezuela linked, this time by a poem written by the Puerto Rican, Luis Lloréns Torres, in honor of Bolívar:

> Poet, soldier, statesman, hero, he stands,
> Great like the countries whose freedom he won;
> He whom no country can claim as son,
> Though as his daughters were born many lands.
>
> His valor was that of he who bears a sword;
> His courtesy was that of he who wears a flower:
> Entering salons, he laid by the sword;
> Plunging in battles, he tossed away the flower.

The peaks of the Andes to him seemed to be
But exclamation points after his stride:
Soldier-poet he was; poet-soldier was he!

Each land that he freed
Was a soldier's poem and poet's deed:
And he was crucified.[1]

The work of Bello, diffused throughout South America, was aimed at teaching the people to speak their language correctly. As an educator, Bello soon realized that learning to read might well be the most urgent need of most of the population of Hispanic America. Not only that, people should also be taught to make reading a habit. As a grammarian, Bello saw that the Spanish spoken in those countries was poor and needed improvement, and diligently set himself to the task.

Andrés Bello was a man capable of giving himself to profound thought without his judgment being clouded by the conflicts of the age. Notice, for instance, his assertion that the revolutionary movement in his America sprang from Spanish cultural elements in those countries, and, therefore, Spain could not be accounted guilty of all the errors and crimes attributed to her. Where so many were blinded by prejudice, he perceived reality with a lucid humanistic view.

Bello had already conceived his immortal message when he was called to Chile in 1826. He was then living in London, where he was publishing his newspaper, *El Repertorio Americano*. There Juan Egaña sent him an invitation to go to serve as an advisor to the Chilean government. The great example of ignoring frontiers and transcending territorial divisions in order to serve a republic not his own was yet to be repeated. While still in London, however, he had published also his "Silva a la agricultura de la zona tórrida." [2]

Broad as the scope suggested by this title is, it still fails to suggest the full greatness of the work. For this is not merely a descriptive poem, nor is it simply a glorification of the soil and flora—the geography and botany—of a new world rich in promise for the new man of the Americas. It is a flowering of warnings, admonitions, and advice, of expressions of hope, unified by the vision of a fatherland common to all, which was to be just, useful, prosperous, and universal. The Colombian critic, Miguel A. Caro, considers that this poem surpasses "the highest and most highly priced gifts of eloquence" to be found in the rest of Bello's poetry. Actually, Bello was more than "the most Virgilian of our poets," as the Spanish critic, Menéndez y Pelayo, called him, including all the Spanish-speaking world in his evaluation.

Bello's experience in England—a country so rich in civic freedom, so appreciative of equanimity, the home of law—taught him day after day that nonmilitary institutions are as worthy of respect and emulation, as deserving of immortality, as the heroic epic of the captains who crossed the Andes and were victorious in the battlefields of Maipó, Boyacá, Junín, and Apurima.

At a time when the glow of the last battle for independence had not yet been extinguished, when the flames of heroism and the fires of war still, after sixteen long years, burned brightly, Bello invoked peace. He predicted a splendid future when men should think: "Liberty sweeter than the empire, / And the olive than laurel lovelier far." [3] For: "There, too, are duties / To be fulfilled: close, close the deep / Wounds made by war." [4]

It will be necessary to restore a spirit of brotherhood, move the mill-wheel, clear the forest, open vital highways toward the future. War had filled the earth with ruins, reduced it to ashes: ". . . tombstone / Of earthly joy, wind's mockery." [5]

But hope lives again, for the first flower of spring, lovely to the sight, has grown from that mistreated soil. The poet, usually cold, expresses at times in this poem the tenderness of one who sees a soul in nature, and loves her in the farmer worthy of divine mercy:

> May his piety, rustic, yet sincere,
> Find grace before thine eyes;

May he never over failed hope shed a tear
Misled by a false dream's flattering lies;
Preserve from unseasonable rain
The delicate embryo in the seed;
Let no vengeful gust the seedlings bruise
Nor the ripening grain
Voracious gnawing insect feed:
And send not a long hot summer's drought
To dry up the tree's maternal juice.[6]

The poet prays repeatedly that wicked war shall be buried in the depths of the deepest abysses; that fearful unrest shall leave men's souls. For the list of the doomed, the tortured, the orphaned, and the dead is already endless.

Bello's "Silva" establishes a parallel between agriculture and peace, rural life and good government, poetry and the hope of civic virtues capable of creating a great America. Seldom has reason reached so high in the Spanish language to serve the whole family of Hispanic peoples.

Did they heed Bello's message in time? Had they done so, the number of conflicts between the republics of the hemisphere, once at peace with Spain, and the civil wars in them would have been considerably reduced. As it is, hardly five consecutive years have passed since the end of the wars of independence without frontier incidents or without a dictator coming to power—as a stain upon that world that Bello dreamed of as one of order and freedom, peace and justice.

The immortal message of Bello is, in fact, still valid today: it should be useful to listen to it. Useful if the poet's work is read not as a model of rhetoric but as a guide to conduct, a standard to live up to. Claims and counter-claims still continue to divide lands made one by geography. The disinterested love for the American continent as a whole that inspired men such as Miranda and San Martín, Bello and Bolívar, Egaña and Alfaro, Hostos and Martí is not triumphant yet.

Bello envisioned the unity of the Hispanic-American countries in a double sense, political and cultural. This latter aspect is kept alive by his own humanistic works on grammar. Bello—like Rufino José Cuervo, Justo Sierra, Marcos Fidel Suárez, Eugenio María de Hostos, and Rafael Angel de la Peña—was a great teacher. The other aspect of the hemispheric unity, however, still awaits the leadership of men of good faith who will not content themselves with the words of Bello's "Silva," but will go deeply into their spirit and give them dynamic and enduring life.

[From *Expresión de Hispanoamérica*, Vol. I, San Juan, Puerto Rico: Instituto de Cultura Puertorriqueña, 1960.]

9

Luis Muñoz Rivera, Civil Poet of Puerto Rico

I

Emerson once said, "Every true man is a cause, a country, and an age." [1]

Regardless of whom the New England sage had in mind, we Puerto Ricans know that these words could apply to no one more exactly than to Luis Muñoz Rivera (1859–1916).

The pro-autonomy movement of Román Baldorioty de Castro was the most spontaneous development in the political conscience of nineteenth-century Puerto Ricans, and the one with widest repercussions. Neither the abnegation of Ramón Emeterio Betances nor the continental reach of Eugenio María de Hostos sufficed to alter the course of Puerto Rico in this respect.

In his article on Baldorioty de Castro, written in New York on May 14, 1892, José Martí said: "The cause of autonomy was not for him a mere exchange of conviviality with those charming generals who are in the habit of hanging tomorrow those with whom they played chess yesterday; it was the true defense —in jail, in poverty, in exile—of the liberties in whose vanguard he was always to be found. For never did freedom advance so far in Puerto Rico that Baldorioty was not ahead of it." [2]

In his *Antología puertorriqueña. Prosa y verso* (New York,

1923), Manuel Fernández Juncos wrote: "No Puerto Rican ever enjoyed in his lifetime a greater popularity than don Román Baldorioty de Castro, and none was ever more affectionately remembered by his fellow citizens after his death."

When this patriot's light began to dim, the ideal of self-government, dear as it was to our forefathers' heart, would have collapsed at that point for lack of a leader with the powerful intelligence and the unwavering will necessary to face up to the realities of the moment. It was at this juncture that Luis Muñoz Rivera became a significant figure in the political life of Puerto Rico. His leadership and proud civic-minded genius breathed new life and vigor into the autonomy movement and made its twilight flare up again into a new dawn of hope. True, it was overcome by shadows almost as soon as it appeared, but only to regain its splendor under new and even more difficult circumstances.

Muñoz Rivera was always in front whenever responsibility was challenged. He was a man who could assert before his judges: "Forty-two times have I been tried, and every time for the crime of patriotism." Yet, he never incited his followers to useless sacrifice; his victories were those to be won by a persevering mind, by rational patience, and by prudent evolution.

As early as 1893, he wrote that "from concession to concession it was possible to go far." With this in mind, he concentrated on looking for an empirical solution for each problem as it arose. The majority of Puerto Ricans understood the dynamics of this carefully planned progress—his method of forwarding the cause of the people without demanding of them a sterile immolation—and expressed their approval of his program and their trust in his leadership. Muñoz Rivera was aware of the weaknesses of a small country such as Puerto Rico; his policy, therefore, was to find a specific remedy for each new crisis—as if showing by this flexibility his agreement with Renan's dictum that our opinions become stagnant at the point where we stop thinking. Like the men of Greece's best period, Muñoz Rivera was not merely willing to face facts: he was interested in meeting and overcoming difficulties, without ever avoiding them or denying their existence.

His private life and political career reveal the painful psychic distortions of a man spurred on by strong rebellious impulses and at the same time checked by the reins of self-imposed moderation. His integrity and sense of civic responsibility forced him to think calmly and speak deliberately while his inner fire blazed. Such self-control was not the least of the sacrifices made by a man who, sternly keeping his passions in hand, was never silent when it was necessary to speak out or to make demands for his country's sake.

None of the military governors imposed by Spain upon Puerto Rico was more cruel or determined to stamp out the autonomy movement than General Palacios. Luis Muñoz Rivera protested vigorously against this man's abuses and instigated the people also to protest. From his poem against General Palacios, we quote the following stanzas: [3]

> Behold him! Look well upon the face
> Of this old overseer of the troop:
> No curve of kindness lends that smile its grace,
> No single gleam of light softens that look.
>
> Sinister soul; congested, brutish face;
> Lips drooping in a gesture of disdain;
> Heart that no plea for mercy ever sways;
> Ear closed to every cry of pain.
>
> . . . .
>
> High among the mountain peaks he plots
> The arbitrary orders he dictates,
> Lurking with his reptiles and his helots
> Behind masses of guns and bayonets.
>
> Fearing the avenging fever, he his tent
> Has pitched far from the sea and there unlocks
> The coffer of his military trials, bent
> On loosing the evils of a new Pandora's box.

Inquisitor! to prey upon our land
Your hordes of myrmidons you send
Like a black and ravenous band
Falling upon us to murder and to rend!

. . . .

Before this monstruous abortion of the abyss,
There are still men who hold their heads up high,
Whose soul with horror rejects his tyrannies
And are filled with sublime contempt of life.

While one heart beats with full integrity,
Red dawns of vengeance still present a threat
And little David with his puny sling
May fell the Iberian Goliath yet.

A general who never saw a fight!
Bereft of honor, of chivalry, of all;
To cut down ideas in their flight—
That is the only use he gives his sword.

Enjoy your peace, O tyrant! for the day
Shall come when your murky solitude
Is broken by a storm yet far away,
The clamor of a distant multitude.

And then a cry of rage shall fill the air:
Roar of a titan that his yoke shall rend;
Cry of a people as their chains they tear;
Cry of a people that their hangman curse! [4]

Like Martí, who made a distinction between the Spanish government, against which he rebelled with all his soul and against which he bore arms, and the people of Spain, whom he wholeheartedly loved, Muñoz Rivera was able to distinguish even among the men sent to Puerto Rico with the authority to rule. He lashed out at Romualdo Palacios, but this did not cloud his judgment of General Contreras, who was a friend of

Puerto Rico. When Contreras' term as governor ended in 1889, the poet, speaking for his people, publicly recognized Contreras' merits. But not without first asserting and confirming the collective decorum of the people for whom Muñoz Rivera spoke:

> Never has Borinquen's sad muse sold
> Her honor, nor profaned her grief
> By rendering, like a lying courtesan,
> A facile tribute to vile flattery.

> Austere and noble in misfortune grave,
> Her laurel-crowned head held high,
> She did once quietly fold her wings
> Like a bird nesting by seething crater's side;
> But never, forgetful of her greatness,
> Did she grovel to seek security
> In the shelter of abrupt fortress walls
> Nor in a palace of wealth and luxury.

> . . . .

> Today Borinquen lifts her voice in grief,
> And fills with echoes her mountains and her plains,
> Coming to bid you, General, Godspeed,
> With her native songs' harsh, untutored strains.

> Heed her, General, she does not lie,
> Nor the purity of her wings does ever stain;
> She cannot falsely make a show of grief,
> Nor the transports of a warm affection feign.

> One day the storm unleashed upon us broke,
> Our people's gaze turned, stunned, to Spain;
> At last the motherland gave hope
> To bring a surcease to such pain.

> You were the dawn that lighted up our heaven;
> You were the rainbow stretched across our sky;

You were the hope that we at length were given
To still our grief and calm our agony.

. . . .

May the gallant vessel of your life
By Fortune's favoring breezes be impelled;
May you live to be the glory and the pride
Of the illustrious land that gave you birth! [5]

The twentieth century was well into its second decade and Spain's sun had long since set in the Greater Antilles when Muñoz Rivera went to Washington as Resident Commissioner from Puerto Rico. While in the capital, he received from Señora Díaz Navarro a postcard with the Spanish flag and coat-of-arms. On the reverse side of the card, Muñoz Rivera wrote:

Yesterday, when that flag hung like a threat
Above my country's battlements,
How gladly my life I would have given
To see it from our shores driven,
Sailing away with its hues of gold and red!
Today, in its flagship drooping somberly,
Leaving, it takes what can never be replaced,
A code of honor and of chivalry.
And now, what would I not give to see
That flag, alas! rule over the whole world. [6]

II

Speaking of his dreams and hopes for Puerto Rico, Muñoz Rivera wrote verses about his program of peaceful affirmation as one engraving in bronze for posterity:

Fiery of heart, serene of soul,
With sinewy arm, will strong and free,
Faith for a guide and reason as control,

> Owning no flag but liberty;
> Without the pariah's cowardly submission,
> Without the brute's innate ferocity:
>
> So, in my dreams of precarious ambition,
> I longed to see my country stand one day
> Not as a mob that in hopeless revolution
> By feckless violence is led astray.[7]

The above lines are from his "Nulla est redemptio," and were written in 1889. In 1901, he reaffirmed their thought in another poem, "París":

> I reject rioting. Yes! I reject
>   Rebellion that unchecked
> To kill, rob, burn, annihilate is made:
> I know that reason has sold out her rights
>   When in the streets she fights,
> Sheltering behind the abrupt barricade.[8]

Never in Spanish America had a people been given norms of orderly political evolution by a man of so virile a temperament as Luis Muñoz Rivera. In this sense, he is unique among those who speak his same language in the New World. Such an image becomes more definite when we recall that he was a poet not of faint hues and shadowy nuances but of direct and fiery expression. That Muñoz Rivera was an independent, sanguine, and energetic man is clearly shown by his actions as well as by these lines:

> And thus, in my verses' turbulence,
> Something answers to the restlessness in me,
> For to their slow unfolding clings a sense
> Of the volcano's fatal blast of heat
> And of the tempest's deadly violence.[9]

That is a stanza from his poem, "Ráfaga," where he also describes himself as "crude and proud." The following lines are from another poem, "Mens divinor":

> Face to the sun, upon the solid language
> Where the ideal has left its mark
> I tame my stanzas as a gaucho
> In the pampas breaks in his wild mustangs.[10]

In still another composition, "Amparo," he shows his awareness that the echo of a woman's voice has given his lyre "the soft note that till then it lacked."

The truth is that if the equanimity of his thinking often made him appear as having the hardness of marble, it was only because he smothered his inner fires with self-discipline. With all his popularity, he could well have instigated the people to bloodthirsty revolt, had it not been for the clarity of his aspirations. He was quite aware of what the clanging bells mean when the motherland demands "wide walls of virile breasts, / exploding gunpowder, and clashing swords." Dwelling on this thought, he would say:

> I know the hoarse shout
> Of the bells
> As they swing in disorderly rout;
> I know they call out:
> "Revenge! Revenge!" as they knell.[11]

But, with the vision of a prudent statesman, he worked carefully and unremittingly on a political system based upon law, order, and justice. Four unforgettable lines bear the stamp of his mental attitude:

> In this valley of misery and mud,
> I care for nothing; here is my philosophy:
> To be at war always and against all,
> With my own conscience being always at peace.[12]

These last two lines embody the living essence of Spanish quixotism exalted to a religion of duty.

As the verses I have been quoting bear out again and again,

we could say of Luis Muñoz Rivera what Alfonso Méndez Plancarte said of the Mexican, Salvador Díaz Mirón, that "his poetry does not invite one to dream, nor does it stir into vague movement the sleeping waters of the spirit." [13]

There is, however, at least one clear-cut difference between Díaz Mirón and this limpid man from Puerto Rico. Of the Veracruzan poet, Francisco Monterde wrote: "For the Mexican poet of the twilight of Romanticism . . . the shortest route to popularity lay across the public square of scandal, the resonance of which measured the stature of genius. Young Díaz Mirón disdained any other yardstick." [14]

Although Muñoz Rivera once fought a duel—in circumstances that according to the norms of his time made it unavoidable—his courage was not usually expressed by means of the natural aggressiveness, augmented by the stimulus of the tropics, that Monterde sees in Díaz Mirón. Often insidiously persecuted, his sensibility wounded by more than one taunt, his printing press destroyed by a cowardly mob, Muñoz Rivera turned every attack upon him into a victory of his spirit. He could honestly declare that though his enemies should be as numerous as the sands of the sea and the stars in heaven, he was the enemy of no man.[15]

III

Being a man of a well-defined and vigorous personality, Muñoz Rivera endeavored to help Puerto Rico develop a character of its own, and never consented to his country being treated without due consideration and respect. Like a sculptor modeling a lump of clay, he worked on the amorphous mass of the colony, striving to give it a shape whose lines and planes would have a distinct image, worthy of being given the permanence of bronze. His words were as effective as weapons as they were as an artist's tools. And so well did he achieve his aim with them that Puerto Ricans have ever since been filled

with such love of their land and its typical features that neither long absence nor exile, poverty, or prosperity have been
able to tear from the heart of those born in that small island
their loyalty to it. Indeed, it is the ardent desire of every
Puerto Rican that his nationality shall endure, as it is his ac-
knowledged duty, too, to glorify it with his devotion in his
memory and spirit.

Let us not confuse, however, Muñoz Rivera's healthy re-
gionalism with the blind nationalism that refuses to seek—or
even to see—what is of value outside its own country. Muñoz
Rivera found nourishment for his spirit not only in the sap of
his own native land but also in the fresh sweetness of that of
other nations. Rather than raise confining walls, he opened
frontiers to the souls of men. We are, inevitably, insular
enough, God knows! Why add to our natural isolation by rejecting contacts that will enrich us as part of the universal
harmony? We need not cut ourselves off from our roots or forget our native idiosyncrasies and earthly passions; but we
should not demand a national identification tag on anything
that may ennoble us. Such was Muñoz Rivera's kind of region-
alism: one that would affirm what defines us among the rest of
mankind without making us a peculiar and eccentric species.

It is revealing in this respect that a book by Muñoz Rivera
like *Tropicales*—so much his own as ours, as well as of the lati-
tudes that gave it its name—should begin with a poem dedicated not to Puerto Rico but to Kosciuzko's immortal Warsaw
—"where the heroes of Poland their honor defend." It is likewise significant that the Marseillaise and the city of Paris
should also provide the themes for two other poems in the
book. Moreover, the book contains still another poem, "Vendi-
miaria," which is a lyrical consecration of the wines of different nationalities—like those of Cyprus, Falerno, Jerez, the
Rhine, Champagne, and Tokay, this last one being called "the
blood of Hungary that nourishes unvanquished patriots."

Muñoz Rivera voiced his solidarity with all persecuted patriots everywhere, well knowing that suffering is the same

through the whole length and breadth of the world, and that identical impulses stimulate the unanimous will of all crusaders for freedom.

More than once he felt discouraged almost to the point of hopelessness. But a man struggling to instill in his people the kind of social conscience that was his own ideal was not apt to capitulate to pessimism. In his poem, "La estatua," Muñoz Rivera prophesied a splendid new dawn for us Puerto Ricans:

> This gentle nymph that to the lullaby
> Of the palm fronds now drowses languidly,
> Shall one day strong and triumphant rise
> Shaking off her anaemic lethargy;
> Feeling a new life surge
> Like fresh blood through her arteries,
> And forever, yes! forevermore her life
> Shall be lived in joy, greatness, and dignity.[16]

And, like a joyful peal of bells, like a hosanna of affirmation, he added, jubilant, sure, trusting:

> *Ese día vendrá. ¡Llegad, hermanos!*

[From *Expresión de Hispanoamérica*, Vol. II, San Juan, Puerto Rico: Instituto de Cultura Puertorriqueña, 1963.]

10❖
My Memories
of Alfonso Reyes,
A Mexican
Savant

I

In Madrid, when I was a very young man, Ramón Gómez de la Serna invited me once to a farewell dinner. The place was not surely to be the crypt of Pombo, the cafe where Gómez de la Serna used to have his literary gatherings. The guest of honor was none other than Alfonso Reyes, that man of universal culture—as had been evident to all from the time his first book was published—who had early found his real self by delving deeply into the treasure trove of the Greek and Spanish classics. Not that this ever prevented him from being essentially and profoundly Mexican.

On February 15, 1911, Pedro Henríquez Ureña had written to Menéndez y Pelayo that Alfonso Reyes, "the youngest writer in Mexico," was already "the one with the most brilliant future."

Alfonso Reyes arrived in Madrid late in the year 1914, having left behind, as he used to say, "the holocaust of his fatherland and the collapse of his family." The day I am speaking of, he was met at the Lhardy restaurant by Ortega y Gasset, Azorín, Eugenio D'Ors, Andrenio, Eduardo Marquina, Enrique Díez-Canedo, Melchor Fernández Almagro, Gómez de la

Serna, and several other Spanish friends. From the Americas, I remember two compatriots of his, Francisco A. de Icaza and Luis G. Urbina, and the Cuban José María Chacón y Calvo.

I listened to Reyes with a devotion aroused in me not only by his ideas but by the way he expressed them. At that time, there were in Madrid two or three Spanish-American ambassadors whose pompous and chauvinistic oratory sounded like a clash of tambourines with a beating of drums, being just plain gibberish. And now here was this man: small-great, outstanding, self-contained, deliberate, and subtle in his finely attuned, thoughtful remarks. After having served his country as chargé d'affaires, he was about to return to Mexico, as free of verbosity as he had come and deserving as ever of unanimous intellectual respect. He would have some rest and then was to be named minister plenipotentiary to other American republics.

His words, spoken in a low voice, were profound, winged, decorous, full of spirit. His farewell speech distilled sincere emotion: "Farewell, Spain, very much my own. Soon it will be eleven years since I left my country. Now they call me back and it is time for me to return. . . ." But there was also in his voice a certain undercurrent accent: that of a man who is going to make himself useful without having any conditions imposed upon him, his own life and work being sufficient proof of his integrity and culture.

Eugenio D'Ors, that good-natured and corpulent humanist with the "studiedly wild" bushy eyebrows, put an unforgettable footnote to the occasion. Reyes, he told us, had corrected the Spanish image of the "golden-tongued" Spanish American. How exact this appraisal was! Reyes did know how to silence the tin songbird and let the nightingale sing out. He was, indeed, putting an end to decades of fatuity and offenses against good taste, replacing them by the tone of a man who would one day write,

> Perfect rose that I adore,
> How shall my words be stressed

> Your perfection to implore
> Save by the beats in my breast? [1]

That day I hardly spoke to Alfonso Reyes, except perhaps a few words of admiration. I felt that I was too young to claim his attention, that he should be left free to give his hand and ear to his important friends.

II

Ten years later, when he was representing his country in Brazil, I sent Alfonso Reyes a small volume of my lyrics. His answer was prompt and, typically, no mere routine acknowledgment. On the flyleaf of a copy of the Madrid edition of his book, *La Visión de Anáhuac* (1923), he had written some very encouraging words: "To José A. Balseiro, in return for his enchanting *Sonetos,* with cordial greetings, Alfonso Reyes. Río, 1934."

At intervals, during the next two years, Reyes sent me several of his other books. Then, on July 1, 1936, he sent me greetings from his home at 397 Laranjeiras Street, advising me that the following month I could write to him at the Mexican Embassy in Argentina, 820 Arroyo Street, Buenos Aires.

I had no doubt that I was corresponding with an eminent man, and eminent not only in the world of literature. His cordiality reminded me of Unamuno's, different as these two men were. Only, when don Miguel initiated his correspondence with me in 1928, he did so to comment on the long essay in my book, *El Vigía* (Volume II), where I discussed and praised his best novels, so undervalued then in Spain. [2]

Encouraged by the "alfonsequence" (the happy coinage was Alfonso Reyes' own) of my cosmopolitan friend from Monterrey, I dared to request that, if after having read my work he found it acceptable, he should write the prologue to my book of poetry, *La pureza cautiva.*

When Reyes had to return to Mexico, the pressing haste of his trip did not cause him to forget the young Puerto Rican professor at the University of Illinois. He asked Pedro Henríquez Ureña, a famous friend of his already mentioned, to return my manuscript. Henríquez Ureña kindly did so, sending me my work with Reyes' prologue.

This episode always reminds me of one expression in Reyes' book, *Cortesía,* so revealing of that delicate human touch of its author: "It does no harm to bring into everyday living the forms of culture."

Naturally, in interpreting what this wise and versatile intellectual meant by "forms of culture," we must not confuse good manners with unreasonable indulgence. A self-disciplined thinker and artist who used to set for himself ever higher standards, Reyes said before the Mexican Academy on March 22, 1955, that he was not in the habit of "proffering his admiration blindly." [3]

(Speaking of Reyes' prologue, I remember that one of our Puerto Rican writers said to me that it was disappointingly brief. How sad that a man should apply himself to measuring length instead of appreciating essence! He must have forgotten Gracián's pithy saying, "What's good, if short, is twice as good." But, after all, my distinguished compatriot's viewpoint was no different from that of Lincoln's contemporaries who failed to appreciate the Gettysburg Address. Real connoisseurs had no such trouble: many of those who have commented upon my work have begun by quoting those words that Alfonso Reyes wrote in Argentina on November 30, 1937.)

Reyes was still very young when he worked out a life-plan for himself, and it was his good fortune that he never once had to stray from his enlightened path. While still in preparatory school, he made a speech advising his fellow-students, "Have an ideal, have an aspiration, and if you can gradually attain them during your life, you will have found a reason for living." Many years later, on the occasion of being awarded the Avila Camacho Prize, he asserted, speaking at the Instituto

Mexicano del Libro on September 10, 1954, that he could still repeat those words without altering so much as a comma.

III

In the spring of 1951, the First Congress of Spanish-American Academies Affiliated to the Spanish Royal Academy met in Mexico. As a foreign member of the Spanish Academy, resident in the United States, I was officially invited by its then director, don Alejandro Quijano. I spoke with Reyes at two of the meetings, but our conversations were so frequently interrupted that nothing worth recording came of them. Reyes invited me to visit him at his home, but I fell ill, and when I was finally able to leave the hotel, it was only to board a Miami-bound plane.

In August, 1953, we held the Sixth Congress of the International Institute of Ibero-American Literature at Mexico City and at Guadalajara. On my arrival at the capital, so highly praised by Bernardo de Balbuena, I was welcomed by a large postal card from Alfonso Reyes. It was a photograph of his extraordinary library (containing over 40,000 volumes) with the humanist himself leaning upon the railing of the mezzanine where he worked. On the reverse side of the card he had written: "Let not my fine friend, don José A. Balseiro, forget that I expect him in this books corner. Telephone 152225. Thank you! (And if you wish to honor me by bringing along some of your friends, excellent!)"

What he so modestly called a "books corner" would have been more appropriately designated, like the library of Father Francisco Javier Clavijero in eighteenth-century Mexico, "a house of wisdom," for such it was to the visitor arriving at that "most transparent region of the air."

Germán Arciniegas, too, recalling Reyes, placed him in that very library when, in March, 1962, he wrote about "The friends of Alfonso Reyes":

To visit again the house of Alfonso Reyes is to continue a dialogue that death has not interrupted. Alfonso was he himself and his books, his papers, his file cards, and, of course, his courtesies. After long years of pilgrimage, he returned to Anáhuac and built himself a hall, big as a church, where he could keep in files, in companies, in battalions, the thousands of volumes he had acquired and treasured in Madrid, Paris, Rio de Janeiro, and Buenos Aires. Halfway up the walls of this enormous library, he built a mezzanine. There he lived— like a sentinel and a soothsayer. Early in the day he was at his command post: his desk. In half an hour he had read through and dealt with all his mail (for he was a man who answered letters!). After that, he gave himself up to his work, like a millionaire.

In a lecture at Nuevo León University, professor Ernesto Mejía Nieto said: "Reyes retired from life and shut himself up with his books. The last twenty years of his life, at least, he spent in his 'alphonsine chapel.' "

As can be seen, it is easy for different people to agree when they all try to appraise the treasure of so rich a personality. My words, written immediately after our friend died, express essentially the same reaction as those of Arciniegas and Mejía Nieto. After all, we had all visited that temple and were speaking of the same high priest.

IV

In the lyric verses of Alfonso Reyes there are many fraternal references to his friend and fellow-poet, Enrique González Martínez. Among them are the four poems in praise of the author of *Las señales furtivas:* "A celebrar los años del poeta," "Dio un paso más el áspero hachero inexorable," "Poeta, médico y . . . poco," and "El alma en soledad está indefensa." As for his tributes in prose, it is enough to cite Reyes' moving words, spoken some two years after the death of the author of *Ausencia y canto,* to appreciate the exemplary closeness, human and creative, that existed between them: ". . . and I want not to fail to mention, at least in passing, our sweet elder brother, whose shadow still walks amongst us: Enrique González Martínez."

These examples, added to the personal tributes to other beloved authors that abound in his poetic works,[4] encouraged me to suggest to him, during a conversation in 1953, that a most charming theme for an essay would be, "Alfonso Reyes and Friendship."

Seldom have I seen a man's face light up as his did then: his forehead seemed to become clearer, his eyes sparkling, his smile ineffable. Reyes' smile was what he himself liked a smile to be: "the brightness of a thought completely filling out consciousness." For it had "the quality of a confession," as the living smile that it was, always immaculate and trustworthy. (In a very limited way, these pages on Reyes are actually fragments of that essay to be written.)

V

At that time, Reyes himself told me that he suffered from a painful heart condition. It is a very curious fact that three friends, as close to each other as brothers, the Dominican Pedro Henríquez Ureña, the Spaniard Enrique Díez-Canedo, and Alfonso Reyes, should have contracted an identical disease and that all three, in that order, died of it.

During the conversation, Reyes gave me a copy of his collected poems, *Obra poética,* published the previous year, with the following inscription: "To José A. Balseiro, poet, writer, and a very dear friend. Most cordially, Alfonso Reyes, 1953."

In the summer of 1959, the Universidad Nacional Autónoma de México invited me to give a series of lectures on Hispanic-American literature. The Academia de la Lengua, of which Reyes was director, was to present me with an honorary diploma. The subject of my lecture was, "Mexicans and

Puerto Ricans." I would be introduced by another illustrious friend, Francisco Monterde, who was to succeed Reyes to the presidency of the Academy.[5]

My wife and I arrived in Mexico on July 25. The following day we went with Monterde to call on Reyes and his wife, *doña* Manuelita Mota.

We found Reyes painfully aged. Having let his beard grow, his face seemed full of gray shadows. Short as he was, his obesity made him look rotund as he sank deeply into his armchair. Near at hand, in the same mezzanine study, was the couch where, to save unnecessary steps, he then slept. We had the sudden impression of looking at a mass of deteriorating flesh. But after we embraced and he began to speak as fluently, harmoniously, and cleverly as ever, with his accustomed wit-seasoned wisdom, his spirit rose, batting its wings to prevail over the ailing body.

Apparently, his whole organism had been affected, and we could not prevent Reyes from referring to the ever more acute crises of his illness. It was not death that he feared. What terrified him was the possibility of a cerebral stroke: "Not that!" he protested emphatically. "To see myself mentally incapacitated with half my body dead—that I couldn't stand."

We all tried to change the subject, but Reyes kept coming back to it. "I once read," he told us, "that a certain tribe of Indians had a really enviable custom. When the cacique became decrepit, but before he was a total physical ruin, one of the tribe's strongest youths would take a club and, first making sure that the cacique was not aware of what he was about to do, ended his life with one well-aimed blow. That is what I would want now, when I'm only kept alive by the science of an eminent heart specialist, Dr. Cháves." (In "Impaciencia del Paciente," from his sonnet sequence, *Charla*, Reyes had written these incontrovertible words: "Techniques improve; the patient never does.") He went on, "They want me to stay here when I'm longing to return to Cuernavaca. There the thick-foliaged trees are my friends, for they are real trees, not those scrubby urban trees that are about the only ones left in Mexico City."

Who, on hearing Reyes speak like that, could have failed to recall a sonnet of his, the first of his book, *Homero en Cuernavaca:*

> To Cuernavaca, sweet retreat, I go
> When fickle or dejected I give in
> To an urge to interrupt my tale
> And give my story a breathing spell.
> To Cuernavaca I go, aspiring only
> To breathe her balmy breezes for awhile:
> A pause for ease and liberty
> At the brief distance of a sigh.
> Not country or city, peak or valley,
> But blessed solitude, quietness that heals
> Or mild, unsurfeiting company.
> Vegetable warmth where the Self
> As in a hammock sways to philosophic poise.
> To Cuernavaca I go, to Cuernavaca! [6]

Seeing Reyes as he was then and hearing him sigh for his Cuernavaca made the association of ideas inevitable. Here was a man who remained singularly sensitive to the natural beauty of every place where he had left a portion of his heart. Years before, for instance, passing through Rio, where he had once lived, on his way to Buenos Aires, he had written a beautiful poem with these meaningful lines: "Landscape is no longer enough: / We want it with memories too."

But Alfonso Reyes was too much of a refined soul to wallow for long in his personal sufferings when in the company of friends. He turned to me. He regretted not being able to make the speech introducing me at the Academy, although he hastened to add that Monterde would do it better: "Of course he will! I have asked, begged, my good colleagues to accept my resignation as director. I can no longer fulfill my duties there —as in this case, when I won't be able to be there to greet you." Our protests that he, being who he was, could not be substituted for were of no avail.

As we said goodbye, Reyes added, as if voicing his inner distress, "It is lamentable, lamentable! I shall be sure to ask Monterde to speak for me as I myself would have spoken." And he did, in fact, call aside the author of *Moctezuma, el de la silla de oro* to insist on this request with affectionate and courteous solicitude.

We had not yet reached the bottom of the steps when, in pressing accents of unforgettable sincerity, he repeatedly said to us, "Don't go away from Mexico without coming back to see me. Promise!"

We did as he wished.

But between our first and second visit—the last!—he developed further symptoms of heart trouble. At noon one day, before my lecture at the University, Monterde told me, "Alfonso was very ill last night."

One morning, however, we had word that Reyes expected us that afternoon.

We did not find him sick in bed but sitting at his work-table with the intellectual dedication he had expressed in Number 53 of his *Confidencias:*

> Never forgetting what long patience
> And resignation the farmer's work requires,
> I apply myself with diligence
> To my daily share of work, hour by hour.
> Never having sensed what difference
> There is between loss and profit,
> I plant without laxness or urgency
> Along the furrow that my hand has traced.
> While waiting for the appointed hour
> The seedlings I protect, the plantings spray,
> Straighten the stalk of my beloved flower,
> Weed well my plot; and when you see the spade
> Drop from my listless hand one day,
> You'll need not ask—you'll know I'm dead.[7]

His expression that day was different, very different. The shade of sadness had lifted from his face. He even laughed rather than smile, especially when a small boy with sparkling black eyes, olive skin, and quick, nervous movements burst into the room. "Ah, here is my Mexican grandson; no one could be more Mexican; see how lively he is." Reyes made these comments while the charming child quickly kissed him and dashed out of the room before his grandfather could finish the sentence. Reyes spoke in the light tone of one who is enjoying himself. His spirit, the spirit of a man who lived in the world of the intellect, like the geniuses of Greece's best period, could also be playful, finding depth in human joy. This quality shows, for instance, in the subtitle of one of his lyrical works, *Minuta,* which he presented as a "poetical game." In his prose, too, we often marvel at his epigrams, which are like gems compounded of wit and imagination. Describing the useful animals of his native Monterrey in a certain passage, he observed that "the horse, rather than a whole animal, is half of a centaur." Peacocks were for him "movable bushes, themes for a landscape." Of a kitten called Juana he said, with critical and epigrammatic intention, that she had taught him "a great lesson: how to tear up manuscripts."

VI

Having almost absolute control over his mental universe, Reyes did not shut himself up to passion—nor to sensuality either. He loathed what he called "that useless and gloomy abstinence that also withers," and confessed that he could be given up for "lost"—for dead, that is—if he ever turned away from "the challenge of a pair of red lips." In his essay, "De cómo Grecia construyó al hombre," we find the following suggestive comment: "In the *Illiad,* Agammemnon still dares to declare openly that he will force upon his home his slave and prisoner of war. Criseis, because he prefers her wit and charms to the less dazzling qualities of his wife, Clytemnestra (and no doubt all lovers of ancient literature share the taste of Agammemnon) ."

Reyes' personality was the closest to Goethe that could be found in the contemporary world. His line—according to the note that precedes his *La filosofía helenística*—was humanism, and he therefore classified himself among the "specialists in universals." He explained once: "We will not be satisfied with studying the objects of culture as isolated objects. We need to submerge ourselves in the historical and philosophical contexts of each age."

Reyes knew that "without love there is no understanding." His method in searching for truth was based on "a delicate equilibrium between joy and knowledge." For him, happily, these extremes complemented each other. He asserted that "if any literary researcher or historian dispenses with emotion, whether from sterility or scientific superstition—which is what tends to make handbooks so depressing—let him not blame the method but his own intractability." He hastened to add, however, that "although emotion is indispensable to method and even precedes it, it should be refined and educated by method as an additional factor in interpretation."

It never escaped Reyes that, "after all, what literature sought in the long run was the heart of men." Writing was for him the breath of life or, as he himself put it, "one of his natural processes." He said: "I write because I live. I have never believed writing to be anything but the discipline of every order of spiritual activity and that, in consequence, it purifies in the process every motive of behavior."

As he told us in his *Reloj de sol*—where we learn so much about Reyes the writer—he was "faithful to an ideal at once ethical and aesthetic, to facts of goodness and beauty." Thus he would go back to "his" Plato.

Poet, critic, thinker, and teacher; conversationalist and lecturer; classical and Romantic; austere and sensuous; cultivator of souls and collector of precious memories; interpreter of fantastic visions and decipherer of symbols . . . Alfonso Reyes was an august master who encompassed the whole scale of aesthetic and human versatility. The following lines give a partial clue to his inner kingdom:

> Uncorruptible thought of mine,
> Unflagging guardian of my care,
> When will you let me step out of line,
> Misapprehend, forget, not care.[8]

When it was time for us to leave, his voice, saying goodbye, suddenly began to choke. Was he already beginning to trim his sails among reefs of doubt? Did he feel, as I did, certain that this was the close of our thirty-five years of dialogue? His eyes, radiant so shortly before, seemed to look not at us but into remote regions foreseen. It was as if we were seeing him against a background of mourning black.

Once we reached the lower level of the library, I whispered to my wife, "Take a good look at him: we shall never see him again."

I waved to him in farewell, and the arc his hand—small, soft, slow—made as he lifted it in answer, was the last physical gesture of his that I was ever to see.

VII

My *Visperas de sombra* has the following dedication: "To three Mexican friends: Alfonso Reyes, Francisco Monterde, Julio Jiménez Rueda."

From Mexico I received the following letter, dated December 19, 1959:

Sr. D. José A. Balseiro
University of Miami
Coral Gables, Florida
U.S.A.

My dear and admired friend:

Let all the bells ring out to celebrate your beautiful book, *Visperas de sombra,* as well as its dedication, which honors and moves me. But, do you really feel already the approach of that dark visitation? Leave that to me, who have been living for many years under the sword of Damocles, and may you go on prospering in health and in poetic skill, and giving us more such admirable fruits of your sensibility and your noble art.

What a time of anguish we live in! Thank goodness that at least there are still men like you left.

I'm sending you a few inconsequential little books as an humble return as well as to convey my wishes for your happiness, now that the year's wheel is completing its turn.

With admiring affection,

ALFONSO REYES

Av. Gral. Benjamín Hill No. 122
México 11, D. F.

Eight days later, shortly before 8:00 A.M., on Sunday, December 27, 1959, Alfonso Reyes died.

The news, although not unexpected, shook the Hispanic cultural world. Its pain-filled echoes were soon heard. In Mexico, Ignacio Chávez said: "He seemed to be not merely a cultured man but culture itself. Now that he is gone, who could replace him? In our own time, no one. These extraordinary men appear only now and then, one or so to a century, and the times are no longer propitious for the long and difficult preparation of a man until he comes to embody the wisdom of his time."

In Argentina, Ezequiel Martínez Estrada commented: "The whole of Alfonso Reyes's work bears the distinctive marks of his lineage. His interest in the problems relating to the life of the spirit, rather than to economics and politics, set him apart from his time and space . . . making him a citizen of the world."

The then ambassador of Columbia in Rome, Germán Arciniegas, remembered him this way: "If Alfonso Reyes was the president of our republic of letters, he ruled us with a light hand. Never was a scholar less dull and pedantic, never more courteous."

Mariano Picón Salas spoke for Venezuela: "It was not only by virtue of his wisdom and the excellence of his style that Alfonso Reyes was perhaps the first humanist and first man of letters in Hispanic America. It was also because of the intention and the moral message with which his work is infused: from his most erudite writings to his most casual essays."

And so we could go on turning the pages of the intellectual geography of the continent to show, in each and every one of its countries, the deeply felt lament for an irreparable loss. My own reaction was expressed, even before I wrote the present essay, in my "Elegía a la muerte de Alfonso Reyes." [9] It consists of seven stanzas in *octavas reales* *—a reference to the seven lustrums that my friendship with Alfonso Reyes lasted:

I know that I shall clasp your hand once more,
Although not in the communion of the clay;
I know your voice upon that farther shore,
Mexican sage, can never fade away;
That latent still, in this our present day
And in the arcane, the genial seed you bore
Shall yield sweet fruit, expression pure
Of your orchard of light, always mature.

The winged words still sound in my ear
That you spoke when life was almost gone,
While, silently acknowledging death near,
I felt your starry self soar in search of dawn.

* *Octava real:* a stanza composed of eight hendecasyllables with a certain rhyme scheme.

Each word a noble vessel, voyage done,
That finds the port in calm, the weather clear;
While in your inner kingdom, cruelly o'ertaken,
Your wounded heart by its long wait was shaken!

Master of friendship, as an example
Of reason, kindness, and of harmony,
Your library was the august temple
Where reigned the science of philosophy.
Yet—O visionary seer!—there fantasy
A place to dwell had too and ample
Scope. How clearly despite pain's scars
I see you yet, inveterate hunter of stars!

Within your breast the raging whirlwind
Augured the sinister hurricane was near;
But in the rich vineyard of your mind
You turned to sweetest wine the salty tear
And, subtle alchemist, set at rest our fear
Distilling honey. For, ever wise and kind,
Never did you allow your face to show
The pain your illness made you undergo.

The best of Greece, in land of Mexico,
Under your care, great Humanist, bloomed and grew
To the full radiance of a perfect rose
As an ineffable ornament of you.
And your wisdom brightly reaped its due;
For, universal specialist, you could cross
All frontiers: their Christian doors to your mind
Opened—of your culture index and most certain sign.

And always was your gravity relieved
By wit, light as the petal of a flower;
For your smile dwelt not only on your lip
But in your daring, playful power
To lay bare what you touched, and in your dower
To raise with to the heights of poetry.
For never was forbidden fruit we did not find,
Delicious, in your banquet for the mind!

Sojourner of the shades, your image clear
Opens a port of warm security;
For it ever was the rule you held most dear
To help those close to you in work or amity.
Witness that I am to your unique nobility,
I know you go before as one who shields.
For long ago the immortal blossom grew
Of your life, made poetry by you! [10]

Even more than by Reyes' death, if this were possible, I was painfully impressed by the arrival of the books he had promised to send me—when the sender was already buried in the Rotunda of Eminent Men in Mexico City! The dedications in these books, brief as they were, had a tone of intimacy and a sad irony. Like this one: "To José Agustín Balseiro, Happy New Year, 1959–1960"; or this one, definitive and irrevocable: "To José Agustín Balseiro—the last drops from my pen—with a cordial embrace."

VIII

Now, more than ever, I read and reread the sonnet, "Ausencias," in which Alfonso Reyes left us a consoling message:

The friends most dearly loved by me
In a short span have gone away,
And now I live surrounded by their shades,
Which brings but meager comfort to my grief.
Their voices mingle with my voice while I
Most urgently desire to be done
With mortality and go where they have gone:
Thus in suspenseful wakefulness I lie.
And yielding to this intoxicating power,
I ponder how time becomes eternity
As it flows infinitely from hour to hour;
And, overflowing the limits of mortal breath,
My heart explores the unknown immensity
And I become familiar yet with death.[11]

Certain as I am that his voice upon that farther shore shall never fade away, my transcendental hope is above all renewed by what Reyes himself wrote in 1954 about his "meetings" with Pedro Henríquez Ureña: "But now I have him beside me, forever, since that day in May, 1946, when he suddenly collapsed during one of his daily trips from Buenos Aires to La Plata. Since then, he is never far from me. I talk with him and ask him questions."

Maestro, tomorrow, may we resume, like the rising of an endless dawn, our interrupted dialogue in your "little books corner"?

[From *Expresión de Hispanoamérica,* Vol. II, San Juan, Puerto Rico: Instituto de Cultura Puertorriqueña, 1963.]

11✤

Gabriela Mistral

As early as 1630, Lope de Vega, in his *Laurel de Apolo*, sang the praises of a mysterious lady from Peru who corresponded with him, signing her letters "Amaryllis Indiana."[1] The foremost poet of Spanish America during the colonial period was a nun, Sor Juana Inés de la Cruz, whom Karl Vossler called "Mexico's tenth muse." Another nun, this one from Bogotà, Colombia, Sor Francisca Josefa de la Concepción—better known by her surname of Madre Castillo—was, according to Anderson Imbert, "the great mystic of our literature." These and other women writers—among them the Peruvian Saint Rose of Lima, the Ecuadoran Jerónima de Velasco, and the Brazilian Rita Joana de Sousa—lacked neither intellectual predecessors nor spiritual sisters in the Iberian peninsula. We have only to recall, among others, Beatriz Galindo, Queen Isabella's Latin teacher; Lucía de Medrano, who probably taught at Salamanca; and the deaf Teresa de Cartagena, the author of *Arboleda de los enfermos* and *Admiración de las cosas de Dios,* who in the fifteenth century decided to "wage war on idleness." But, above all, let us remember the greatest of them, Teresa de Ávila, admirable for her moral courage no less than for her reforms of Spanish convent life; for her highly individual prose as much as for her poetry, so intense in its mystical devotion and so passionate in its human feeling. When Teresa was beatified, another woman, Cristobalina Fernández de Alarcón, had the honor of dedicating a poem to her.

Nineteenth-century Hispanic America saw two renowned female writers: the Cuban Gertrudis Gómez de Avellaneda, who wrote poetry, novels, and plays; and the Peruvian Clorinda Matto de Turner, who in her novel, *Aves sin nido,* ardently denounced the exploitation of the Indians by the worst of the "conservative" forces.

With such precedents, it is surprising that the *modernista* movement in Hispanic America should not present any outstanding feminine figure. Yet, if we were to judge by the notable group that followed that movement in time, we would conclude that the women allowed the men to initiate it in order that they might reemerge later with their message of fresh emotions and intimate revelations.

Three countries stand out particularly for their female writers during this period: Chile, with Gabriela Mistral; Argentina, with Alfonsina Storni, born in Switzerland of parents of Italian ancestry; and Uruguay, with Delmira Agustini—her father, born in Uruguay, was of French ancestry, possibly from Corsica, her mother was Argentinian of Gallic-German ancestry, and her grandfather was German—and Juana de Ibarbourou.

It has been observed that, although in these republics women have lacked both the personal freedom and the civil rights enjoyed by their North American sisters, their writings have been a frank and astonishing revelation of their most intimate emotions and most ardent desires. This note they never even toned down. Take, for instance, a composition like Delmira Agustini's "Plegaria":

> Eros, have you never chanced to feel
> Pity for statues?
>
> .   .   .   .
>
> For ice-gloved hands, powerless to pluck
> The delicious fruits of the flesh or the fantastic
> Flowers of the soul?
>
> .   .   .   .

Pity for sacrosant features of sex
Armored in ghostly fig leaf by chastity? [2]

It would be almost impossible to find women more feminine than these in their tenderness, their sensitivity, the sincerity of their passionate love. And yet, more than one of them
confessed that she wished she had been born a man. Why? It
was their belief that men are not subject to repressions, that
for them the world is open. Alfonsina Storni, who in her "Sa-
ludo al hombre" laid down her shield "in simple and valiant
condition of defeat," wrote in her poem "La que comprende":

> She kneels, with dark head drooping,
> Past youth and lovely in her maturity,
> Before a dying Christ who from his Cross
> Looks down on her with pity.
>
> Her eyes are heavy with the weight of sorrow,
> Heavy as her womb is with child unborn,
> To the pale, bleeding Christ she pleads,
> "Let not my child be a daughter . . . not a
>   daughter, Lord!" [3]

Just as obvious and suggestive is the following composition
of Juana de Ibarbourou, ironically titled "Mujer":

> If I were a man, of darkness and moonlight,
> Of peace and silence I would take my fill.
> Night after night, alone I'd go
> Through the quiet fields, by the restless sea.
>
> If I were a man, what a strange, wild,
> Inveterate vagabond I would be!
> A friend of all roads that invite to range,
> Never to go back but onward endlessly!
>
> When I'm beset by these restless fancies,
> What deep sorrow being a woman is to me! [4]

Of all these women, Gabriela Mistral was the one who traveled more widely. She had also the toughest moral fiber among all of them. She lived and died single, and with her deep maternal instinct forever unfulfilled, she was like a slowly drained vessel. A great love crushed her early in life. After that, she went on filling the deep cistern of her soul with diverse manifestations of universal love: love of children, of the weak, of the oppressed.

Gabriela was born in Vicuña (valley of Elquí), in northern Chile, on April 7, 1889, to Jerónimo Godoy and Petronila Alcagaya, and was baptized with the name Lucía. She was hardly more than a child when she became a schoolteacher, like her father and a sister. Driven by her missionary spirit, she went to Patagonia, "the land that has no spring," which, to her, was a foretaste of loneliness and death: "To whom can turn she who has wandered so far / If farther than this none have gone but the dead?" [5]

It was still Chilean land, but not the one she had called "softer than roses and honey."

Painfully wounded by the death of her lover (Romelio Ureta Carvajal), who committed suicide in 1909, Gabriela fell into desperation by the horror of a God who denied his mercy to those who took their own life:

> Is there no ray of sun will ever reach them?
> No water laves the red shame of their blood?
> To them alone your eyes are ever blinded,
> Your fine ear deaf, your heart forever cold?
>
> So men assert, in error or malice,
> And, to others, You may be justice, Lord;
> But I, who once tasted wine from Your chalice,
> Shall never call You anything but Love! [6]

In thus appealing to a merciful God, Gabriela drew far away from Vargas Vila, the iconoclastic Colombian writer whom she professed to admire, earlier in her life, in her letter to Carlos Soto Ayala in 1907.

After she moved to Punta Arenas, still busy teaching, she began to compile the poems for her first book, *Desolación.* She really had no intention of publishing it, but rather of putting it secretly away. "I have written as one who talks to herself," she said, "for I have been lonely everywhere."

Among the poems in this book is the sonnet sequence, "Los sonetos de la muerte," which in 1914 won first prize in a nationwide contest and made her known to her own people.

Her experience, acquired in Chile as a teacher, was further enriched in Mexico when President Obregón's Minister of Education, the famous writer José Vasconcelos, invited her, in 1922, to collaborate in the educational reform in that country.

Gabriela Mistral loved children, especially poor children; she loved the mistreated and neglected Indians; she loved the Jews, whom she called "suffering flesh." (She claimed that one of her grandmothers was Jewish and read to her from the Bible, so dear to Gabriela.) To the Jewish race she sang:

> The world has played with your strings of tears
> And with your sobs has lulled itself to sleep.
> The lines upon your face I hold so dear,
> Like scars cut in the mountains are deep.
>
> . . . .
>
> O Jewish race, yet to praise your home
> Your voice is sweet and your breast strong,
> To sing the Song of Solomon
> With shattered heart and lip and tongue.
>
> . . . .
>
> O Jewish race! O tortured flesh!
> O blood of bitter waters!
> Like heaven and earth you endure, and grows afresh
> Your clamor like a forest! [7]

Like José Martí, whose spiritual influence and moral example are so evident in the thought and the style of Gabriela Mistral, she, too, might well have said: "With the poor of this earth / I wish to cast my lot." [8]

For Gabriela Mistral, wherever there was human misery, there Jesus was suffering also. And this suffering of Christ would bring upon her the pains of the Crucifixion. Then she hated the bread that nourished her, the verses she wrote, her very joy. As a Christian, she believed that integral democracy, with a deep sense of social justice, could save the world.

It was the Old Testament, not the New, that she loved. Indeed, there was a considerable degree of Hebrew fire in her passions. The impression of the world gave her a thirst for God, for beauty, for love. Her devotion to children was a manifestation of this thirst for God. God and children appear related, now in the words, now in the spirit of her poems:

> Little children's feet,
> Blue with the cold,
> How can they see and not cover you,
> Dear God! [9]

And in another one:

> Little children's hands,
> Little hands that beg,
> To you belong the valleys
> Of the world.
>
> . . . .
>
> Poor little hands,
> Hungrily outstretched;
> Blessings on those that fill you.
> Blessings on them!
>
> Blessings on all that give you
> Back the world,
> Feeling you like a cry.
> Blessings on them! [10]

Even thinking of her own death, Gabriela imagined children playing with her ashes:

After many years have passed, when I shall be just a small heap of silent dust, play with me. Play with the earth of my heart and of my bones. If a mason gathers me, he will make me into a brick and then I shall be forever imprisoned in a wall; I, who hate quiet niches. If they made me into a brick for a jail, I would blush with shame on hearing a man weep. And as a brick in a schoolhouse, I would be unhappy too, not being able to sing with you in the morning.

I would rather be the dust you play with by the roadside, in the country. Press me hard: I have been yours; scatter me: I shaped you. Trample on me because I did not give you all of truth and all of beauty. Or just scamper over me, singing, that I may kiss the soles of your beloved feet.

. . . .

And when you mold images with my clay, break them at every instant; for at every instant was I broken by the pain of my tenderness for children.

Her maternal instinct moved her deep inside. Gabriela went through life alert and sensitive, as a woman who "cared for other people's children" and who "looked at the mothers of all the children in the world." Never has anyone entered with such tenderness and understanding into the feelings of a woman about to become a mother:

I grow pale if he suffers in me; I walk in pain from his hidden pressure, and he who is in me, unseen, could kill me with one movement.

But never think that it is only while my body shelters him that he can pierce me and be entangled in my entrails. When he shall walk the roads freely, however far he should go, the wind that beats against him will tear at my flesh, and his cry will sound also through my throat. My weeping and my smiles shall have their beginning in your eyes and on your lips, my child!

In her "Plegaria por el nido," her prayer begged:

Soft be your breeze that makes it sway,
Sweet be your moonlight silvering it,
Strong be your bough that is its stay,
Dazzling your dew bejeweling it.

From this small, delicate shell,
Woven from strands of rough gold,
Turn away the elflocks of the rain,
The sharp crystals of the cold.

Turn away the brusque wing of the wind
Whose caress would tear it apart;
Hide it from him who would find
It with greed in his heart.

You, who made ugly to me
The torture of your creatures fine,
Of the fragile snowflake of the lily
And the little columbine,

Tenderly shield this fragile form,
Let your light touch deep love impart.
Childlike it shivers in the storm;
It is so like a heart! [11]

The second thirst of this poetess, her thirst for beauty, takes expression not through the form but through the content of her work. As regards the former, ever since *Desolación* appeared in 1922, the critics pointed out its technical defects. Another poet, Gerardo Diego, cites the following comments of the Chilean scholar, Julio Saavedra Molina, on those verses:

These poems are seldom impeccable in form. The language, in some instances, is not correct; the prosody, in others, leaves something to be desired: certain little crutches subtract elegance and cleanness from the expression; certain harsh colors strike the eye disturbingly; the dissonance of certain stresses shocks the ear or spoils the harmony . . . For these very reasons, in spite of the formal shortcomings of her work and of its almost total lack of "art," in the scholarly sense of the word, these poems of "desolation" have won the admiration of those who appreciate sincerity in works of art and know how to value a diamond, even in the rough, that shines with passion, genuinely expressed, unschooled sorrow, and, in short, sincere feeling transposed into verbal discoveries.

And the Spaniard Gerardo Diego adds his own comments:

There is some justice in this judgment, as there would be if one applied rigid standards to the supposedly most perfect poets mentioned later by Saavedra: Rubén [Darío] and Fray Luis [de León].

(And, by the way, may I point out that the Master, León, was censured for centuries, especially by critics in Seville, for lack of correctness and for sloppiness. Not to mention the attacks that have been directed at Darío.) But, aside from that, one can detect the underlying professorial or academic prejudice in these objections. And the strange thing about it is that the poetess herself is infected with these scruples to the point of remorse. One finds in her confessions an abundance of references to her uncultured crudeness, apologies for the fact that she was self-educated, and even blushes for her unconquered natural limitations and rusticity. In this both she and her severe critics err.

. . . As a volcanic upheaval in her native Chile, so erupts in the verses of Gabriela Mistral the essential unconventionality, the abrupt interior flame that involves and breaks her. To call this outburst—at once free and inevitable—an imperfection, is to misunderstand.

The thirst for beauty in Gabriela Mistral was, essentially, nobility of thought. For her, as for Miguel de Unamuno and Antonio Machado, words were a means, not an end. Her work characterizes itself by its intensity of emotion in the expression of life's dramatic aspects. Remember how, in her poem on the death of Amado Nervo, she called herself "mud and sad ashes." How often her lyrical expressions seem indeed to be

compounded of these elements because of the suffering and
hopelessness behind them! In that same poem she invoked the
Mexican poet with these words:

> Under the shadow of God, cry out what you know:
> That we are orphaned, we walk alone, you saw us so;
> That all flesh with anguish cries out for death! [12]

Then the thirst for love. It appears in two predominant aspects in the work of Gabriela Mistral. One looks back into the
past: to her tragic frustration. In such instances, her expression was haunted by the somber specter of death. Seeing herself irrevocably abandoned by her beloved, she realized that "a
great love" had "overturned" her and that she would nevermore be fulfilled. And she felt ashamed of living like a coward,
without the courage either to go and look for him or to forget
him:

> I have no other task on hand,
> Aside from loving you silently,
> Than this hard labor of tears
> That you have left to me.
>
> . . . .
>
> I am so ashamed
> To live in this cowardly way!
> Not seeking you out
> Nor driving your memory away! [13]

Thinking of the beloved dead one, she found a certain morbid consolation in reminding herself that no other woman
would descend into his grave and dispute her the remains of
the suicide:

> I shall walk away singing the beauty of my revenge,
> Because to this hidden depth no woman's hand shall reach
> To snatch away from me your handful of bones! [14]

She seemed pleased that the lips of her lover could no longer enjoy lascivious kisses, nor his eyes reflect the erotic image of other women:

> Ah, nevermore shall your two eyes
> Staring blindly, mirror a flushed,
> Desire-distorted face!
>
> . . . .
>
> Ah, never again shall your lips
> Taste the shameful kiss dribbling
> Concupiscence like thick lava! [15]

This atmosphere of anguish she maintained through many of her poems, concluding that love was but a "bitter exercise." Yet, she could not hate the man who deceived her: "Hate is but brief, and love immeasurable." [16]

A new problem arose for her, however: that of the salvation of a suicide's soul. Desperately she implored God to overlook the sin of one who made away with himself—¡*Di el perdón, dilo al fin!*—for even if the man who committed suicide treated her cruelly, she never stopped loving him:

> Lord, you forget that I loved him,
> That he knew himself master of the heart he hurt.
> He poisoned my springs of joy: no matter!
> I loved him! I loved him, don't you know? [17]

In its other manifestation, love in Gabriela Mistral turned toward the world of the senses, although here it was much less obvious.

When the lovers became conscious of their passion, she suffered, believing herself to lack the physical beauty that would make a man take delight in looking at her.[18] Her mouth, her voice, her body were, if we take some of her verses at face value, one of her obsessions:

I am ashamed of my sad mouth,
My broken voice, my rough-hewn knee;
You looked, you came to me, and now
I feel my nakedness and know my poverty.[19]

In "El poema del hijo," written when she was thirty, her
hair, already sprinkled with "the premature ashes of death,"
we have an allusion to "my tired lips, my bitter heart, my defeated voice." Heart-rending words these, when we think of
the latent capacity for tenderness and caressing so often revealed in her work! Take, for example, this invocation to a
clay pitcher, "El cántaro de greda":

Pitcher of clay, brown as my own cheek, how
available to my thirst you are!

Better than you is the lip of the waterfall
that opens in the brook; but that is far away
and I cannot go to it this summer night.

Every morning I slowly fill you to the brim.
At first, the water sings as it flows down
into you; when it becomes silent, I kiss its
trembling lip to repay its merciful kindness.

You are graceful and strong, brown pitcher.
You are like the breast of the peasant woman
who suckled me when I was weaned from my own
mother's breast—and looking at you I think
of her.

Can you feel how dry my lips are? They are
lips that have known many thirsts: of God, of
beauty, of love. None of these things was
simple and docile like you; and all still
make my lips grow pale.

Do you feel my tenderness?

In summer I put fine damp golden sand under
you, that the heat may not crack you, and
once I tenderly mended one crack in you with
fresh clay.

I have been awkward in many tasks, but I
have always wished to be the sweet housewife
who handles things with a tremor of tenderness
because perhaps they feel, perhaps they suffer
as she does . . .

Tomorrow, when I walk on the fields, I shall
cut sweet peppermint leaves for you and sink
them into your water.

Clay pitcher, you have been kinder to me than
those who called themselves kind.

I wish that all the poor could have, as I do
in this burning afternoon, a pitcher of fresh
water to slake their bitter lips!

We feel a freshness as of a cool breeze when this woman
turns aside, however briefly, from her fevered love. She comes
from her labyrinth of anxieties, from her incandescent halluci-
nations, unbroken by fatigue. She arrives, calm of voice and serene of heart, determined to understand. And even, sometimes, with the purpose—which she cannot always achieve—of
sounding a new note, a note of joyousness, in the orchestration
of her inner world: [20] "Let us now turn to the smiling verse /
From verses striped with gall and blood." [21]

In her poem, "Mis libros," Gabriela sang the praises of her
favorite books: the Bible, Dante, Saint Francis of Assissi, Kem-
pis, Amado Nervo, and the Provençal poet, Frederic Mistral.
Alluding to the latter and to his poem, "Mirèio," published in
1859, Gabriela wrote:

Poem of Mistral, the heady fragrance
Of new-plowed furrow you have brought to me!
I have seen Mireille press love's gory fruit
And through the horrid desert flee.[22]

Does her admiration of "Mirèio" and its creator explain
how Gabriela chose the second part of her pen name? Possibly.
"Gabriela" is the feminine form of the Archangel Gabriel's
name. It has been said of this pseudonym that it is "the name
of an archangel and the surname of a wind," since "mistral" is
how they call, in some Mediterranean countries, the northwest
wind.

In Gabriela Mistral's list of favorite authors, I miss two:
Rabindranath Tagore and José Martí.

The poetess herself made, in another page, some comments
on a poem of Tagore. She took a line from this Oriental poet
—"I know that I shall also love death"—as a point of departure for her own: "Neither cold nor unloving, as other see her,
does death appear to me. It seems to me rather like an ardent
force, a tremendous passion that claws and tears at our flesh to
pour out the soul like a swollen torrent." (I happen to have
an autograph of Tagore, written aboard the "Rotterdam" on
October 30, 1920, that would have fascinated Gabriela. It
reads: "Only that life is precious which is worth dying for.")

The relationship, spiritual and effective, between the Chilean schoolteacher and the Cuban apostle of freedom was close
and irrevocable. Gabriela Mistral made frequent public state-
ments of her veneration for Martí. In a lecture delivered in
Havana on October 30, 1938, she said: "Reading his work with
the passion with which he inspires us, we enthusiastic Martí-
ans dig as busily as beavers in his prose and in his poetry."
And further on: "I know by heart the difficulties of Martí's
speeches and of one whole section of his poetry. I know them
from having read the work of this man as one examines the
texture of a cloth against the light: observing it and enjoying

its complexity, so revealing of manual dexterity or technical knowledge."

Juan Marinello suggested that in this woman Martí had a clear and authentic resonance. But one can go further than that. Let me point out a few specific parallels.

In his *Ismaelillo* (1882), Martí gave proof of the lyrical grace with which he was able to reach the heart and mind of a child. Seven years later, in his magazine, *La Edad de Oro,* he showed again his devotion to the life and dreams of children. There we have the precedent, in Spanish-American literature, for the children's world that Gabriela Mistral carried in her heart.

One of Martí's favorite authors was Teresa de Ávila, whose richly personal style gave a new tone to Castilian prose. Moved by his own creative originality, Martí likewise contributed his unique characteristic accent and personal expression to the enrichment of the Spanish language.

Martí was in his day the most notable champion of Hispanic-American fraternity. Only his scope was universal. No one equalled him in the defense of the ethical solidarity of those peoples; no one felt as deeply as he did the moral obligation of returning the Indian his dignity and of giving the Negro a constructive place in the development of the new political society. And so does Gabriela enter, passionately eager to give guidance, into the heart of that Indian-white-neo-African America. This thought was well expressed by Gregorio Marañón when he said: "Gabriela Mistral is autochthonous America infused with universality. Two dimensions—the profoundly regional and the inexhaustibly human—meet in her without friction, in supreme harmony."

In chronicles and articles written in New York, Martí sent to his America, along with his own message, the message of the world. In her writings for the Hispanic-American press, Gabriela sent her *recados* from one and another city where she lived as consular agent for Chile—the same post in which

Martí served Argentina, Uruguay, and Paraguay while resid-
ing in New York.

There was for a number of years a difference between Gabriela Mistral and José Martí. Although an unrelenting fighter
against the Spanish government, Martí loved the Spanish people; Gabriela, on the contrary, kept alive for a long time her
prejudice against the Spaniards and her intense aversion to
them. In the mind, at times distrustful, sometimes dry, often
lost amid confusions and contradictions, of this otherwise
warm and generous woman, the Spanish were merely the exploiters of the Indians. She would not stop to reason. She did
not make the right distinction between avarice and Christian
spirit; between the aggressiveness that characterized the Conquest as a whole and the magnanimity—dating from the time
of Queen Isabella—of those who decreed laws making amends
for injuries inflicted, who expounded doctrines based on con-
cepts of universal justice and gave compassionate protection to
the oppressed. Hating the Spaniards for their harshness, Gabriela overlooked the historical fact that the Hispanic Americans, once free, were not, in general, less harsh with the Indians than the encomenderos had been. And this despite the fact
that the Indians had helped win the wars of independence.
Let us add, however, that, no less than among the Spanish in
the past, the Indians have and always have had defenders
among the Hispanic Americans.

During the Spanish civil war, Gabriela turned over the
copyright of her third book, *Tala,* on behalf of the orphans of
Spanish Loyalists, the *republicanos,* in exile. The printing
costs of the first edition of this book were borne by another
woman of the Americas, the Argentinian Victoria Ocampo,
outstanding representative in her own country of cosmopolitan intellectual values.

In 1924, Gabriela Mistral's second book of poems, *Ternura,*
was published in Madrid. In this book she sang to all children
in the child she always dreamed of as her own:

God the father his thousands of worlds
Moves silently.
Feeling his hand in the darkness,
I rock my baby to sleep.[23]

Ternura was reprinted in Montevideo in 1925. When a third printing came out in Buenos Aires in 1945, it included a "colophon that looked like an excuse," which she had written in Petropolis, Brazil, that same year. Here is its closing thought: "A love that stumbles when it speaks, a love that stutters, is apt to be the most loving of loves. Something like this is the love I have given the little ones."

Two years later (1947), again in Buenos Aires, the second printing of *Tala* appeared. Apropos of it, Gabriela wrote to me (January 21, 1948) from Santa Barbara, California, "This book has little unity, and I like unity." And, with her characteristic courageous candor, she added, "In Chile they hate it."

Tala seemed to me particularly interesting for various reasons. For one thing, it did not repeat the theme of her famous first book. Sixteen years had gone by (1922–1948). The author wrote now about different countries as if they were persons. Gabriela captured the hemispheric American spirit with visions of fresh originality. She gave us the human warmth of the sun of the Incas, of the corn of Anáhuac, of my own island of Puerto Rico,

Whose speech is sweet
As that of infancy;
Its songs as holy
As a hosannah! [24]

The "Nocturno de la consumación" is one of the most intimate things its author ever wrote; it is, at the same time, one of her most universal poems:

. . . .

So long have I gnawed on the darkness
That joy I can never relearn;
So often have trodden on lava
That my feet all softness forget;
Such long years I have fed on the desert
That the name of my country is Thirst.

. . . .

I have learned a terrible love
That brought my joy to an end;
I have earned the love of Nirvana,
The desire nevermore to return
But to cling to the Earth hand in hand,
With my silence answering hers:
Bereft of my very Father,
And severed from Jerusalem! [25]

Clearly one can see that her pristine passion, the central axis of her drama and her prosody, had not lost its edge. We have here, intense and unmistakable, the quality of suffering that purifies and lays itself bare through years of being shaken to its vital roots. An existence without daylight is described, overwhelmed by early grief, by the anguish of incurable bitterness. The destiny of adolescent Gabriela was to become a universe of pain, an unchangeable pain for which, even as a mature woman, she would find no remedy. The intimate texture of her soul was woven, fatally and definitively, by abandonment and loneliness; by unremitting tension in the face of a world that inflicted on her, time and again, tearing, irreparable wounds. First, her sweetheart; then the nephew she called Yin-Yin, who, when he committed suicide in Petropolis, killed the last of Gabriela's personal loves and tore the last of her affective ties.

Later, in her poem, "La caída de Europa," from her book, *Lagar* (1945), she was to call herself: "Your sister who has no child, / Nor mother, nor any present kin." [26]

In this her fourth book with a one-word title—*Desolación,*

Tala, Ternura, Lagar—Gabriela was like the shadow of a
shadow: "What hand shall I lend that is not mourning?" [27] She
saw herself as suffocating:

> Still they come to me
> Calling my name, seeing my face;
> But I, suffocating, see that I am
> A tree, devoured and rotten,
> Enclosure of darkness, coal consumed,
> Thick-leafed juniper, deceitful cypress,
> Real to the eye, to the hand elusive.[28]

The symbols of exhaustion and extinction succeeded one
another in pathetic accumulation. She had attained now, as
perhaps never before, the acceptance of renunciation. But, although she believed her memory had burned out "like a needy
hearth," she returned to her old theme: the nagging thirst of a
frustrated love. Tortured, knowing that "love is a wonder to
end all wonders," she let out her prolonged, remote cry of anguish: the complaint that "without the grace of love, how
heavy earth weighs on us!" Even a feeling of agonizing farewell can be detected in one stanza from her poem, "Atardecer":

> I feel my heart in sweetness
> Melt like waxes:
> My blood like sluggish oil,
> Not wine, flows in my veins,
> And I feel my life escaping,
> Silent and sweet as a gazelle. [29]

I met Gabriela Mistral in Madrid, at the home of the
Cuban short-story writer, Alfonso Hernández Catá. The PEN
Club had invited her to speak, and it was on such one occasion
that she, showing a subtle and yet profound insight of the
Spanish soul, called Spain "a good loser." Years later, in 1945,
Gabriela was granted the Nobel Prize for Literature. The fol-
lowing year, a book appeared in Madrid bearing the title
Homenaje a Gabriela Mistral. It was a 126-page volume with

works in verse and prose by fifteen writers.[30] It was prefaced by a page from Gabriela's own hand, "El cielo de Castilla," from which I here transcribe the following passage:

> Let the traveler take the measure of this sky; in itself, it may well be worth the trip. Perhaps such a sky is nowhere else to be found. A fantastic dryness of the land is required before the atmosphere can attain this total chastity, before it can devour mists and fogs like this.
>
> . . . .
>
> Exiled from rural America, and neither able nor willing to forget it; habituated to green lands and acid greens, a creature born amidst joyous botany, in Castile can find a part of herself only in its sky.

The first edition of *Desolación* is a disinterested fruit of the cause for better cultural relations between the United States and the spiritual values of the countries to the south. In 1922, a number of North American professors and students, encouraged by the late Federico de Onís, on learning that Gabriela was a teacher and that her collected poems had never been published, paid the cost of publication of such an edition by the Instituto de las Españas in New York. Since then, a number of Gabriela Mistral's compositions have been translated into English. She was invited to teach or lecture by more than one institution. And, on December 11, 1950, The Academy of American Franciscan History, in Washington, D.C., conferred upon her the Serra Award of the Americas.

The same misgivings with which Gabriela at one time regarded Spain, as we have already seen, also characterized her feelings toward the United States, influenced by the imperialistic errors of the past.[31]

This is what Professor Alfred Coester refers to, in *Literary History of Spanish America*, when he remarks that "among [Gabriela Mistral's] articles are frequent flings at the United States." But, just as the Argentinian Manuel Ugarte had declared that hatred of the United States is "an inferior feeling that leads nowhere," so did Gabriela write:

> I, hate the Yankees? No! They are defeating us, they are overcoming us because of our tropical languor, our Indian fatalism. They are alienating us because of a few of their virtues and all of our racial vices. Why should we hate them? Let us rather hate what there is in us that makes us vulnerable to their nails of steel and of gold: their willpower and their opulence.
>
> Let us direct every activity like an arrow to this ineluctable future: Latin America made one, unified by two stupendous things: the language God gave her and the pain inflicted upon her by the North . . .

Serving Chile in consular and diplomatic capacity, Gabriela Mistral traveled widely. And, as mentioned above, in 1945, this woman—who up to the age of twelve had lived in the humblest of rural dwellings and who was accused falsely as a thief by her teacher, Adelaida Olivares, a blind woman, and stoned by her classmates—received in Stockholm, from the hands of King Gustav V of Sweden, the most universal literary honor, the Nobel Prize. But wherever she went, despite resentments and never wholly forgiven years of bitterness, Gabriela carried her native land in her heart and in her conscience. Good evidence of this is found in her *Recados,* selected in 1957 by Alfonso M. Escudero, who rightly stated: "Near or far, Gabriela had a feeling for Chile, especially for the valley of Elqui, that very few of our writers have."

However, Gabriela Mistral was not always in high esteem in her own country. In addition to what I had already read on this matter, I heard some Chilean writers speak of her with indifference or contempt. Such remarks arose occasionally from personal reactions; at times they came from thin-skinned people who remembered only her remarks on national defects, which she was only anxious to see corrected. "The motherland," she wrote, "can be served in various ways, except in the childish and honey-tongued manner of the conventional chauvinist."

However, there were, too, very prominent Chilean writers who sang her praises. I remember also the affection with which, in our last conversation, she spoke to me of José de los Santos González Vera, Hernán Díaz Arrieta ("Alone"), Eduardo Barrios, and Arturo Torres-Rioseco. In his *Interpretación de Gabriela Mistral,* Hernán Díaz Arrieta brought up significant distinctions:

> Let us, then, say it without reticence.
>
> Gabriela Mistral did not love Chile. She loved her native Monte Grande and, by extension, the valley of Elqui, the countryside and the mountain, the country and mountain people, her childhood days. Beyond that, she looked with suspicion at a strange and hostile people, for whom she could feel no affection and to whom she felt opposed. . . .
>
> Only outside Chile did Gabriela Mistral become acquainted with any kind of peace, beginning with the not least important one: financial peace. Neither the prize granted her *Sonetos de la muerte* in the 1914 contest nor her successive promotions as a teacher had liberated her from the professional yoke.
>
> Strangers' eyes discovered her, other people's houses sheltered her, admirers and friends from distant lands gave her, at long last, the most basic element for the good nutrition of the soul: a feeling of her own superiority. . . .
>
> She was, it must be admitted, predisposed to alienation and rebellion. Whether as an effect of her paternal heritage, which inclined her to wander, whether because of the hostile environment in which her childhood and youth were spent, whether from deeper impulses difficult to diagnose, there was in her an almost morbid propensity to exclude happy memories and bring forth the painful ones.

To understand better these subtle observations of Díaz Arrieta, let us compare them with what González Vera wrote in his *Comienzos de Gabriela Mistral:*

When her sister Emelina, who was a schoolteacher, had taught Gabriela what she knew, their mother, a small slight woman, took her to Vicuña to finish her last year of elementary school. Gabriela was bored there. Save for a little astronomy, she found herself repeating everything she had learned at Monte Grande. The principal called the mother and told her that her daughter was stupid, advising her to employ the child in housework.

And let us now listen to the reverent words of Pedro Prado:

You will see her come and awake in you the obscure nostalgia one feels on seeing a strange ship come into port . . . Last echo of Mary of Nazareth, an echo coming from your high mountains, she, too, is filled with the divine stupor of knowing that she is the chosen one. Never desecrated by a man's hand, she is virgin and mother: no mortal eyes did ever see her child, but we all have heard the lullabies with which she sang him to sleep.

You will recognize her by the nobility she awakens!

Her whole being emanates a sweet and pleasant balm. O soft invisible rain that softens the hard earth and makes the hidden, waiting seeds germinate. Make no noise near her, for she comes battling for simplicity.

Gabriela Mistral spent her last years—years of physical deterioration: anemia, arteriosclerosis, cancer—in Roslyn, New York, writing out in pencil her most ambitious poem, "Recado de Chile." Her fellow countryman, the journalist, Carlos Santana, described it with these words:

[This poem] is an extensive lyrical geography in verse of her distant homeland. . . . In this work Gabriela sings the praises of her land, evoking the men of the mountains, the countryside, the sea. From each region of Chile's lengthy geography, she extracts, recreating it, what most strongly engages her inspiration.

Gabriela's somber, lonesome green eyes closed forever in Room 420 of the General Hospital at Hempstead, Long Island, on January 12, 1957. Her remains were flown by the United States Air Force to Lima, Peru, where another airplane waited to take her on the last lap of the journey to her native land of Chile. She lay in state at the Teacher's Mausoleum on January 22, which was proclaimed a day of national mourning by the Chief Executive of the Republic, don Carlos Ibáñez, and his cabinet. Later, as had been her wish, Gabriela was buried in Monte Grande, in the northern desert where she had spent her childhood.

[From *Expresión de Hispanoamérica*, Vol. I, San Juan, Puerto Rico: Instituto de Cultura Puertorriqueña, 1960.]

12✤
Heitor
Villa-Lobos:
the Man and
his Music

Brazil has many attractions: the temperament of its people—
sensitive, friendly, with a subtle sense of humor; the magic of
its landscape; its many enchanting cities . . . But what perhaps charms me the most is what Erico Verissimo noted—and
I accept as true—that Brazilians dislike mathematical precision: they despise numbers and formulae and are fascinated by
words, colors, forms. For not everyone can emulate Euclydes
da Cunha, who, as a military engineer, was acquainted with
numbers and—although he wrote during the *raros intervallos
de folga de uma carrera fatigante*—was able, while building a
bridge in São José de Rio Pardo, to finish one of the literary
masterpieces of our hemisphere.

In my schooldays, arithmetic, algebra, and geometry were
to me stormy seas whose wild breakers overwhelmed a defense-
less youngster. On the other hand, the sound of music, the
play of light and shadow, and the symbol that conveys far
more when it suggests than when it explains were my refuge
from the harshness of the world and lent wings to my develop-
ing imagination.

One day I learned about a poet born in São Paulo in 1831.
He was Álvarez de Azevedo, a lyricist give to uncertainty
who died almost before becoming a full-grown man. When I
read his epitaph, I thought that although the work left by

other Brazilian Romantics might be more important, no one of them, perhaps, sang with words so candidly moving as he had. In the style of Musset, Alvarez de Azevedo told us that in twenty-one years of life he had become a poet, had dreamed, and had learned what it is to love:

> By the cross upon my last and solitary bed,
> In the forest, remote from human strife,
> Rest in the shade, O traveler, and write:
> "He was a poet, he dreamed, and he loved life." [1]

Despite its flourishing cities, equipped with almost all the technical advantages of civilization, Brazil is one of the few lands where the folklorist can still make new discoveries. He may even come upon mysterious rites in magical, out-of-the-way, almost inaccessible places, as happened to the Uruguayan, Alberto Soriano, when he went deep into Macumba, of aspect "at once angelic, daemonic, and pathetic." Although music was the latest of the arts to yield cultivated fruits in Brazil, the richness of Brazilian popular melodic themes, with their surprising, original rhythms, proved to be a gold mine in addition to great joy to its composers.

Mário de Andrade claims that sound was from the beginning a factor in the religious experience. In Brazil, it is a fact that the initial manifestations of Catholicism are intertwined with music. The first attempts at musical composition there were made in connection with popular religious plays, or "mysteries," in the medieval manner, written by Jesuit, José Anchieta. Born in Tenerife, Canary Islands, this man became an outstanding figure in the history of Brazil, where he arrived when barely nineteen years of age. In his zeal to convert the aborigines and make Christianity strike deep roots in their nature, Anchieta even had recourse to a Guarani dance as an aid in his apostolic mission. As Fagundes Varella exclaimed, evoking him: "Spirit of the apostle of the wilderness! / Singer and sage. Lodestar of the future!" [2]

The first musician of universal stature produced by Brazil was also a priest, Father José Mauricio Nunes García, born in Rio de Janeiro in 1767 and ordained in 1792. There are a number of similarities between his life and that of Heitor Villa-Lobos. The humbleness of their origin, for instance. Both men, like Camargo Guarnieri at a later date, knew poverty in their childhood. A further similarity exists in the fact that it is not known whether Father José Mauricio was trained by the pupils of the Jesuits who had been expelled from the country in 1759, or was—as L. H. Correia de Azevedo believes—a self-taught genius. For Villa-Lobos, although he had three highly competent teachers whom he never forgot—Agnello Franca, Francisco Braga, and his own father—did actually learn more by himself than through any outside tutoring.

A product of the eighteenth century, Father Nunes developed within the tradition of Haydn and Mozart. There was not, in his time, the devotion for Bach that Villa-Lobos so reverently came to feel. In the first quarter of that century, polyphony had already lost followers, and the melodic style based on homophony prevailed. It was even sarcastically said that music was made for the ears, not for the eyes. Bach's artistry in the handling of voices, contrary to the manner imported from Italy, estranged from his sacred music the public of the so-called Age of Reason and of Light, whose lack of appreciation of baroque polyphony showed that they were in darkness. Even by the time of Beethoven's death in the nineteenth century, the edition of the complete works of Bach, which the genius of Bonn so eagerly looked forward to, had not yet appeared. It was not until 1829, the year Father José Mauricio died, that Mendelssohn conducted *The Passion According to Saint Matthew*. And not until Brahms proclaimed it was the excelling value of the first genius of the "Three B's" fully recognized.

Aside from the intrinsic merit of his music, Father Nunes García was the archetype of the colonial period. The fact that he was born in America affected his career. Officially, creative artists from European birth were preferred. Such was the case when Marcos Portugués, protégé of the King of Portugal, Dom Joan VI, arrived in Brazil in 1811. Nineteenth century Brazil was a model of hospitality to outstanding foreigners, as evidenced by the artistic mission that arrived from France in 1816 under the direction of Joaquín Lebreton (although later on, in trying to make itself predominant, it gave rise to inescapable rivalries).

Brazil knew how to nourish its culture with outside contributions. Witness the Swiss botanist, Jacques Huber; the founder of the museum at São Paulo, Herman von Ihering; the naturalist Fritz Müller; the Danish paleontologist, Peter Wilhelm Lund; his United States colleague, Charles Frederick Hartt; the Belgian astrologist, Luis Cruls; the architect Pezerat; the painter Polierre . . . and with many others, including the Austrian writer, Stefan Zweig, who in grateful tribute dedicated one of his books to Brazil, and the Cuban short-story writer, Alfonso Hernández Catá, who left his life there, the list shows the great number of foreigners who, honored in Brazil, liked the country and loved the cordial spirit of its people.

The fame of Father José Mauricio continued in that of his disciple, Francisco Manuel da Silva, who composed the music for the Brazilian national anthem, the words for which were written by Osorio Duque-Estrada.

After religious music lost its splendor, there were other philharmonic manifestations. Manuel Araújo Porto-Alegre called the Rio of his time "the city of pianos." Arturo Napoleão, virtuoso of this instrument, completed his training there, while Luis Chiafarelli founded the music school of São Paulo.

European standards and styles were still predominant in 1836 when Carlos Gomes was born in Campinas de São Paulo. With Gomes, Brazilian musical nationalism had its first faint dawn. It was later accentuated by the *Suite Brasileira* of Alberto Nepomuceno, who was born in Fortaleza in 1864. This, too, was the year of birth of Alexandre Levy, whose *Samba*, although orchestrated in the European manner, features a native Brazilian dance.

While Father José Mauricio followed German models, Gomes, who studied in Milan, a disciple of Verdi, was an innovator in Brazil, bringing there a new musical genre. In his opera, *O Guarani*—which opened at La Scala in 1870 and in Rio the following year—Gomes did not seek to interpret a foreign environment. His libretto was based on a novel about Indian life by his compatriot, José de Alencar, whose language attempted to reproduce the native speech and whose inspiration was Romantic. Although opinions of the novel ranged from the generous acceptance of Machado de Asís to the harsh judgment of Montenegro that it was false and contrived, the art of Gomes brought Brazil worldwide honor.

Enrique Oswald, born in 1852, is considered by some to be the best trained and, by others, the most sensitive musician of his generation. But it is generally stressed that he lacked the ethnic roots of true Brazilian character.

These men, with others of perhaps lesser importance, were the last representatives of Brazil's belated Romantic movement. Glauco Velázquez, who died in 1914 although he was born three years after Villa-Lobos, was seen by Renato de Almeida as immersed in an atmosphere of vague images leading from symbolism to impressionism. It was Villa-Lobos who initiated a whole new era, which he dominated with his vigorous personality.

When an artist is capable of saying of himself that he has created his own independence, as Villa-Lobos did, and declares that he prefers the worst of his work to the best of others, those who study his life and listen to his music must realize that they are dealing with a most vital creative force as well as one of the most extroverted personalities of our time.

Should we need more evidence that Heitor Villa-Lobos was an individualist, both as a man and as a composer, it would be enough to remember that, on his arrival at Paris in 1922, he told his colleagues that he had not gone to France in order to study with any of them. "If you don't like my compositions," he said, "I will go; if you do, I'll stay for a while."

This remark is the key to a complete understanding of his advice to the young musicians of the New World to cease looking up to Europe for inspiration. "When I write music," he explained, "I do it in the style of Villa-Lobos."

The exact date of Villa-Lobos' birth is not known. In his *Music in Latin America*, Nicolas Slonimsky states that, according to *Riemann's Dictionary*, the composer was born in 1890; *Who's Who in Latin America* gives the date as 1884. Villa-Lobos himself never clarified the question. In a calendar of his life published in 1941 by the Brazilian magazine, *Música Viva*, he claimed to have been born in 1888. But during his tour of the United States in the spring of 1945, he gave the date 1886 to those in charge of writing up the programs for the orchestras he was to conduct. The Brazilian musician, Burle Marx, affirms categorically that Villa-Lobos was born in 1881, and this is the date accepted by most Brazilian musicians.

Personally, I am inclined to think that such contradictions may be understood partly as a wish to appear younger and partly as a sort of practical joke. When, on February 12, 1954, in a lecture to the Miami Symphony Club, I alluded to the statement of Slonimsky in the Maestro's presence, Villa-Lobos laughed like a little boy caught in a prank. But not even in our private conversation afterwards did he correct the date given by Burle Marx: March 5, 1881.

These contradictions are important, however, in that they contribute to our attempts to establish a closer relation between Villa-Lobos' biography and the history of his country. It is not easy to think of the former without in some way relating it to the latter; and it would be difficult by now to imagine Brazil without the products of Villa-Lobos' art.

When was the land of Brazil truly discovered? When was it, in fact, born to European civilization?

History tells us that it was Pedro Álvares Cabral who, with a large Portuguese fleet under his command, claimed this immense territory for his country on April 22, 1500. However, we also know that the Spaniard, Alonso Pinzón, had previously landed north of the Amazon River. There are rumors, too, of a possible voyage by Amerigo Vespucci before the landing of Álvares Cabral.

Aside from chronological data, it has been definitely established that Vespucci was not merely uttering high-sounding words about Brazil when he asserted that, "If earthly Paradise exists anywhere on earth, it can't be very far from that place."

Foreign as well as Brazilian writers of different periods agree in their praise of Brazil's exceptional beauty. Eugenio María de Hostos, influenced by his own notion of nature, once said that he disliked "excessively picturesque descriptions." However, after he arrived in Santos, he told in his first letter to *La Tribuna* of Buenos Aires—March 21, 1874—how he had climbed up a tortuous path to the summit of a medium-height peak called Montserrat, and described his impression of the view with words like these: "As one climbs, how the narrow variety of the landscape becomes a unit! As one looks, how one's understanding of that wild beauty expands! As one listens, how one's ears are filled with woodland music!"

Euclydes da Cunha was right when he said that in Brazil nature is an interplay of antithetical elements. Well could he have referred to enthusiastic descriptions that "make of this country a privileged region, where nature has set up her most impressive headquarters."

Another exaltation of the Brazilian natural wonders is this one from Professor Silvio Lugo: "Wherever you turn, richness of coloring, bacchanals of fragrance, lyrics of beauty. Above, mountain ranges covered with herculean vegetation agitating its muscular arms. Below, golden wheat fields playing tunes of wealth and peace. Everywhere, landscapes of beauty and riches, riches and inspiration, inspiration and encouragement, as if Brazil were the compendium of the universe, eternally reproducing beauty."

It was by gathering, synthetizing, and stylizing the natural elements of his land—its people, its birds, its jungle, its mountains, its native dances, even the happy shouts and tumult of its carnival—that Villa-Lobos created his music.

Three of his most ambitious and best series of works— *Bachianas Brasileiras, Choros,* and *Memoprecóce*—could not be torn from their own proper and characteristic background, and neither could most of his other works. Villa-Lobos was almost as prolific as his country is rich in natural wonders. So abundant was his musical production that he himself did not know for sure how many musical scores he had written. Some investigators put the number over 1,400.

Such creative fertility brings to mind the overwhelming waterfall at Iguassú, which dwarfs Niagara by comparison, or the vastness of the Amazon river, whose currents surpass those of twenty Mississippis and whose basin is larger than the whole European continent. The visual elements of Brazil are an inevitable and vital aspect of her famous son's music.

Villa-Lobos felt that folk music was the expansion of a people's spirit, its vital development revealed in tones. To him, folklore was a kind of "biological expression" of nationality. In this connection, it is pertinent to recall some of the opinions of Louise Peppercorn, published in the number of February, 1943, of the London *Music Review.* She wrote that Villa-Lobos liberally borrowed from and harmonized folk melodies, creating genuine compositions with a folkloric base. He deliberately reproduced, Miss Peppercorn said, popular themes in otherwise original compositions or made arrangements of these tunes for the vocal parts.

We often find in Villa-Lobos' music, therefore, an amalgam of what has been described as opposing forces. It could be a manifestation of the multiplicity of racial and cultural elements, in addition to the Indian, that have become more or less established in Brazil since colonial times: Portuguese, French, Spanish, Dutch, and African. But, as Burle Marx reminds us, no matter what its sources, the music is still Villa-Lobos' own.

Villa-Lobos regarded his musical career as a kind of ideo-logical mission—which reminds us of the teacher in him. He pondered passionately on the subject of musical education for the masses. This, by the way, shows that he was in touch with practical realities, not isolated in an ivory tower.

He advocated reform in musical education, arguing that the first step should be to develop a method of teaching music appreciation that would free us from existing confusions. Making good his word, he began in Brazil a conscientious modification of traditional methods, casting aside their false values.

Villa-Lobos believed that if music is not kept alive in sound, its essence is lost, no matter how much time is given to its academic study. To him, music was a living force, not mere aesthetic theory. It should be learned, he insisted, as a child learns his native tongue. The child, he explained, becomes fa-miliar with the words, the pitch, and the expressive forms of the vernacular long before he is required to learn even the simplest of grammatical rules. Harmony, for example, should not be taught to children by means of written rules but by ear, "then, later on, teach him the rules if he has need of them."

The heterodoxy of his opinions shows that Villa-Lobos was, by temperament, a romantic. Romantic, too, was his passion for local color, his fascination for the exotic, even for the ex-travagant.

As a creator, Villa-Lobos had resources of winged fantasy and a fertile imagination to draw from. How, for instance, did he compose his score on the Manhattan skyline before he ever saw it? Simply by placing on the pentagram-lined paper a sil-houette drawing of the skyscrapers and transposing the latter to the former.

In Paris Villa-Lobos met Natalie Koussevitsky, who at that time was married to the famous orchestra conductor. She left in the memory of the Brazilian a lasting impression of kind-ness. This impression was translated into music by the Mae-stro. Let him explain how he did it: "As it would be impossi-

ble for me to describe her in a long, drawn-out, objective, or
concrete dissertation, I rely on the mysteries of sound as they
are incarnated in the free songs of the birds of my native land
and in its natural and folkloric backgrounds. They inspire my
musical imagination. I do not worry much about the rules and
logic of form; instead, I prefer the aesthetics of my art."

That was the genesis of his symphonic poem, *Madona*, of
December 29, 1945. As many others of his works, this poem
proves that Villa-Lobos was frequently a programmatic composer, in the sense given to this term since Berlioz and Liszt.

An anecdote typical of Villa-Lobos circulates in the United
States. In one of his scores, in the part for the bassoon, appeared a note impossible to play. How was the sound of low A
to be produced? "Stick a roll of paper in your instrument,"
Villa-Lobos instructed the musician, "and you shall find your
note." The trick achieved what musical technique had failed
to produce.

This takes us to another aspect of the teacher in Villa-Lobos. In conducting a musical work, he would not be satisfied
with anything but perfection. But, in order to attain his high
standard of excellence, he would previously drill the orchestra,
at every laborious rehearsal, on the phrasing of themes and
subthemes, the attainment of tonal exactitude, the expression
of the nuances of light and shade, the accentuation of a given
rhythm, how to reach the full expression of a passage . . . To
illustrate his points, Villa-Lobos would often take in his own
hands one instrument after another and show the musicians,
by on-the-spot demonstrations, how to achieve, technically and
expressively, what he had in mind. In short, to the authority
of a conductor who revealed faithfully the soul of a composition, Villa-Lobos added the ability of a teacher who knew, in-
timately and effectively, the registers and the possibilities of
the strings, woodwinds, brasses, and the percussion instruments. He was a living lesson in which the artist and the ar-
tisan went hand in hand, thus permitting the score to reach

full expression, with each of its components operating with deliberate authenticity in the re-creation of its character.

All of this enabled Villa-Lobos, when he conducted before an audience, to do so with such economy of gesture, such serenity and self-control that he always left the impression of one of the least conspicuous of conductors, but one who, essentially, achieved more. His appearance, so reminiscent of Beethoven's, had no need of the aristocratic poses of Karl Muck or of the solemn severity of Serge Koussevitsky. He did not become, as Felix Weingartner, an actor with the gestures of a dancer; nor, as Toscanini, did he turn into an electrical whip relentlessly striking whomever commited the slightest error. Nor was he either, like Stokowski, the incarnation of a contagious, imaginative, and sensitive dynamism. Without implying any qualitative comparison of the artistic measure of these men, but rather of their personalities and human characteristics, it is only pleasant to remember the atmosphere of self-confident gravity and orderly composure that the Brazilian created from his podium.

That was the classical manner of Villa-Lobos. But the romantic one appeared in still another of his aspects. And also in his creed—to which Beethoven would have agreed—was that the function of art is to serve mankind. One cannot imagine Villa-Lobos selecting as the motto for any of his works that phrase of Henri Regnier that Ravel chose for his *Valses nobles et sentimentales,* "The delicious and ever renewed pleasure of a useless occupation." For Villa-Lobos, the true ideal of an artist was to serve the masses, giving them what is only in the artist's power to give. He went even farther in this direction, asking, "What is so-called 'art' if not the expression of humanity and of everything concerning human beings?" Villa-Lobos reminds us of Tolstoi, who believed that to be happy a man must keep intact his link with nature; must love the sky that covers him, the fresh clear air, the rural life.

Now we can understand in all its implications what Villa-

Lobos had in mind when, in 1930, he submitted to the government of Brazil a project, at once revolutionary and constructive, utopian and naive, on the means of keeping public order during elections. Villa-Lobos offered to provide the authorities with a formula for carrying out this difficult task and to inspire understanding and civic responsibility as well. "I can," Villa-Lobos affirmed, "achieve with my art what the government cannot with all its soldiers."

In 1931, he was appointed supervisor and director of musical education for the public schools of Rio de Janeiro. Among his innovations was the creation of the "Orfeão de Profesores." Within the short period of four months he founded a 12,000-voice choir. He also developed in other cities throughout the country numerous choral groups that celebrated September 7, Brazil's Independence Day, with song. In 1936, Villa-Lobos represented Brazil at the International Congress of Musical Education in Prague. For a number of years, the Maestro increasingly occupied himself with pedagogical endeavors at the national level and composed very little. Under his system, children learned the basic elements of music through singing. As Robert Sabin wrote, "They are taught to think of and feel music as an integral part of their lives." This was precisely Villa-Lobos' aim. He saw music not only as a manifestation of a high level of education, or as a soothing diversion, but as "something affecting us in more potent, mystic, and profound ways."

In this sense, it can be categorically stated that no composer anywhere did ever do for his country what Villa-Lobos did for his.

It was Villa-Lobos' deep conviction that the composer should not allow any mask or pretense of any kind to interpose itself between his personality and the beautiful revelation of his soul. He respected only the composer who writes music because life without it would be meaningless to him. Moved by sincere motives, such a composer works for an ideal. His music, therefore, will flourish as a vital element throughout the whole social structure.

In 1835, Alfred de Musset said in his *Nuit de Mai:* "Nothing makes us great as a great sorrow does; do not allow yours to make you mute: desperate songs are the loveliest."

More than one hundred years later, Villa-Lobos was not afraid of speaking as a Romantic when he said: "Through sorrow, people become conscious of spiritual needs that can never be satisfied by music as an academic discipline. They will demand a music from the heart, wherein lies the true expression of humanity."

If one puts together the underlying sense of Villa-Lobos' words with his endeavors in the field of education, his unshakable belief in democracy emerges.

His harmonies and rhythms are at times impulsive, as coming from a passionate champion of the progress that leads to the social emancipation of human beings and to their emotional beautification as well. As in Beethoven, nobility in Villa-Lobos emanated both from his heart and his mind. He was a man who refused to pay undue respect to conventionalities. In him we find some of the qualities that characterize Schiller's heroes. Indeed, the more we think of names like Beethoven and Schiller, the more we feel inclined to see Villa-Lobos, because of his passionate and rebellious nature, as essentially a Romantic.

Villa-Lobos maintained that "in music, patriotism and its exploitation is something very dangerous. Great music cannot be produced that way—instead, we will have propaganda."

On the other hand, he favored that kind of nationalism that was "the strength of the land": the geographical and ethnical influences from which, in his opinion, no composer could escape: the temperament of the people and the environment in which they live. Villa-Lobos believed that such "sources" were indispensable for the creation of genuine and vital art.

The history of music presents quite a few examples that invalidate this opinion but it contains also as many that bear it out. And Villa-Lobos, in the field of music—as Euclydes da Cunha, Gilberto Freyre, and Caio Prado, Jr. in that of sociology and sociological history—studied Brazil in the living reality of its people, against the background of their own land. He did it, as da Cunha said of himself, *animado do culto da personalidade humana.*

The art of Villa-Lobos, exuberant and intoxicating at times, is like a magic mirror that reflects exclusively Brazilian motifs. Yet, it shows how rich and audacious its tonal language can be precisely when it explores the soul of the people and the natural wonders of the land. In this regard, Villa-Lobos might well have quoted Borodin's proud words, "We are self-sufficient." For it can be said that the composer had whatever he needed within the geographical scope and the mystery of Brazil, whose territory occupies 3,290,564 square miles, one-fourth of which is virgin forest.

Villa-Lobos' orchestration is unique in its use of native Brazilian instruments: *xucalhos, reco-reco, caxumbu, puita.* Not in vain did he, at eighteen, travel inland familiarizing himself with primitive songs, dances, and musical instruments. He himself said that it was as a result of that expedition that his art was born. Yet, despite his emphasis on all that was national, Villa-Lobos freed himself from isolationist tendencies. Moreover, he breathed cosmopolitan inspiration into his work and never attempted to export provincial airs. On the contrary, he enriched the national character of his music with the adoption of international accomplishments. He did, in short, what Martí had advised Hispanic Americans to do: "Let the world be engrafted in our republics, but our republics must still be the tree trunk."

If I mentioned Borodin a while ago, it was not only because his phrase was applicable to Villa-Lobos, but also because, even in so original a work as Villa-Lobos' *Choros Number 6,* one can detect here and there echoes of passages from *Prince Igor.* And yet, what other piece could bring to us the jungles of Brazil as that of Villa-Lobos does? There the enigmatic murmurs, with voices sometimes thin, as if wrapped in leaves, sometimes of complex emotional structure, as a conflict of lights and shadows, finally resolved; there the sound, now present, now emerging as if from remote insinuations, now weightless, now dense, at once inert and alive like the everlasting drama of nature. But take also *Momoprecóce*. Its author warned that "it cannot be classified . . . in any known musical genre, not even in regard to its form." Yet, it seems to me that, although in general terms this is true, had Villa-Lobos never heard Debussy's music, some of his motifs, as well as the technical means he used to present and resolve them, would have been different. Consider that the original version of this fantasia, written in 1919, one year after Villa-Lobos became acquainted with the Debussy of the *Préludes* for piano, was first written for piano only. In this case, as in many others, Villa-Lobos' originality did not grow from the inside out.

Besides Borodin and Debussy, we should not forget Stravinsky among those who definitely influenced Villa-Lobos. But being much more prolific and less pure, Villa-Lobos neglected at times the quality of his work, indulging in bombastic vulgarities that only the richness of his color made tolerable. At such times, his facility for composing—one might almost say improvising—loosened his style, which sagged and fitted itself upon the technical substructure rather than follow purely aesthetic lines.

Returning to the theme of Villa-Lobos' universality, consider also *Bachianas Brasileiras,* his tribute to the genius of Johann Sebastian Bach, whom Villa-Lobos revered as a sort of archetype because Bach knew so well how to draw inspiration from the folk songs of his country. Remember, too, Villa-Lobos' enthusiastic acceptance of United States jazz and of the genuinely North American works of Gershwin. All of this is evidence of the eager curiosity and eclectic and cosmopolitan tastes that, as a man and a composer, characterized Villa-Lobos.

Examining the programmatic outline of *Momoprecóce*—since we have already referred to this work—we note that its objective elements predominate, but without noticeable imitation. It is a kind of realism that affects the inner world but lacks emotional expression. There is even at times a hint of the gentle irony that we also recognize in the toccata of the little rural train in the *Bachiana Number 2*. But once and again and many times in the work of Villa-Lobos, we find that the melodic line is laden with emotion. Such is the case in the aria based on a Brazilian song, from that same *Bachiana*, also in the loveliest part of the *Number 5*, for soprano and strings with a violoncello solo. As for the re-creation of Brazilian rhythmic expressions, his *Choros Number 8* stands out.

What Villa-Lobos did in *Momoprecóce*—conceive it first for piano and enlarge it later for piano and orchestra—he repeated in *Rudepoéma*, originally composed in 1926 and completed, in its final version, in 1932.

Like George Gershwin, Heitor Villa-Lobos began his career loving and cultivating the popular themes, which he glorified in the *Cirandas*. Being poor, Villa-Lobos used to earn his living by playing the piano at a cinema. Then destiny intervened romantically in his life, not, however, to bring him tragedy but splendorous fame. During a concert tour of South America, Artur Rubinstein went one night to the theater where he was most pleased by a piece new to him. When he asked who had written it, Villa-Lobos, incredulous, appeared. An hour or so later, as Rubinstein himself recalls, the composer paid a surprise visit to the virtuoso at the hotel. Villa-Lobos had come with a full orchestra, to play his music for Rubinstein. From that occasion on, they were friends.

Rubinstein took such a generous interest in Villa-Lobos that soon he used his influence to send the composer to Europe. I have already told how Villa-Lobos arrived in Paris in 1922. Less than five years later, a Villa-Lobos festival was held in the French capital with the participation of the Lamoreaux Orchestra. A similar program was again offered there in 1929.

In the United States there has been frequent evidence of admiration for Villa-Lobos. Many articles in his praise have appeared in the most important publications, and the composer was repeatedly invited to conduct some of the most famous orchestras in the country. In February 23 and 24, 1945, the Boston Symphony Orchestra interpreted a whole Villa-Lobos program. More than one academic institution has honored itself by honoring Villa-Lobos. The last one to do so was the University of Miami, which granted Villa-Lobos a Ph.D. in Music in February, 1954. On that occasion, the Maestro conducted a symphony orchestra that had at other times played compositions of his.

Heitor Villa-Lobos has made millions of friends for Brazil in Europe and the Americas. With many of his compositions, he has enhanced his country's prestige.

November 17, 1959, was a day of mourning for Brazil—and for music: Heitor Villa-Lobos died of cancer in Rio de Janeiro.

[From *Expresión de Hispanoamérica*, Vol. I, San Juan, Puerto Rico: Instituto de Cultura Puertorriqueña, 1960.]

13

The Pampa,
the Horse, and
the Song

Reading books in which Argentina is mentioned, whether by
native or foreign authors, makes us immediately aware of that
country's territorial immensity.

El lazarillo de ciegos caminantes dates from 1773. It is attributed to a certain Calixto Bustamante Carlos Inga. Who
was this chronicler who called himself "Concolorcorvo"—with
a crow's color? Alonso Carrión de la Vandera, maybe? Was he,
as some hint, a Spaniard passing as "an authentic Indian"?
Was he a Peruvian, this writer with the humorous and sometimes sarcastic manner? [1]

Among the places described by him are lands of Tucumán,
in the northeastern region of Argentina. In Chapter VIII, he
noted that "one single landowner's property has a circumfer-
ence of twelve leagues albeit he and his family are unable to
work even two of them." Here he anticipated the problems of
a vast territory without a population large enough to settle it
and make it productive.

Rimas, a book of verse by Esteban Echeverría, was published in 1837. The most important poem in this collection is
"La cautiva," not only because of its relation to the land and
its Romantic nature, new in Argentina at that time, but also
because it was the first verse legend published by a Hispanic
American.

The poem begins like this (italics are mine) :

> *It was evening, the hour*
> *When the sun with golden shower*
> *Bathes the Andes.* Below stretched
> Mysterious and measureless
> The desert . . .[2]

In Chapter I of Sarmiento's *Facundo* (1845) there is this passage: "The immense tracts of land at this country's borders are uninhabited, and some of its navigable rivers have never known even of the most fragile and smallest of barks. The most troubling problem of the Argentine republic is its vastness; the desert surrounds it and sneaks into its interior; solitude, stretches of land without a single human dwelling, are the usual, unquestioned frontiers between one and another province."

The sensation of solitude at the far, wide horizon and the impressive reality of the unpeopled plain, so well recorded by these authors, contribute to a desolate feeling of individual helplessness.

But to those who are lonely song is good company. It is born of man but it envelops him with its music and encourages him with its words; it acquires an autonomous existence, yet it reincorporates finally to the singer.

In his book, *Una excursión a los indios ranqueles* (1870), Major General Lucio V. Mansilla said that to cross the pampas "the horses are the main thing." To travel that immeasurable emptiness, the gaucho knew no other vehicle. Anxious to communicate with other human beings, he went to remote settlements only to always return to his home premises. Wherever the gaucho went he sang his own ballads or learned the ballads of others—it all came to the same thing.

That is how the art of the *payador* * was born.

In his *Muerte y transfiguración de Martín Fierro,* Ezequiel Martínez Estrada wrote: ". . . a spontaneous art with a tradition going back to the soldiers of the Conquest, without any

---

* *Payador:* name given in the Rio de la Plata region to a wandering singer of folk songs.

significant contribution from aboriginal poetry or music. The Viceroyship of Rio de la Plata re-created, as if he had never existed before (although following the general lines of that type of poetry) the wandering minstrel, whose glorious ancestors were troubadours and jugglers."

Jorge M. Furt, in his *Cancionero popular rioplatense,* recognized the Spanish roots of some of the songs of Argentine *payadores,* but added: ". . . the pristine origin is not sufficient to erase the indigenous imprint left in these ballads by our gauchos, who adopted them as if they were a creation of their own nature, translating them into their own manner of thought and speech, and infusing them, through their songs, their words, and even their personal meanings, with the absolutely Creole character of their race."

Without his horse, the gaucho would be bounded by the horizon he could reach with his eyes. He would be unable to participate in dialogue, confined by the almost limitless steppe. He needed his horse to overcome his isolation. "To gallop is to lessen distance," said Ricardo Güiraldes in *Don Segundo Sombra* (1926). And one way for a man to compensate for what little he has—which he will always need as an extension of his own being—is to give many names to a single object. *Overo, flete, potro, parejero, pingo, jaca, repiso, redomón* were only a few of the many gaucho synonyms for "horse."

To the gaucho, a horse was not only useful, he was also his owner's best companion: in fighting and at peace, in the everyday work and on holidays. The man and the animal grew and developed lives parallel to each other, both enriched by unforgettable experiences. Bartolomé Mitre expressed it this way in *El caballo del gaucho:*

> By my side he has grown old
> And his blood, like mine, runs cold
> With age and weariness;
> But in summer he's my shade,
> And my compass on the plain,
> And my friend in loneliness.

> Very soon we'll speed away
> Through the vast and lonely plain,
> For we are old.
>
> Oh, my *moro,* Heaven grant us
> That when death comes it shan't part us
> But we'll go together both! [3]

Life, for both man and horse, was just that: a race. For the true gaucho scorned everything static and instinctively loved the dynamic. But it was a race whose mechanical elements were not significant, but rather the adventurous emotion of suffering and joy hazardously shared.

The horse gave wings to the song, for it was on horseback that the payador wandered about. How could one think of Martín Fierro other than as Azorín visualized him, that is, with its essential roots in another Hispanic myth? In his essay, *En torno a José Hernández,* Azorín subtly observed that Martín Fierro could stay still no more than Don Quixote could. How, then, could one evoke Martín Fierro if not astride his *moro,* eating up the miles?: "For me the earth is small / And I well could wish it bigger." [4]

But, even more than a consummate horseman, Martín Fierro was really a payador, a singer of inexhaustible inspiration: "The verses come flowing from me / Like clear water from a fount." [5]

Here are the opening stanzas of *Martín Fierro* as Hernández published it in 1872:

> To the tune of my guitar
> I here burst into song
> For he whose night is made long
> By extraordinary sorrow
> From the lonely bird may borrow
> And console himself with song
>
> . . . .

As I die, I'll still be singing,
Singing they shall bury me,
And singing I still will be
At the Eternal Father's feet:
For singing I was conceived
And I left the womb to sing.

May my tongue not ever falter,
May my words come tripping free.
Singing brings glory to me
And when I burst into song,
You shall hear me going strong
Though the earth crack under me.

. . . .

With my guitar in my hand,
I drive e'en the flies away;
No one dares bar my way,
And when my heart is in tune,
I make the bass cry as I play
And the treble throb and swoon.[6]

And, what was the worst thing that could happen to a payador when he was inducted into the army? Once again his relationship with his horse became apparent:

But the worst was yet to come,
For they took my *moro* away;
I'm no dope, pal, but one day
The Commander comes to me
Saying he wants to see
My horse learning to eat grain.

Well, figure out if you can,
How your humble friend now fared:
On foot, with his navel bared,
Tired, ragged, broke, and sore . . .
They could hardly have done more
If to punish me they'd cared.[7]

This feeling of being punished by the loss of his horse is tragically magnified in the work of Benito Lynch, *Romance del gaucho* (1933). In Chapter LV, we find the following dialogue between the protagonist, Pantalión, and Oros, the messenger his mother sends to him:

> "Ahah . . . Tell me one thing . . . Horses . . . Do you have horses for such a long trip? I only brought this one and the cart horse I told you about, and this heat kind of gets you down."

> "Sure I have, and it's a swell one too!" answers Pantalión, real happy-like. "I have my big 'badface,' and that's saying I have the best horse in this settlement—or any other settlement, far's that goes . . . Ahah!"

> "That's good! . . . I thought maybe you'd sold it or gambled it away . . ."

> "You're crazy! . . . I'd sooner sell myself . . . I love that animal better than my own hide . . . Ahah!" [8]

But later on, in spite of this love, in his eagerness to get to the place where *doña* Julia, the woman he so passionately and wholeheartedly loves, awaits him, he spurs the exhausted horse on and on until the poor beast stumbles and slows down:

> Like a madman, the young man threw himself off the horse again and, pulling out his knife while holding the 'badface's' bridle, plunged the knife up to the hilt into him, shouting, as if the horse had been human: "Take this, you damn good-for-nothing!"

Then Pantalión tries to go the rest of the way on foot, hurrying on, obsessed with the idea of getting there soon:

> He had hardly walked more than a few yards this time when he suddenly shrank into himself. A gust of cold air on his shoulder blades made him stop and turn around once more.

This time he had to believe it: a horse, a riderless horse, was galloping after him, making the ground ring with its hoofbeats and filling the night with the noise of its whinny . . .

"Blessed Virgin!" thought Pantalión, "that must be my 'bad-face' coming to punish me." Then he saw, or thought he saw, in the moonlight, the bulk of an enormous horse furiously bearing down upon him, with blood spurting from a chest wound and eyes shooting fire. Pantalión took off, losing his hat in his haste, and ran like a madman across the plain, until, worn out, he fell and rolled on the ground . . .

. . . And people say that the following morning some men passing by found him, stiff and dead, on a heap of straw.

There we have again, only in a different way, a gaucho and his horse finishing the race of life together, as in Mitre's poem. But what in Mitre was a cordial sentimentality, in Lynch acquired the tragic dimension of fate.

It is significant that Mitre, author of *El caballo del gaucho,* should also be one of those who sang to the payador par excellence, Santos Vega, previously glorified by Hilario Ascasubi. Toward the end of Mitre's composition, his vision of the horseman crossing the plain merges with that of the famous *coplero* * who was buried there:

> Sleep! while the herder awakes,
> Vigilant, with the morning star
> His voice echoing near and far
> Between forest and lagoon
> From the round-up and the forge,
> From the whole land rising strong
> As others take up the song
> Like a choir singing in tune.

> And the errant gaucho the while,
> In his crossing of the plain,
> Has pulled in his sorrel's rein,

* *Coplero:* a singer of country ballads.

> Dismounted to take his ease,
> Spread out his poncho on the ground,
> And in the sheltering shade,
> His humble prayer has made:
> Santos Vega, rest in peace! [9]

In "Los gauchos," a poem by Leopoldo Lugones, we find once again the same suggestion of thematic unity, only this time it is the horse and the guitar:

> His poetry is the early
> Glory of the country's green,
> Where the light whinny of a pony
> Rejoices the morning scene.
>
> . . . .
>
> His memory is like the vague
> Cry of an old, unused guitar . . . [10]

Even the city bred poet, when dealing with the gaucho theme, expresses in many ways his love of the horse and of everything relating to horses. Ricardo Rojas, discussing gaucho literature in his book, *Literatura argentina,* commented on Estanislao del Campo and his *Fausto* (1866): "The fame of this poem has so much eclipsed the other works of its author that his literary reputation rests almost solely upon it. His *Fausto* has given him a well-defined position among gaucho poets, indisputably putting him in the same class as Hidalgo, Ascasubi, and Hernández."

In *Fausto* one can see the fondness with which the poet spoke of the horses of his characters:

> Ah, that Creole! He seemed to be
> Pasted right onto his beast,
> Which, though lively, to say the least,
> Obey the rein you could see.
> Biddable it seemed to be,
> As a town young girl's horse, say,

Or a hack hitched to a dray.
Christ! I would give any amount
To be owner of such mount.
Oh, what a beautiful bay!

Prancing all along the way,
Tossing its head in its pride,
You could hear, far and wide,
The silver clink on that bay.
For silver made its gear gay:
Poitrel, spurs, buckle, and bit.
On its headpiece, for all to see,
It had more silver than Potosí.
Why, even its *bolas,** for me,
Were of silver, yes siree! [11]

At a later date, another poet, Rafael Obligado, added to the
glorification of Santos Vega, "the one of great fame." In his
poem, "El alma del payador," the horseman and his guitar are
once again brought together:

In drowsy afternoons in summer
When the mirages seem
Like bright waters in a dream
With vast and fantastic rollers;
Silent, somber, and absorbed,
A horseman rides down the slope.
Leaving the emerald height,
He reaches the lonely shores
And leads his mount to the waves
With his guitar on his back! [12]

The publication of *Fausto* provoked some objections from
Juan Carlos Gómez to the gaucho genre. Writing then to del
Campo, he said, as if in recrimination: "Throw far away from
you the gaucho's guitar, which, if it does touch our hearts at
times, at the ranch door, under the stars, does so only because,
in certain states of the soul, a single melodious note is enough

* *Bolas:* the gaucho's "lasso" and weapon, consisting of two or more
iron or stone balls attached to the end of a cord.

to move us deeply and pursue us for a long time with its lingering vague memory."

Note how "the guitar" is constantly joined to the theme of "the gaucho."

Needless to say, Estanislao del Campo rejected the advice of Juan Carlos Gómez. He admitted that the gaucho was disappearing, but replied that at least "the memory of his language and means of expression" should not be allowed to vanish with him.

In Chapter VII, "La tristeza del gaucho," from his book, *Nuestra América,* Carlos Octavio Bunge wrote harshly that the Argentinians of his time had "no throat for song."

Martínez Estrada indirectly agreed with this opinion when he said: "Toward the middle of the past century, the singer's profession was on the decline. He was already a legendary figure when Hernández rehabilitated him in his poem and a mere symbol when Obligado disinterred him. Today, very few peasants can tune a guitar, and they look upon singing as a gringo custom that they would be ashamed to follow."

Today's inhabitant of the pampas is too far from being able to boast with Martín Fierro that "with the baptismal water he received the gift of song." Only literature still keeps alive the payador, who is one of the characters richest in local color ever produced by any land. However, although physically extinct, the gaucho, as Madaline Wallis Nichols noted, has become a symbol of the national spirit and the prowess of his country.

In a paper on *La poesía gauchesca vista por don Miguel de Unamuno* (Salamanca, 1956), Manuel García Blanco quoted from a letter of Unamuno to Juan Arzadun (August 3, 1892), as follows: "Have you heard about José Hernández' gaucho poem, *Martín Fierro?* If I should have the pleasure of seeing you, I will lend it to you. It is written in the gaucho argot and consists of *décimas* * to be sung to the accompaniment of the guitar. . . . To my mind, he is the first-ranking poet in the

---

* *Décima:* a stanza made by ten octosyllabic verses. But, as a matter of fact, the stanzas in *Martín Fierro* are not décimas.

Spanish language (or any similar language) now alive. He has the power of the primitives: astounding."

On September 1, 1935, the London *Observer* published a review by Ronald Fraser of one adaptation into English of *Martin Fierro* by Walton Owen, illustrated by Alberto Güiráldez. Fraser described the hero of this poem as "a cowboy with a guitar, who gathered up the sadness of those endless plains into song . . ."

There we have the synthesis, and the image, of the whole of a literature whose symbols are the payador, the pampas, and the horse.

Aside from literature, were we to look for another artistic expression of this already dead era, we could find it perhaps in the illustrations of the painter Molina Campos, who depicted scenes of gaucho life with lines at once dignified and subtly caricaturesque.

The cattle-raising plain is not, however, the only region of song in Argentina. In another of his books, Ricardo Rojas rightly observed that one must define two zones: that of the singing gaucho and that of the troubadour, the latter extending from the valleys of the great rivers to the first swell of the foothills. Said Rojas:

> Both are the melodious expression of the society to which they belong; but the gaucho singer's style is rather epic, whereas the troubadour's is lyrical. The theatre of the one is the *pulpería* —the neighborhood food and liquor store. And if his guitar of conceited payador does not lack the subjective note, its vibration is lost in the convivial hurly-burly of the revels or in the ballads that solemnly deal with the exploits of the bad gaucho. The troubadour of the woods, on the other hand, is taciturn and intense like the race that has him for a genius. His main preoccupations are love, suffering, and death. . . . A people of artists, they see these cultivators of poetry and music as their most genuine representatives. Suffering suggests to their muse the maxims, generally rhymed, of a wise philosophy of resignation and anguish. In the midst of this bitterness, however, their humor often breaks through smiling, like a star reflected in the depths of a tenebrous lake.

This same author told us in *El país de la selva* that one rarely finds "a popular verse that does not speak of the *sonckoy*—the heart—of anguish, of sadness, of death." Rojas pointed out that these poems "are born from illiterates who lack instruction of any kind, and their value resides in their expression of the collective soul or of individual passions." He proved—all this in Chapter VI, "El trovador"—that some of the songs of northern Argentina, composed in the Quetchua language, show that "the fount whence flows this hidden torrent of inspiration is to be found in the remotest Indian traditions."

If this is true of the region "where the Salado and the Dulce rivers flow murmuring God's blessings on that peaceful Mesopotamia," it does not seem that one could say the same of Argentinian poetry in general.

In a lecture on *El espíritu y la cultura hispánica en la expressión popular argentina,* on November 16, 1939, Carlos Ibarguren asserted that a considerable portion of the folklore of this land bore its flowers and fruits from an authentically Spanish seed. And he added: "To prove this, one has only to glance quickly through our collections of popular songs and proverbs published with pithy studies, like the notable work of Juan Alfonso Carrizo and the interesting studies of Ciro Bayo, Jorge M. Furt, Lehman-Nitsche, and Draghi Lucero. The erudite study on *Martín Fierro* by my distinguished colleague in the Academy, don Eleuterio Tiscornia, so rich in literary and philological data, confirms my assertion."

Basing his theory on the most authoritative sources, Ibarguren cited numerous Castilian poems that have influenced the poetry of Buenos Aires and other Argentinian provinces. Said he: "If we leave the pampas region and go to the Andes, we shall still find Spain in our folklore. Juan Draghi Lucero, in his *Cancionero popular cuyano,* includes many poems that are just like those collected by Menéndez Pidal in his book, *Flor nueva de romances viejos.* . . . The Creole guitarist's repertoire includes not only anonymous verses but also poems by

some of the greatest geniuses of Spain: Lope de Vega, Que-
vedo, Calderón, Montemayor, Moreto . . . without, of course,
knowing anything about these poets . . .''

Dwelling further on his point, Ibarguren went on: "Eleuterio Tiscornia's thoughtful and profound study on *Martín
Fierro* gives evidence of the genuinely Spanish filiation of this
poem from its very first stanza. . . . Together with the guitar,
Tiscornia observes, the gaucho received from Andalusian folk
music his style of expressing his inspiration in song."

But Ibarguren made also a necessary and conclusive eluci-
dation about the true Argentinian nature of this masterpiece
among national poems: "The verses of *Martín Fierro* were not
the result of an erudite search for literary and ideologic elements of Spanish popular expression. They sprang sponta-
neously like wild flowers from the character and the speech of
our people, and Hernández admirably observed and recorded
them."

There is in the annals of Argentina a fact that singularly reveals the love and respect of that people for poetry and song.
But, before coming to it, let us ask, when did the war of independence of the Thirteen Colonies end? The answer is, in
1783. And we are at once struck and astonished by the fact
that "The Star Spangled Banner" was not written until the
war of 1812, and only much later adopted as the young republic's national anthem. Moreover, we in the twentieth century
can read three works on the history of the United States—
James Truslow Adams' (five volumes), Charles and Mary
Beard's (two volumes), and John D. Kicks' (two volumes) —
without finding the name of either the patriotic song or of its
composer, Francis Scott Key (1780–1843).

Now, among the literary studies of Juan María Gutiérrez
(1809–1878), there is one titled "La literatura de mayo" in his
book, *Los poetas de la Revolución*. Gutiérrez, a former rector
of the University of Buenos Aires highly praised by Menéndez
y Pelayo, evoked in this study the first years of armed struggle

against Spain in the United Provinces. We quote the following passage:

> Once our arms had been favored by victory, it was necessary to remind the people of the triumphs attained on both shores of the River Plate and in the farthest frontiers of the republic, comfort them with the hope of further glory, and anathematize the enemy that resisted the torrent of Argentine pressure.
>
> To this end, the Assembly, whose wise and courageous decisions so largely contributed to pave the way for independence, appealed to the talent and patriotism of Father Rodríguez and Dr. Vicente López, inviting them to compose a popular song to encourage our soldiers in battle and keep the ardent love of liberty alive in the breast of every citizen.
>
> At the Assembly's May 11, 1813, session, both compositions were read, and that of López was solemnly proclaimed as "the only song of the United Provinces."

Three days later, on May 14, the song was "printed in the paper and with the format of the *Gaceta ministerial del Gobierno de Buenos Aires.*" Thus the Argentinian national anthem was born. It was set to music by the Maestro Blas Pereda. It begins, "Hark, mortals, the sacred cry . . ."

In his *Canto a la Argentina* (1910), Rubén Darío, as if anticipating in a lyrical synthesis all we have been saying, made the almost inevitable allusion to the immensity of the pampas, called Argentina "land of harmony," and evoked the "inspired payador": "Who sighs his deepest sorrow / Or weeps with his *vidalita.*" * [13]

Darío went on to predict that the melodies of the payador would have a permanent place in literature:

> The gaucho will have a part
> In the joys the future brings,

* *Vidalita:* a type of Argentinian popular song to be accompanied by the guitar. Its theme is usually love, and its mood is sad.

> For the simple old songs he sings
> Shall enter the kingdom of Art.[14]

The whole poem is permeated by the themes of liberty and fraternity:

> Argentina, region of sunrise!
> O dynamic and creative land,
> Open to all who thirst
> For liberty and life!
>
> . . . .
>
> Hail, fatherland, which are also mine
> Since you belong to all mankind:
> Hail in the name of Poetry
> And in the name of Liberty! [15]

To Darío, Argentina is "homeland of brotherhood," a country open "to the activity of all men."

From her earliest beginnings as a nation, as we have seen, there arose simultaneously in Argentina the consciousness of its enormous physical extension, the cult of poetry and music, and the cult of the horse, which is a primitive symbol of nomadic freedom.

It is not surprising, therefore, that a people capable of initiating their national life that way should name their country after silver and song.

We gain in wisdom the more we penetrate into its vital spirit—as Leopoldo Lugones said in one of his "Odas seculares":

> A joyful friendship of the Argentinian soul
> Like the bright greeting of an open hearth.[16]

[From *Expresión de Hispanoamérica*, Vol. I, San Juan, Puerto Rico: Instituto de Cultura Puertorriqueña, 1960.]

Notes

Chapter 1

1. Byron did not consistently keep a diary throughout his life. He started several very brief ones at different times. However, more than one thousand of his letters have already come to light.
2. Peter Quennell, outstanding authority on the life of Byron, expresses the following in Chapter II of *Byron, the Years of Fame* (London, 1935): "Undoubtedly there is a great deal to be said for the suggestion that Byron's deformity had a nervous and deep-seated rather than a localized and merely physical origin." He precedes this statement with a quotation from H. Charles Cameron's article, "The Mystery of Lord Byron's Lameness" (The *Lancet,* March 31, 1923).
3. It is a curious fact that, in the sequence of Byron's amorous conquests, Lady Carolina was succeeded by Lady Oxford, twenty years his senior. Although still sexually desirable, it could be perhaps that the poet found in her the type of woman with the tender love, the intelligence, and the culture that his own mother so patently lacked.
4. It should not be assumed from what Byron said here of the Anglo-Americans that he did not esteem them or that their praise failed to flatter him. In fact, he admired the United States as a model of vigor, freedom, and moderation (letter to Hobhouse, October 12, 1821). And in *Childe Harold* (IV, xcvl) he paid the tribute of his praises to George Washington. Two years before, writing from Angostura, Bolívar had referred to the United States as "a unique model of political virtues and moral culture . . . brought up in freedom and nourished on pure freedom."
5. It is quite important in this context to remember that Lord Byron had told Hobhouse (letter of October 3, 1819) that "My affairs in England are nearly settled or in prospect of settlement; in Italy I have no debts and I could leave it when I choose."

6. Martí's worship of Bolívar flares up now and then throughout his works like a burning torch. The words quoted (in translation) are from his speech on Bolívar of October 29, 1893.
7. There is no doubt that, almost exactly six months before—on October 16, 1809—a heroic revolutionary uprising took place in the small town of Funes, Ecuador. But it is a fact too that, failing to attract many followers, it could not succeed and did not, therefore, have the transcendent importance of the one that exploded in Venezuela—which was followed by the uprisings in Buenos Aires, on May 25, and in Bogotá, on July 20, 1810.
8. There are those who believe that Byron alluded to Napoleon in the following lines from Canto IV, stanza lxxxix, of *Childe Harold:* "Save one vain man, who is not in the grave, / But, vanquished by himself, to his own slaves a slave." See *Century Readings for a Course in English Literature,* edited and annotated by J. W. Cunlifee, J. F. A. Pyre, and Karl Young (New York: 1920), vol. II.
9. On August 23, 1819—the very year of his full and almost domestic intimacy with Teresa Guiccioli—Byron ended a letter to Hobhouse begging him to believe in and correspond with him "as long as I can keep my sanity."

Chapter 2

1. *The Writings of Benjamin Franklin,* 10 vols. (New York, 1905–1907); letter to David Hartley (1789).
2. Except the following: Rome, Naples, the Spanish College at Bologna, and Coimbra.
3. In his essay, "Franklin en el Mundo Hispano," Professor John E. Englekirk has written: "In the history of cultural relations between the Hispanic- and Anglo-American worlds, Franklin is the only one to stand out as a living human being in the gallery of great men of our Independence epic. . . . And already before the end of the eighteenth century, his *Autobiography* was read by the whole western world as that of the most representative figure of the young American Republic."
4. Y el pueblo primogénito dichoso / de libertad, que sobre todos tanto / por su poder y gloria se enaltece, / como entre sus estrellas / la estrella de Virginia resplandece, / nos da el ósculo santo / de amistad fraternal.
5. Miró la Europa ensangrentar su suelo / al genio de la guerra y la victoria . . . / Pero le cupo a América la gloria / de que el genio del bien le diera el cielo.
6. Bolívar based his attitude on the desirability of "not incurring the ill will of Albion."
7. There was one other difference: the *fueros* were still operating. As an institution, the *fueros* (a word derived from the Latin *forum*)

originated in the Middle Ages and were widespread throughout Latin America during the colonial period. Under this arrangement, only a part of the population was subject to the common courts. Privileged classes, including certain government, army, and church officials, were judged by special courts of their own, both in civil and criminal cases. Such privileges, enjoyed by these favored classes as against those of lower social status, were known as the *fueros*.

8. The position of Darío and Rodó respectively in regard to the United States is thoroughly discussed in Chapter III.

9. Y la América debe, ya que aspira a ser libre, / imitarles primero e igualarles después.

10. As late as 1957, boundary disputes were still with us, as witness the one between Nicaragua and Honduras over the Mosquitos region: a difference that Honduras had considered settled since the year 1906.

11. Some grant an even greater significance to the Conference of Bogota (1948). Luis Quintanilla, for instance, delegate from Mexico at the O.A.S. Council, states: "Until the Bogota Conference Pan-Americanism was formless . . . it lacked a constitutional structure."

12. In 1955, the United States signed agreements with several Latin-American nations for collaborating in the investigation of peaceful uses of atomic energy.

Chapter 3

1. Rubén Darío, *Obras poéticas completas* (Madrid: M. Aguilar, 1945), p. 805.
2. *Ibid.*, "Dilucidaciones," *El canto errante*, p. 765.
3. *Obras completas, Los raros* (Madrid: Afrodisio Aguado, 1950), II, 257.
4. *Ibid.*
5. *Ibid.*, p. 259.
6. E. K. Mapes, ed., *Escritos inéditos de Rubén Darío* (New York: Instituto de las Españas en los Estados Undios, 1938), pp. 160–161.
7. *Ibid.*
8. *Ibid.*
9. *Ibid.*
10. José Enrique Rodó, *Ariel* (5th ed.; Montevideo: Claudio García y Cía., 1944), pp. 21–22.
11. *Ibid.*
12. Darío, *Los raros*, p. 259.
13. Rodó, *op. cit.*, p. 85.
14. Instituto Nacional de Investigaciones y Archivos Literarios, *Fuentes* (Montevideo, August, 1961), Year I, No. 1, p. 70.
15. Rodó, *op. cit.*, p. 85.
16. Mapes, *op. cit.*, p. 162.

17. Rodó, *op. cit.*, p. 160.
18. Mapes, *op. cit.*, p. 162.
19. Rodó, *op. cit.*, p. 89. (Despite Rodó's silence about Darío in this particular instance, Darío was always grateful to him for his essay on *Prosas profanas.* Generous to the end, he wrote about Rodó and his book, *Ariel,* saying that "it marks a new triumph of his spirit and one more conquest made by his precepts for the beauty of existence, for the elevation of Hispanic-American intellects." See, Rubén Darío, "José Enrique Rodó," *Cabezas: Obras completas,* II, 963.)
20. Rodó, *op. cit.*, p. 91.
21. Darío, *Los raros,* p. 257.
22. Darío, "En París," *Autobiografía* (5th ed.; Madrid: S. H. A. D. E. [w. d.]) , Chap. xxxii, p. 139.
23. *Ibid.*, pp. 139–140.
24. Darío, "Los anglosajones," *Peregrinaciones: Obras completas,* III, 423.
25. A quarter of a century later, a Mexican intellectual, José Vasconcelos, was to write in his book, *Indología:* "The United States is not merely a useful Martha but also a dreaming and creative Mary . . ." See, José Vasconcelos, "El asunto," *Indología,* preface and selection by Fernández MacGregor (Mexico: Ediciones de la Secretaría de Educación Pública, 1942) , p. 177.
26. Darío, *Peregrinaciones,* pp. 426–427.
27. *Ibid.*, p. 427.
28. Walt Whitman, *Leaves of Grass* (New York: Doubleday, Doran and Co., 1940) , pp. 228, 229. (Whitman wrote three other poems to Lincoln: "O Captain! My Captain!" "Hush'd Be the Camps To-Day," and "This Dust Was Once the Man," all of them expressive of heartfelt devotion.)
29. José Martí, *Obras completas* (Havana: Editorial Lex, 1946) , II, 1815.
30. See Donald F. Fogelquist, *The Literary Collaboration and the Personal Correspondence of Rubén Darío and Juan Ramón Jiménez* (Coral Gables, Florida: University of Miami Press, February, 1956) , p. 19.
31. Darío, *La caravana pasa: Obras completas,* III, 614–615.
32. Y me volví a París. Me volví al enemigo / terrible, centro de neurosis, ombligo / de la locura, foco de todo *surmenage* / donde hago buenamente mi papel de *sauvage* / encerrado en mi celda de la rue Marivaux, / confiando sólo en mí y resguardando el yo. / Y si lo resguardara, señora, si no fuera / lo que llaman los parisienses una *pera.* / A mi rincón me llegan a buscar las intrigas, / las pequeñas miserias, las traiciones amigas / y las ingratitudes. Mi maldita visión / sentimental del mundo me aprieta el corazón, / y así, cualquier tunante me explotará a su gusto.—Darío, "Epístola," *El canto errante: Obras poéticas completas,* p. 818.

    In that same year, 1907, in *Poema de otoño y otros poemas,* Darío left another note of great human interest concerning Paris. It is entitled "Poema de carnaval" and was addressed also to Señora

Lugones. The very first stanza reveals the Argentinian poet's concern for the Maestro's state of mind. Darío, in these verses, was trying to deny that he was panicky, disappointed, or splenetic: "Ha mucho que Leopoldo / me juzga bajo un toldo / de penas, al rescoldo / de una última ilusión. / O bien cual hombre adusto / que agriado de disgusto / no hincha el cuello robusto / lanzando una canción." (Leopoldo has long thought / I'm saddened and distraught / and can warm myself with naught / save one last fantasy. / Or else I'm a man crossed, / embittered by disgust, / who won't swell his throat robust / in song and jollity.) Darío then assured them that Paris was the only city in the world where, in dreams, he sank in "the sweetest depths of joyous life." But let us not forget the words "in dreams," that this was a "carnival poem," and that Darío himself confessed that he was just pretending. In another line he said that he had sung with a mask on ("y puesta la careta / ha cantado el poeta"). Darío, *op. cit.*, pp. 868–873.

33. Darío, "Augusto de Armas," *Los raros: Obras completas*, II, 389.
34. Darío, *Letras: Obras completas*, I, 389.
35. Alfred de Musset, "Rolla," *Oeuvres Complètes* (Paris: Edition et Librairie, Imp. Ramlot et Cie., 1932) , p. 69.
36. Darío, "Palabras liminares," *Prosas profanas: Obras poéticas Completas*, p. 606.

Chapter 4

1. Rubén Darío, Preface, *Cantos de vida y esperanza: Obras poéticas completas*, p. 690.
2. De la América ingenua que tiene sangre indígena, / que aún reza a Jesucristo y aún habla en español.—*Ibid.*, "A Roosevelt," p. 705.
3. ¿Seremos entregados a los bárbaros fieros? / ¿Tantos millones de hombres hablaremos inglés?—*Ibid.*, "Los cisnes," p. 715.
4. Abominad la boca que predice desgracias eternas, / abominad los ojos que ven sólo zodíacos funestos, / abominad las manos que apedrean las ruinas ilustres, / o que la tea empuñan o la daga suicida.—*Ibid.*, "Salutación del optimista," p. 695.
5. Inútil es el grito de la legión cobarde / del interés, inútil el progreso / yanqui si te desdeña.—*Ibid.*, "¡Carne, celeste carne de mujer!" p. 736.
6. Mas la América nuestra, que tenía poetas / desde los viejos tiempos de Netzahualcoyolt, / que ha guardado las huellas de los pies del gran Baco, / que el alfabeto pánico en un tiempo aprendió; / que consultó los astros, que conoció la Atlántida / cuyo nombre nos llega resonando en Platón, / que desde los remotos momentos de su vida / vive de luz, de fuego, de perfume, de amor, / la América del grande Moctezuma, del inca, / la América fragante de Cristóbal Colón, / la América católica, la América española, / la América

en que dijo el noble Guatemoc: / "Yo no estoy en un lecho de rosas"; . . . —*Ibid.,* "A Roosevelt," p. 706.

7. Un desastroso espíritu posee tu tierra: / donde la tribu unida blandió sus mazas, / hoy se enciende entre hermanos perpetua guerra, / se hieren y destrozan las mismas razas. / Al ídolo de piedra reemplaza ahora / el ídolo de carne que se entroniza, / y cada día alumbra la blanca aurora / en los campos fraternos sangre y ceniza. / Desdeñando a los reyes nos dimos leyes / al son de los cañones y los clarines, / y hoy al favor siniestro de negros Reyes / fraternizan los Judas con los Caínes. / . . . / Las ambiciones pérfidas no tienen diques, / soñadas libertades yacen deshechas: / ¡Eso no hicieron nunca nuestros caciques, / a quienes las montañas daban las flechas! / . . . / ¡Pluguiera a Dios las aguas antes intactas / no reflejaran nunca las blancas velas; / ni vieran las estrellas estupefactas / arribar a la orilla las carabelas! / . . . / La cruz que nos llevaste padece mengua; / y tras encanalladas revoluciones, / la canalla escritora mancha la lengua / que escribieron Cervantes y Calderones. / . . . / Duelos, espantos, guerras, fiebre constante / en nuestra senda ha puesto la suerte triste: / ¡Cristóforo Colombo, pobre Almirante, / ruega a Dios por el mundo que descubriste.— *Ibid.,* "A Colón," *El canto errante,* pp. 782–784.

8. *Ibid.,* "Dilucidaciones," p. 761.

9. *Ibid.,* p. 765.

10. Bien vengas, mágica Águila de alas enormes y fuertes, / a extender sobre el Sur tu gran sombra continental, / a traer en tus garras, anillas de rojos brillantes, / una palma de gloria, del color de la inmensa esperanza, / y en tu pico la oliva de una vasta y fecunda paz.—*ibid.,* p. 787.

11. Darío, "Manuel Ugarte," *Cabezas: Obras completas,* II, 1005.

12. Yo panamericanicé / con un vago temor y con muy poca fe / en la tierra de los diamantes y la dicha / tropical.—Darío, "Epístola," *El canto errante: Obras poéticas completas,* p. 816.

13. Darío, "Roosevelt en París," *Cabezas: Obras completas,* II, 672.

14. *Ibid.,* pp. 672–673.

15. *Ibid.*

16. *Ibid.,* pp. 675–676.

17. *Ibid.,* p. 677.

18. Alto es él, mirada fiera; / su chaleco es su bandera / como lo es sombrero y frac; / si no es hombre de conquistas / todo el mundo tiene vistas / las estrellas y las listas / que bien sábese están listas / en reposo y en vivac. / Aquí el amontonamiento / mató amor y sentimiento; / mas en todo existe Dios, / y yo he visto mil cariños / acercarse hacia los niños / del trineo y los armiños / del anciano Santa Claus. / Porque el yanqui ama sus hierros, / sus caballos y sus perros, / y su *yacht* y su *foot-ball;* / pero adora la alegría, / con la fuerza, la harmonía: / un muchacho que se ría/ y una niña como un sol.—Darío, "La gran cosmópolis," *Lira póstuma: Obras poéticas completas,* pp. 988–990.

19. ¡Oh pueblos nuestros! ¡Oh pueblos nuestros! Juntaos / en la esperanza, y en el trabajo y la paz. / No busquéis las tinieblas, no per-
sigáis el caos, / y no reguéis con sangre nuestra tierra feraz. / Ya
lucharon bastante los antiguos abuelos / por Patria y Libertad,
y un glorioso clarín / clama a través del tiempo, debajo de los
cielos, / Washington y Bolívar, Hidalgo y San Martín. / Ved el
ejemplo amargo de la Europa deshecha; / ved las trincheras fúne-
bres, las tierras sanguinosas; / y la Piedad y el Duelo sollozando
los dos. / No; no dejéis al Odio que dispare su flecha; / llevad a
los altares de la Paz miel y rosas. / Paz a la inmensa América. Paz
en nombre de Dios. / Y pues aquí está el foco de una cultura
nueva, / que sus principios lleve desde el Norte hasta el Sur, /
hagamos la Unión viva que el nuevo triunfo lleva: / *The Star
Spangled Banner,* con el blanco y azul.—Darío, "Pax," *Versos oca-
sionales: Obras poéticas completas,* pp. 1064–1070.
20. Sangre bebió el suelo del Norte / como el suelo meridional. / Tal a
los siglos fue preciso. / Para ir hacia lo venidero, / para hacer, si
no el paraíso, / la casa feliz del obrero / en plenitud ciudadana, /
vínculo íntimo eslabona / e ímpetu exterior hermana / a la raza
anglosajona / con la latinoamericana.—*Ibid., Canto a la Argentina,*
pp. 936–937.

Chapter 5

1. Alonso de Ojeda's words, on arriving at the Antilles in 1509, are significant in this context. He told the Indians: "God . . . created
Heaven and earth and one man and one woman from whom you
and I, and every man who has ever been or ever will be in this
world, are descended."
2. Cieza de León was barely thirteen years old when he sailed to America; Hernán Cortés was nineteen; one of his captains, Gonzalo de
Sandoval, twenty-two. And there are many other similar cases.
3. I refer here to members of aristocratic families who accompanied the
conquistadores rather than to the latter themselves. Pizarro, Balboa, and Valdivia, for instance, were of humble origin. Of Valdivia,
Rosa Arciniega says that he did not object to carrying out menial
tasks, especially in agriculture.
4. Let us bear in mind on this point that, after putting down the uprising of the *Comuneros* in Aragon, Philip II of Spain himself concluded that his subjects were ungovernable.
5. The *indigenista* (pro-Indian) group in Peru includes among others,
Manuel González Prada, José Carlos Mariátegui, Pedro S. Zulen,
Dora Mayer, Haya de la Torre, César Vallejo, Castro Pozo, López
Albújar, César Falcón, Manuel Seoane, Carlos M. Cox, Luis Heysen,
etc. The pro-Spanish group includes José de la Riva Agüero, Al-

berto Wagner Reyna, Carlos Pareja, Paz Soldán, Raúl Porras, Víctor A. Belaunde, and Guillermo Hoyos Osores, etc.

6. Among the worst horrors perpetrated upon the Indians are the actions of the Peruvian Amazonas Company Limited, denounced by Pío Jaramillo in his book, *El indio ecuatoriano*, Quito, 1922. On the other hand, any foreign capitalist, no matter how liberal his conduct or reasonable his profits, provides an ever present pretext for the Communists' unceasing exploitation of the narrow nationalism of some of those countries.

7. As when the extreme Left in Brazil accused Foreign Minister Joao Neves de Fontoura of servile subservience and of having made his country "a satellite" by agreeing to sell petroleum to the United States during the Korean war. To this charge, Fontoura replied, "What they want is to see us leave all [our natural resources] buried and thus display our political and economic inferiority. . . . It is a way of making us poor and weak . . . of making us an easy prey to the world revolution the Kremlin wants to bring about." The sociologist Gilberto Freyre, in his book, *New World in the Tropics*, warns that, "One thing is certain: for the first time in the history of the relations of Brazil with the United States, Yankeephobia is becoming a potent factor . . ."

8. Indio que labras con fatiga / tierras que de otros dueños son: / ¿ignoras tú que deben tuyas / ser por tu sangre y tu sudor? / ¿Ignoras tú que audaz codicia, / siglos atrás te las quitó? / Ignoras tú que eres el amo? / "¡Quién sabe, *señor!*"

9. Crece la desdicha, hermanos hombres, / más pronto que la máquina, a diez máquinas, y crece.

10. Ah, desgraciadamente, hombres humanos, / hay, hermanos, muchísimo que hacer.

11. La indiada lleva la mañana / en la protesta de sus palas.

12. Adelante, campanas populares, / adelante, regiones de manzana, / adelante, estandartes cereales; / adelante, mayúsculas del fuego, / porque en la lucha, en la ola, en la pradera, / en la montaña, en el crepúsculo cargado de acre aroma, / lleváis un nacimiento de permanencia, un hilo / de difícil dureza. / Mientras tanto, / raíz y guirnalda sube del silencio / para esperar la mineral victoria: / cada instrumento, cada rueda roja, / cada mango de sierra o penacho de arado, / cada extracción del suelo, cada temblor de sangre / quiere seguir tus pasos, Ejército del Pueblo: / tu luz organizada llega a los pobres hombres / olvidados, tu definida estrella / clava sus roncos rayos en la muerte / y establece los nuevos ojos de la esperanza.

13. Chile, / dominó la materia, / apartó de la piedra / el mineral yacente, / éste se fue a Chicago / de paseo, / el cobre / se convirtió en cadenas, / en maquinaria tétrica / del crimen, / después de tantas luchas / para que mi patria lo pariera, / después de su glorioso, / virginal nacimiento, / le hicieron ayudante de la muerte, / lo endurecieron y lo designaron / asesino.

14. Compare Neruda's position with that of *don* César Battle Pacheco, who, speaking to Uruguay's House of Deputies on June 21, 1945, said, referring to the United States: "What country have we ever known to respect others more than [the United States]? Did not Artigas have the protection of North America in his struggle for independence? Did not Argentina receive her first arms for her war of independence from the United States? Yet, we, to a people of this caliber, respond time and again with insults and injuries."

15. La diana de madrugada, / va, con alfileres rojos, / abriendo todos los ojos. / La diana de madrugada. / Levanta en peso el cuartel / con los soldados cansados. / Van saliendo los soldados. / Levanta en peso el cuartel. / Ay, diana, ya tocarás / de madrugada algún día, / tu toque de rebeldía. / Ay, diana, ya tocarás. / Vendrás a la cama dura / donde se pudre el mendigo. / —¡Amigo!—gritarás—¡ Amigo! / Vendrás a la cama dura. / Rugirás con voz ya libre / sobre la cama de seda: / —¡En pie, porque nada os queda! / Rugirás con voz ya libre. / Fiera, fuerte, desatada, / diana en corneta de fuego, / diana del pobre y del ciego, / diana de la madrugada.

16. Todos estos yanquis rojos / son hijos de un camarón, / y los parió una botella, / una botella de ron.

17. De dos en dos / las maracas se adelantan al yanqui / para decirle: / —¿Cómo esta usted, señor? / Cuando hay barco a la vista, / están ya las maracas en el puerto / vigilando la presa excursionista / con ojos vivos y ademán despierto. / ¡Maraca equilibrista, güiro adulón del dólar del turista! / Pero hay otra maraca, con un cierto / pudor, que casi es antimperialista. / Es la maraca del artista, / que no tiene que hacer nada en el puerto. [*Maraca*, a round gourd rattle, typical Antillean rhythm instrument; *güiro,* an elongated gourd with grooves cut on its surface, also typical rhythm instrument of Antillean popular music.]

18. See Eugenio Chang-Rodríguez' evaluation of Mariátegui in *La literatura política de González Prada, Mariátequi y Haya de la Torre.* According to Chang-Rodríguez, Mariátegui's was an "incomplete" Marxism, because it had not totally freed itself from the influence of religion. The same author points out, however, that Mariátegui's essay on the Indian question was written for the Russian news agency, Tass, in New York.

19. Y como tú comprendes por qué el héroe bolchevique es / imprescindible para, en carne y sange, entrar a / la historia, entendiéndola, etc.

Chapter 7

1. Para Aragón en España, / tengo yo en mi corazón, / un lugar todo Aragón, / franco, fiero, fiel, sin saña.

2. Early in July, 1893, the following comments on Martí were published in San José, Costa Rica, as part of a description by Emilio Pacheco of a gathering at the Law School in that city: "Martí entered the room leaning on the arm of his friend, Dr. Zambrana; he was pale and stooped slightly as he walked over to the chair reserved for him. Martí was sick."

3. Cultivo una rosa blanca, / en julio como en enero, / para el amigo sincero / que me da su mano franca. / Y para el cruel que me arranca / el corazón con que vivo, / cardo ni oruga cultivo; / cultivo la rosa blanca.

Chapter 8

1. Político, militar, héroe, orador y poeta. / Y en todo, grande. Como las tierras libertadas por él. / Por él, que no nació hijo de patria alguna. / Sino que muchas patrias nacieron hijas de él. / Tenía la valentía del que lleva una espada. / Tenía la cortesía del que lleva una flor. / Y, entrando en los salones, arrojaba la espada. / Y, entrando en los combates, arrojaba la flor. / Los picos del Ande no eran más a sus ojos / que signos admirativos de sus arrojos. / Fue un soldado poeta. Un poeta soldado. / Y cada pueblo libertado / era una hazaña del poeta y un poema del soldado. / ¡Y fue crucificado! [Translation by Muna Lee.]

   Lloréns also pays homage to Bolívar in his only play, *El grito de Lares*. One of the leaders of this local revolutionary movement that took place in a small Puerto Rican town was the Venezuelan Manuel Rojas, to whom Lloréns attributes the following speech as he stands by the hero of the play, Manolo el Leñero, who has been mortally wounded:
   Of Venezuela, my land, / You bring memories to me, / Because you fought with a plainsman's / Unrelenting bravery. / Now that you are at death's door / Your fevered hand give to me / And on reaching Heaven's threshold / Bolívar's embrace receive. (De Venezuela, mi patria, / evoco en ti los recuerdos. / Luchaste con la indomable / intrepidez de un llanero. / En el umbral de la muerte / tu mano febril aprieto, / en el umbral de la gloria / Bolívar te dará un beso.)

2. *Silva,* a metrical composition, usually of alternating endecasyllabic and heptasyllabic lines, some of which, in either meter, may be "free" (not rhyming with any other line) while the remainder rhyme without being subject to any predetermined rhyme-scheme.

3. La libertad más dulce que el imperio / y más hermoso que el laurel la oliva.

4. Allá también deberes / hay que llenar: cerrad, cerrad las hondas / heridas de la guerra.

5. . . . monumento / de la dicha mortal, burla del viento.

6. Su rústica piedad, pero sincera, / halle a tus ojos gracia: no el ri-
   sueño / porvenir que las penas aligera / cual el dorado sueño /
   visión falsa, desvanecido llore: / intempestiva lluvia no maltrate /
   el delicado embrión: el diente impío / del insecto roedor no lo
   devore: / sañudo vendaval no lo arrebate, / ni agote al árbol de
   materno jugo / la calorosa sed de largo estío. . . .

Chapter 9

1. Ralph W. Emerson, *Essays on English Traits*, "Self-reliance."
2. *Obras completas de José Martí* (Havana: Editorial Lex, 1946), I, 554.
3. All quotations from Luis Muñoz Rivera's poems appearing in this
   chapter are from his *Obras completas* (Poetry) : *Retamas, Tropicales, Versos Selectos*, edited and with an introduction by Eugenio
   Fernández Méndez (San Juan de Puerto Rico: Instituto de Cultura Puertorriqueña, 1960) .
4. Mirad: frente por frente se divisa / al viejo capataz de la mesnada; /
   ni un pliegue de bondad en su sonrisa; / ni un destello de luz en
   su mirada. / Alma siniestra: su rostro abotargado; / labio en un
   gesto de desdén caído; / el corazón a la piedad cerrado / y a la
   doliente súplica el oído. / Allá, sobre las cumbres de la sierra, /
   con sus turbas de ilotas y reptiles, / para dictar sus úkases se en-
   cierra / entre nubes de sables y fusiles. / Miedoso de la fiebre ven-
   gadora / plantó su tienda lejos de los mares / y abrió, como una
   caja de Pandora, / el cofre de sus juicios militares. / Inquisidor,
   a sus esbirros manda / que a los hombres apliquen la tortura / y
   caigan en los pueblos como banda / negra y feroz a la que el ham-
   bre apura. / Ante ese monstruo, aborto del abismo, / aún hay
   quien pasa con la frente erguida; / en el alma el horror del despo-
   tismo / y el desprecio sublime de la vida. / Mientras aliente un
   corazón entero / pueden lucir auroras de venganza; / hasta las sie-
   nes del Goliat ibero / la débil onda de David alcanza. / Es general
   sin luchas ni peleas, / sin hidalguía, sin honor, sin nada; / para
   cortar el vuelo a las ideas: / para eso sirve el filo de su espada. /
   Goza en paz oh tirano! que algún día / irá a turbar tus negras
   soledades / lejana, estrepitosa gritería: / zumbido de remotas tem-
   pestades. / Grito de rabia que los aires llena; / rugido de un titán
   que quiebra el yugo; / voz de un pueblo que rompe su cadena; /
   voz de un pueblo que execra a su verdugo.
5. Jamás la triste musa borincana / vendió su honor ni profanó su luto /
   rindiendo, fementida cortesana, / a la lisonja vil fácil tributo. / Se-
   vera y noble en su infortunio grave, / alta la frente de laurel
   ceñida, / pudo plegar su vuelo, como el ave / que junto al cráter
   del volcán anida; / pero nunca, olvidando su grandeza, / se arras-
   tró, por lograr seguro asiento, / al amparo de abrupta fortaleza /
   ni a la sombra de alcázar opulento. / Hoy la voz de Borinquen,

conmovida, / los ecos llena de los patrios lares, / y aquí viene a
arrullar tu despedida / con el áspero son de sus cantares. / Oyela,
general: ella no miente, / ni mancha de sus alas el armiño, / ni
fingir sabe la ansiedad ardiente / ni los vivos transportes del cariño. / Un día la tormenta desatada / sobre nosotros con furor
rugía; / todo un pueblo su atónita mirada / hacia la egregia España convertía. / Con la aurora boreal de la esperanza / la madre,
al fin, calmaba tanto duelo . . . / y en ti vimos el iris de bonanza /
que iluminó el confín de nuestro cielo. / ¡Que el gallardo bajel de
tu existencia / impela con sus auras la fortuna! / ¡Que a ser lle-
gues la augusta providencia / del pueblo ilustre que arrulló tu
cuna!

6. Ayer, amenazante, esa bandera / flotó de mi país en los castillos. / Y
habría dado yo mi vida entera / por mirarla salir, mares afuera, /
con sus matices rojos y amarillos. / Hoy, que en sus reales se plegó
sombría, / se va con ella un ideal fecundo: / un símbolo de honor
y de hidalguía. / Y, creedlo: no sé lo que daría / ¡ay! para verla
dominar al mundo.

7. Alma fogosa, corazón sereno; / brazo nervudo, voluntad entera; / la
fe por guía, la razón por freno; / la libertad por única bandera; /
sin la cobarde sumisión del paria; / sin el brutal instinto de la
fiera; / así, en mis sueños de ambición precaria, / quise en mi patria contemplar un día, / no la turba rebelde y tumultuaria / que
en algarada inútil se extravía . . .

8. Yo condeno el motín ¡sí! yo condeno / la rebelión sin freno / que
mata y roba, incendia y anonada: / yo sé que la razón sus fueros
vende / cuando a luchar aprende / al amparo de abrupta barri-
cada.

9. Por eso en mis estrofas turbulentas / hay algo que responde a mis
afanes: / a veces guardan, al plegarse lentas, / el soplo abrasador
de las tormentas / y el hálito fatal de los volcanes.

10. De frente al sol, sobre el macizo idioma / en que su huella el ideal
estampa, / domo mis versos cual el gaucho doma / sus salvajes
corceles en la pampa.

11. Yo sé lo que dicen / las roncas campanas / cuando vibran en brusco
desorden: / yo sé lo que dicen: ¡Venganza! ¡Venganza!

12. En este valle de miseria y lodo, / nada me importa al fin, y ésta es
mi ciencia: / estar en lucha siempre y contra todo / estando siempre en paz con mi conciencia.

13. Alfonso Méndez Plancarte, "Díaz Mirón, gran poeta y sumo artífice,"
Memorias de la Academia Mexicana, XV (1956), 15.

14. Francisco Monterde, *Díaz Mirón: El hombre. La obra* (Mexico,
1956), pp. 8–9.

15. *Poemas y pensamientos de Luis Muñoz Rivera* (San Juan de Puerto
Rico: Instituto de Cultura Puertorriqueña, 1959), p. 19.

16. Y esta ninfa gentil que ora se duerme / al lánguido arrullar de sus
palmares, / sacudirá su anémico letargo; / se alzará triunfadora y
formidable; / sentirá en sus arterias / circular otra vida y otra

sangre, / y será para siempre, para siempre! / feliz, y digna, y grande.

Chapter 10

1. Perfecta rosa que adoro: / para implorarte no encuentro / sino medir las palabras / con los latidos del pecho.
2. In his prologue to the second edition of *Abel Sánchez*, published that same year by the Editorial Renacimiento, Madrid, Unamuno wrote: ". . . this novel, which has been translated into Italian, German, and Dutch, has been quite successful in the countries where people think and feel in these languages. And it began to meet with some success in our Spanish-speaking countries too, especially after the young critic, José A. Balseiro, in the second volume of his *El Vigía*, wrote an acute and sensitive essay on it. So much so that a second printing has become necessary."
3. See "José Gorostiza en la Academia," *Memorias de la Academia Mexicana de la Lengua*, vol. XV (Mexico, 1956).
4. See, in the index to Alfonso Reyes' poetic works, his tributes to Amado Nervo, Xavier Villaurrutia, Gabriel Méndez Plancarte, Carlos Pellicer, Francisco Monterde . . . to mention only a few of the Mexicans among the number of illustrious authors from different countries.
5. Monterde's speech and mine were published in vol. XVII (1960) of the Academy's *Memorias*.
6. A Cuernavaca voy, dulce retiro, / cuando, por veleidad o desaliento, / cedo al afán de interrumpir el cuento / y dar a mi relato algún respiro. / A Cuernavaca voy, que sólo aspiro / a disfrutar sus auras un momento: / pausa de libertad y esparcimiento / a la breve distancia de un suspiro. / Ni campo ni ciudad, cima ni hondura; / beata soledad, quietud que aplaca / o mansa compañía sin hartura. / Tibieza vegetal donde se hamaca / el ser en filosófica mesura . . . / ¡A Cuernavaca voy, a Cuernavaca!
7. Sin olvidar un punto la paciencia / y la resignación del hortelano, / a cada hora doy la diligencia / que pide mi comercio cotidiano. / Como nunca sentí la diferencia / de lo que pierdo ni de lo que gano, / siembro sin flojedades ni vehemencia / en el surco trazado por mi mano. / Mientras llega la hora señalada, / el brote guardo, cuido del injerto, / el tallo alzo de la flor amada, / arranco la cizaña de mi huerto, / y cuando suelte el puño del azada / sin preguntarlo me daréis por muerto.
8. Insobornable pensamiento mío, / atento celador de mi cuidado, / ¿cuándo me dejarás algún desvío, / desaprensión, olvido, desenfado?
9. Published, one year later (unfortunately full of errata), in *Cuadernos americanos*, year XX, No. 1 (Mexico, January–February, 1961).
10. Sé que otro día estrecharé tu mano / aunque no más en comunión de arcilla; / sé que tu acento, sabio mexicano, / apagarse no puede

en la otra orilla: / que, reposada la genial semilla, / latirá en lo
presente y en lo arcano / para el fruto en sazón, modelo puro / de
tu huerto de luz, siempre maduro. / Aún recojo en mi oído el soplo alado / de tu palabra de postrera hora: / cuando sentía, en
esperar callado, / tu ser de astro en busca de la aurora. / Cada
palabra, como egregia prora / que encuentra el puerto en orden
sosegado; / y en tu reino interior—estremecido / por larga vela—el
corazón herido. / Maestro de amistad para el ejemplo / de razón,
de bondad y de armonía, / tu biblioteca fue el augusto templo /
donde la ciencia de pensar vivía. / Mas también la quimera allí
tenía / su visionario. ¡Cómo te contemplo / —aunque sufriendo del
dolor las huellas—apasionado cazador de estrellas! / En la nave
del pecho el torbellino / que ya auguraba el huracán siniestro; /
pero la vid del pensamiento fino—creando mieles de alquimista
diestro— / convertía la sal en dulce vino / para descanso del pre-
sagio nuestro: / ¡que nunca, por tu rostro, se diría / lo que tu
entraña de aflicción sentía! / La mejor Grecia en tierra mexicana /
gracias a ti, virtud del humanismo, / abrió su rosa en perfección
lozana / como ornato inefable de ti mismo; / y especialista de uni-
versalismo / no hubo frontera ya que su cristiana / intimidad ne-
gara a tu cultura: / índice cierto de señal segura. / Siempre, junto
a lo denso, la ironía / como pétalo leve: que tu boca / no sólo con
los labios sonreía, / sino también con la pirueta loca / y sutil que
desnuda lo que toca / para elevar la gracia a la poesía. / ¡Que
jamás hubo prohibida fruta / sin sabroso lugar en tu minuta! /
Huésped de sombras ya, tu visión clara / nos abre el puerto de
cordial abrigo: / que siempre fue tu regla más preclara / apoyar
al colega y al amigo. / De tu nobleza singular testigo, / sé que
antecedes como quien ampara: / ¡que ha mucho tiempo se cuajó
la yema / inmortal de tu vida hecha poema!

11. De los amigos que yo más quería / y en breve trecho me han aban-
donado, / se deslizan las sombras a mi lado, / escaso alivio a mi
melancolía. / Se confunden sus voces con la mía / y me veo sus-
penso y desvelado / en el empeño de cruzar el vado / que me se-
para de su compañía. / Cedo a la invitación embriagadora, / y
discurro que el tiempo se convierte / y acendra un infinito cada
hora. / Y desbordo los límites, de suerte / que mi sentir la inmen-
sidad explora / y me familiarizo con la muerte.

Chapter 11

1. She may have been María de Alvarado, born in León de Huanuco
   and a descendant of the conquistador Pedro de Alvarado. On the
   other hand, nothing—except that she was born in Peru—is known
   about the woman who wrote *Discurso en loor de la Poesía* and

deserved the praises of Diego Mejía, the Sevillian who translated
Ovid's *Herodias* into Spanish.

2. Eros: ¿acaso no sentiste nunca / piedad de las estatuas? / Piedad para
las manos enguantadas / de hielo, que no arrancan / los frutos de-
liciosos de la carne / ni las flores fantásticas del alma; / piedad
para los sexos sacrosantos / que acoraza de una / hoja de viña
astral la castidad.

3. Con la cabeza negra caída hacia adelante / está la mujer bella, la de
mediana edad, / postrada de rodillas y un Cristo agonizante /
desde su duro leño la mira con piedad. / En los ojos la carga de
una enorme tristeza, / en el seno la carga del hijo por nacer, / al
pie del blanco Cristo que está sangrando reza: / —¡Señor, el hijo
mío que no nazca mujer!

4. Si yo fuera hombre, ¡qué hartazgo de luna, / de sombra y silencio me
había de dar! / ¡Cómo, noche a noche, solo ambularía / por los
campos quietos y por frente al mar! / Si yo fuera hombre, ¡qué
extraño, qué loco, / tenaz vagabundo que había de ser! / ¡Amigo
de todos los largos caminos / que invitan a ir lejos para no volver! /
Cuando así me acosan ansias andariegas, / ¡Qué pena tan honda
me da ser mujer!

5. ¿A quién podrá llamar la que hasta aquí ha venido / si más lejos que
ella sólo fueron los muertos?

6. ¿No hay un rayo de sol que los alcance un día? / ¿No hay agua que
los lave de sus estigmas rojos? / ¿Para ellos solamente queda tu
entraña fría, / sordo tu oído fino y apretados los ojos? / Tal el
hombre asegura, por error o malicia; / mas yo, que he gustado,
como un vino, Señor, / mientras los otros siguen llamándote Jus-
ticia, / no te llamaré nunca otra cosa que Amor!

7. Con tus gemidos se ha arrullado el mundo, / y juega con las hebras
de tu llanto. / Los surcos de tu rostro, que amo tanto, / son cual
llagas de sierra de profundos. / Raza judía, y aún te resta pecho /
y voz de miel, para alabar tus lares, / y decir el Cantar de los Cantares / con lengua, y labio, y corazón deshechos. / ¡Raza judía,
carne de dolores, / raza judía, río de amargura: / como los cielos
y la tierra, dura / y crece tu ancha selva de clamores!

8. Con los pobres de la tierra / quiero yo mi suerte echar.

9. Piececitos de niño, / azulosos de frío, / ¡cómo os ven y no os cubren,
Dios mío!

10. Manitas de los niños, / manitas pedigüeñas, / de los valles del
mundo / sois dueñas. / Manitas extendidas / manos de pobreci-
tos, / benditos los que os colman / ¡benditos! / Benditos los que
oyendo / que parecéis un grito, / os devuelven el mundo / ¡benditos!

11. Dulce tu brisa sea al mecerlo, / dulce tu luna al platearlo, / fuerte
tu rama al sostenerlo, / bello el rocío al enjoyarlo. / De su conchita
delicada / tejida con hilacha rubia, / desvía el vidrio de la helada /
y las guedejas de la lluvia; / desvía el viento de ala brusca / que
lo dispersa a su caricia / y la mirada que lo busca, / toda encen-

dida de codicia . . . / Tú, que me afeas los martirios / dados a tus criaturas finas: / al copo leve de los lirios / y a las pequeñas clavellinas, / guarda su forma con cariño / y pálpala con emoción. / Tirita al viento como un niño; / ¡es parecido a un corazón!

12. A la sombra de Dios, grita lo que supiste: / que somos huérfanos, que vamos solos, que tú nos viste, / ¡que toda carne con angustia pide morir!

13. Yo no tengo otro oficio / después del callado de amarte, / que este oficio de lágrimas, duro, / que tú me dejaste. / ¡Tengo una vergüenza / de vivir de este modo cobarde! / ¡Ni voy en tu busca / ni consigo tampoco olvidarte!

14. Me alejaré cantando mis venganzas hermosas, / porque a ese hondor recóndito la mano de ninguna / bajará a disputarme tu puñado de huesos!

15. ¡Ah! ¡Nunca más conocerá tu boca / la vergüenza del beso que chorreaba / concupiscencia como espesa lava! / ¡Ah! ¡Nunca más tus dos iris cegados / tendrán un rostro descompuesto, rojo / de lascivia, en sus vidrios dibujado!

16. Es breve el odio e inmenso el amor.

17. Olvidas, Señor, que lo quería, / y que él sabía suya la entraña que llagaba. / Que enturbió para siempre mis linfas de alegría! / ¡No importa! ¡Tú comprende: yo le amaba, le amaba!

18. There was a certain peasant crudeness in Gabriela's appearance, but her speech was of unique womanly warmth and her glance was mildness itself.

19. Tengo vergüenza de mi boca triste, / de mi voz rota y mis rodillas rudas; / ahora que me miraste y que viniste, / me encontré pobre y me palpé desnuda.

20. I remember that the late Cecilia Meireles, the exquisite Brazilian poetess, told me that among the numerous letters Gabriela wrote her, only one was written in a joyful mood: one expressing her happiness at being able to revisit Rio de Janeiro.

21. Mudemos ya por el verso sonriente / aquél listado de sangre con hiel.

22. Poema de Mistral, olor a surco abierto / que huele en las mañanas, yo te aspiré embriagada! / Vi a Mireya exprimir la fruta ensangrentada / del amor y correr por el atroz desierto.

23. Dios Padre sus miles de mundos / mece sin ruido. / Sintiendo su mano en la sombra / mezo a mi niño.

24. Tan dulce de decir / como una infancia; / bendita de cantar / como un hosanna!

25. Hace tanto que masco tinieblas, / que la dicha no sé reaprender; / tanto tiempo que piso las lavas / que olvidaron vellones los pies; / tantos años que muerdo el desierto / que mi patria se llama la Sed. / He aprendido un amor que es terrible / y que corta mi gozo a cercén: / he ganado el amor de la nada, / apetito de nunca volver, / voluntad de quedar con la tierra / mano a mano y mudez a mudez, / despojada de mi propio Padre, / rebanada de Jerusalem!

26. Tu hermana que no tiene / hijo ni madre ni casta presente.
27. ¿Qué brazo daré que no sea luto?
28. Todavía los que llegan / me dicen mi nombre, me ven la cara; / pero yo que me ahogo me veo / árbol devorado y humoso, / cerrazón de noche, carbón consumado, / enebro denso, ciprés engañoso, / cierto a los ojos, huido en la mano.
29. Siento mi corazón en la dulzura / fundirse como ceras: / son un óleo tardo / y no un vino mis venas, / y siento que mi vida se va huyendo / callada y dulce como la gacela.
30. Isabel de Ambía, Consuelo Berges, Gerardo Diego, Antonio Espina, Gregorio Marañón, Clemencia Miró, Antonio Oliver, Almira de la Rosa-Ginés de Albareda, Concha Zardoya, Vicente Aleixandre, Dámaso Alonso, Carlos Bousoño, Carmen Conde, Angel Valbuena Prat, Josefina Romo Arregui.
31. Very few people in Hispanic America learned in time about the liberal, anti-expansionist opposition presented by so many nationally prominent men in the United States. (See Chapter II, "The Americas Look at Each Other.") Actually, Hispanic Americans knew only about one sector of North American opinion.

Chapter 12

1. Descansem o meu leito solitario / Na floresta dos homens esquecida, / A' sombra de una cruz, e escrevam nela: / Foi poeta, sonhou e amou na vida.
2. Espirito do apostolo das selvas! / Sabio e cantor. Iuzeiro do futuro.

Chapter 13

1. The Peruvian professor, Augusto Tamayo Vargas, suggests, by means of a question, that Concolorcorvo might have been Father Calixto San Joseph Tupac Inga, born in Tarma to Pedro Montes and Dominga Tupac Inga. See *Revista Iberoamericana* (July–December, 1959), XXIV, no. 48, 333–339.
2. Era la tarde, y la hora / en que el sol la cresta dora / de los Andes. El desierto / incomensurable, abierto / y misterioso a sus pies / se extiende.
3. A mi lado ha envejecido, / y hoy está cual yo rendido / por la fatiga y la edad; / pero es mi sombra en verano, / y mi brújula en el llano, / mi amigo en la soledad. / Ya no vamos de carrera / por la extendida pradera, / pues somos viejos los dos. / Oh, mi moro, el cielo quiera / acabemos la carrera / muriendo juntos los dos!
4. Para mí la tierra es chica / y pudiera ser mayor.

5. Las coplas me van brotando / como agua de manantial.
6. Aquí me pongo a cantar / al compás de la vigüela, / que el hombre que lo desvela / una pena extraordinaria, / como la ave solitaria / con el cantar se consuela. / Cantando me he de morir, / cantando me han de enterrar, / y cantando he de llegar / al pie del Eterno Padre: / dende el vientre de mi madre / vine a este mundo a cantar. / Que no se trabe mi lengua / ni me falte la palabra. / El cantar mi gloria labra, / y poniéndome a cantar, / cantando me han de encontrar / aunque la tierra se abra. / Con la guitarra en la mano / ni las moscas se me arriman; / naides me pone el pie encima, / y cuando el pecho se entona, / hago gemir a la prima / y llorar a la bordona.
7. Y pa mejor, hasta el moro / se me jue de entre las manos. / No soy lerdo... / pero, hermano, / vino el comendante un día / diciendo que lo quería / "pa enseñarle a comer grano." / Afigúrese cualquiera / la suerte de este su amigo / a pie y mostrando el umbligo, / estropiao, pobre y desnudo. / Ni por castigo se pudo / hacerse más mal conmigo.
8. —¡Ah, ah! ... Y diga una cosa... Caballos... ¿Tiene caballos pa un viaje tan largo? ... Yo no truje más que éste y el de tiro que le digo, y el calor está pesadazo... / —¡Claro que tengo y macanudo!—contesta Pantalión lo más contento—. Tengo mi malacara grande, que es como quien dice el mejor caballo del pago y de toditos los pagos... ¡Ah, ah! / —¡Ta güeno! ... Pensé que tal vez lo hubiera vendido o jugao... / —¡Ta fresco! ... Primero me vendo yo... Lo quiero más al animal que a mi mesmo cuero... ¡Ah, ah!
9. ¡Duerme! mientras se despierte / del alba con el lucero / el vigilante tropero / que repita su cantar, / y que de bosque en laguna, / en el repunte o la hierra, / se alce por toda la tierra / como un coro popular. / Y mientras el gaucho errante / al cruzar por la pradera / se detenga en su carrera / y baje del alazán, / y ponga el poncho en el suelo / a guisa de pobre alfombra, / y rece bajo esa sombra, / ¡Santos Vega, duerme en paz!
10. Su poesía es la temprana / gloria del verdor campero / donde un relincho ligero / regocija la mañana. / Su recuerdo, vago lloro / de guitarra sorda y vieja...
11. ¡Ah criollo!, si parecía / pegao en el animal, / que aunque era medio bagual / a la rienda obedecía, / de suerte que se creería / ser no sólo arrocinao, / sinó también del recao / de alguna moza pueblera: / ¡Ah Cristo! ¡Quién lo tuviera! / ¡Lindo el overo rosao! / Como que era escarciador, / vivaracho y coscojero, / le iba sonando al overo / la plata que era un primor; / pues eran plata el fiador, / pretal, espuelas, virolas, / y en las cabezadas solas / traía el hombre un Potosí: ¡Qué! ... ¡Si traía, para mí, / hasta de plata las bolas!
12. Cuando en las siestas de estío / las brillazones remedan / vastos oleajes que ruedan / sobre fantástico río; / mudo, abismado y

sombrío, / baja un jinete la falda / tinta de bella esmeralda, / llega a las márgenes solas. . . / ¡Y hunde su potro en las olas, / con la guitarra a la espalda!

13. Que lanza el sollozo triste / o el llanto de la vidalita.

14. El gaucho tendrá su parte / en los júbilos futuros, / pues sus viejos cantares puros / entrarán en el reino del Arte.

15. ¡Argentina, región de la aurora! / ¡Oh, tierra abierta al sediento / de libertad y de vida / dinámica y creadora! / ¡Salud, patria, que eres también mía / puesto que eres de la humanidad: / salud en nombre de la Poesía, / salud en nombre de la Libertad!

16. Una alegre amistad de alma argentina / como salutación de hogar abierto.

Index

VERMONT COLLEGE
MONTPELIER, VERMONT